# art
## school

art

# school

An instructional guide
based on the teaching of
leading art colleges

*Consultant editor* Colin Saxton

M

*Consultant editor*
Colin Saxton

*Contributors*
David Phillips
Barbara Moss
John Hostler
Victor Hawkins
John Yeadon
David Clifton
Dick Whall
Stan Smith

101

This book was designed and produced by
QED Publishing Limited
32 Kingly Court
London W1

*Art director* Alastair Campbell
*Production director* Edward Kinsey
*Editorial director* Jeremy Harwood
*Senior editor* Kathy Rooney
*Editorial* Nicola Thompson, Julian Mannering, Judy Martin
*Illustrators* Bob Chapman, Edwina Keene, David Mallot,
David Staples, John Woodcock

*Photographers* Clive Boden, Ian Howes, Roger Pring, Paul
Sawyer, John Wyand

*Picture research* Linda Proud, Ellie Player

*Artwork* Dennis Lloyd Thompson

Phototypeset in Great Britain by Tradespools Limited
Frome, Somerset

Colour origination in Hong Kong by Hong Kong Graphic
Arts
Printed in Hong Kong by Leefung Asco Limited

A QED BOOK

First published 1981 by
**MACMILLAN LONDON LIMITED**
London and Basingstoke

Associated companies in Auckland, Dallas, Delhi, Dublin,
Hong Kong, Johannesburg, Lagos, Manzini, Melbourne,
Nairobi, New York, Singapore, Tokyo, Washington and
Zaria

ISBN 0 333 32306 8

Copyright © 1981 QED Publishing Limited

# CONTENTS

# SPECIAL ACKNOWLEDGEMENT

We would like to thank all the students who kindly allowed us to illustrate and comment on their work. From the Lanchester Polytechnic, Coventry we would like particularly to thank students in the Foundation Year and on the Colour and Figure Drawing courses. From the Ruskin College of Art in Oxford, special thanks go to all the students who provided material for photography. Although we were unable to include all the material, we would like to thank particularly the following: Alison Jones, Chris Rushton, Elaine Heckles, Rachel Reeves, Ken Briggs, Sharon Essor, Jonathan Waller, Vicky Marchant, Fiona MacDonald, Ann Gay, Russ Stephenson, Keith Davis, Anu Patel, Ian Marchant, Mark Hedger, Alan Pounder, Tracey Dranfield, Martin Taylor, Simon Fitzgerald, Alison Jones, Jackie Coulter, Piers Wardle, and Susan Hart. We would also like to thank all those people involved in art education in Britain and elsewhere who have given so much help in the preparation of this volume.

# FOREWORD

Many people who value and practise drawing and painting have not attended art college. This book provides – in as practical a way as possible – a course based on those offered at art colleges today. The many projects in the book which the reader can follow are accompanied by the work of actual art students together with commentaries compiled by art school tutors, similar to the type of constructive criticism which students at art college receive. From these comments, the reader can develop a critical awareness of their own work. *Art School* devotes its main coverage of the main disciplines of drawing and painting and provides an introduction to the climate of ideas in art schools today.

*Art School* enables readers to become 'fellow travellers' on a fine art course, to extend their own creative horizons and technical skills and also to review their own creative development against a wider perspective.

*Colin Saxton*

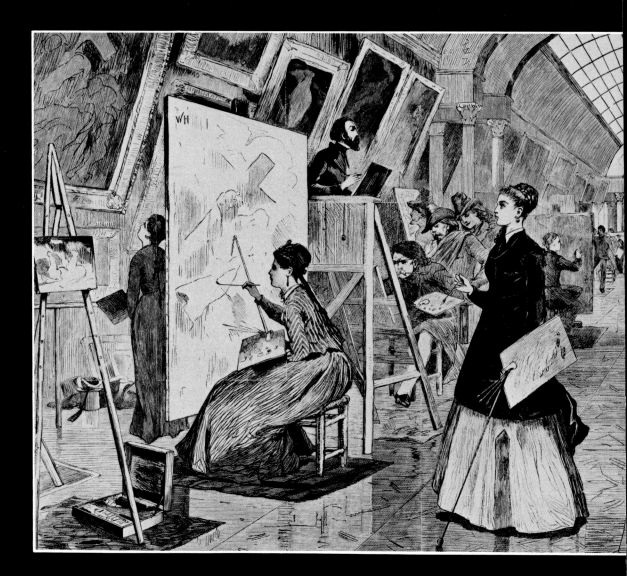

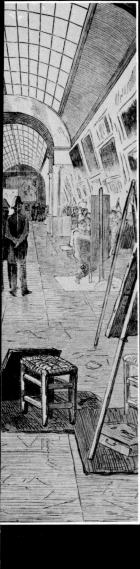

•

HISTORY

•

THE ACADEMIES

•

MODERN ART SCHOOLS

•

THE ARTIST TODAY

•

# THE BACKGROUND

Art has become a substantial part of the cultural fabric of society, and the art world a complex international network consisting of professional artists, dealers, collectors, curators, historians, critics, art students and amateur artists among others. A variety of organizations are devoted to housing, displaying, exhibiting, disseminating and generally encouraging awareness of art as well as its production. Today there are numerous art schools and other institutions which educate aspiring artists. The student body is made up of both men and women of varying ages but predominantly in their early twenties who show talent and commitment in their desire to express themselves through pictorial means. It is the responsibility of the staff in the art school to cherish and develop their students' talents and foster their commitment.

## Art schools today

For students entering art school today, the emphasis in their studies on individuality and self-motivation, even within the confines of a relatively structured course, can be daunting after years of application within more clearly defined and ordered educational frameworks. Usually the first year offers a foundation or an introduction to several of the disciplines which may be studied in subsequent years. It is expected, therefore, that, since most students have a limited and general knowledge of art and design, everyone is usually given the opportunity to experience a number of disciplines which they may take up as specialized areas of study. Typical areas might be fine art, textile design or three-dimensional design.

Therefore, during their first year, students have the opportunity both to acquire new skills and to experience new creative processes which will help them explore their own potential. To liberate and encourage this creativity is of primary importance, but, at a more down-to-earth level, students are, of course, expected to show evidence of the work and enquiry that has taken place, the best examples of which, along with sketchbooks and working drawings, may be presented as a portfolio which is assessed before the student may move on to the following years of the course. At this stage it is usually not necessary for a student to have decided to specialize in any particular subject area, such as painting or sculpture, and an early decision about this may actually be discouraged. Instead, a variety of work is appreciated—quantity as much as quality—as evidence of the commitment and self-motivation necessary for the student to continue. Attention to technical detail

at this stage is encouraged, but is not as important as the students' drive, together with their natural talent or individuality of approach and expression. However, even in the best of artists, this is unusual at such an early stage.

Today art education emphasizes the need to stimulate the creativity of the individual, and this guiding principle applies broadly, irrespective of where the art school is located. The most important factor is the development of the full imaginative potential of the student within a wide range of media, encompassing the more traditional skills of drawing, painting and sculp-

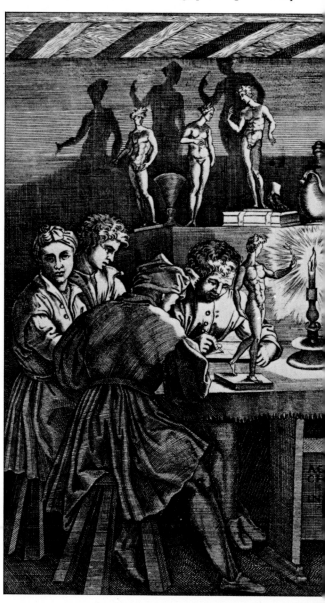

ture and the more contemporary areas of performance, electric media and video, as well as knowledge of the work of mature and established artists in the overall perspective of art history. These types of ideal differentiate the approach of the art school or an art faculty from those of other educational establishments. The emphasis on the personal exploration of individuals' creative ideas is born from the freedom to dare to try anything over a wide range of media. Students can explore whichever areas may be most suited to carrying out their ideas successfully. Usually such attempts show a relationship between works carried out in different

media, an inter-relation of thoughts and cross-fertilization. Art education therefore offers individuals the opportunity to diversify their approaches to art in order to gain excitement, stimulus and a greater knowledge and understanding of various methods and techniques. It also allows students to analyze in depth one particular facet which has stimulated their imagination and seems to offer an expressive possibility worth exploring.

Students need not feel restricted or inhibited, for what counts most is the idea realized in as strong a visual way as possible. They should be prepared for frustrations and disappointments in the fulfilment of

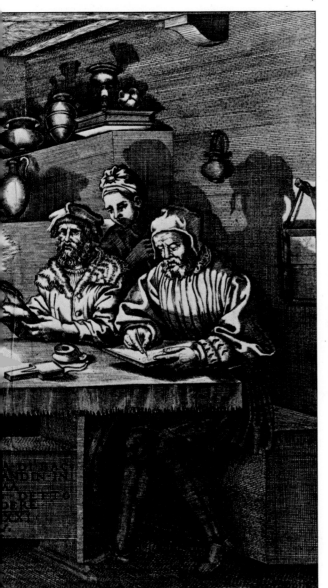
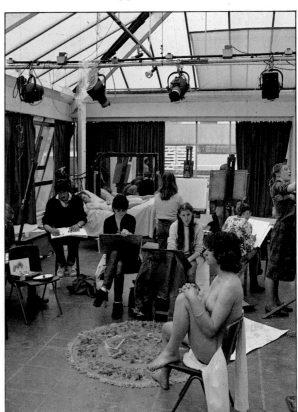

Art schools today have a much freer atmosphere than the academies of previous centuries. In the life studio (ABOVE), for example, students work from a life model in natural light. They are encouraged to experiment with media and approaches, whereas in the equivalent class shown in Veneziano's painting The Academy in Rome (LEFT), the students are working from a cast and drawing it with light from only one source. Only much later in their studies, when they had passed several examinations and competitions, would students of the academy work from a life model. No such restriction applies today.

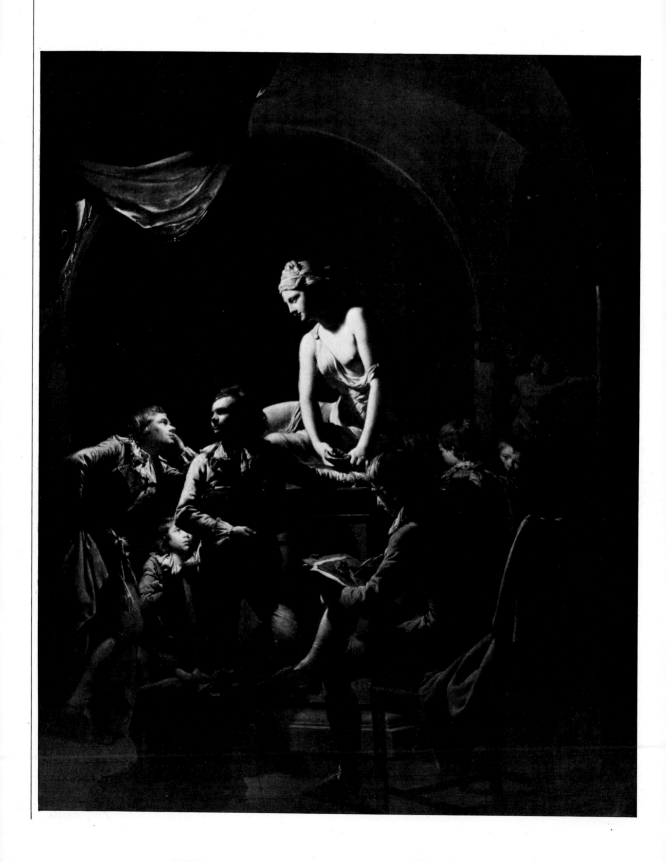

schemes, and they will need an awareness of weaknesses that need to be rectified by study and application. It is widely acknowledged that at the beginning of a career in art for the majority of students quantity is more important then quality, because the desired quality emerges through trial and error from the drive to do, to make, to create, coupled with guidance and encouragement.

This process may seem unstructured. Modern art education relies heavily on the individual tuition or small-group teaching, and demands a great deal of self-motivation from students to pursue interests and ideas stimulated from their own desire to create. Work is appraised by a tutor who subjects it to scrutiny and criticism, students' ideas are challenged and they are asked to justify their lines of enquiry from a pictorial as well as philosophical viewpoint.

This kind of interchange is meant to help the students to form and clarify their ideas about what they are doing and the direction in which they should develop. Most students have experience of putting paint on canvas, or have used and know the effects of various media, such as charcoal, pencil, crayon, or ink for drawing. But discussion about the sources from which an image rises, the form it takes and the reasons why it takes that particular form, helps and encourages the student to be self-critical in a constructive way. Students' ability to be self-critical and self-aware, and yet also to have the courage of their own convictions is a most important aspect of development in art education, and one relevant to every area of work. For example, recent renewed interest in drawing and painting from the figure is just one indication of the re-assessment of the importance of draughtmanship in both drawing and painting. However, to produce a successful figure drawing or painting requires more than the ability to perceive correctly how the figure is structured. This would simply produce an accurate diagram. Figure drawing or painting requires a 'feel' for line, colour, and form as well as a sensitivity to mood, in short, an ability to think and feel in terms of the medium being used and the two-dimensional surface on which the work is being done. The art student must be prepared to make constant corrections and changes no matter how painful this may be, after perhaps hours have already been spent in the first effort.

Some information about colour and the use of paint may be taught—for example, that red and yellow make orange, and that layers of pigment must be graduated from thin to thick, so that surface paint does not crack in drying. While the ability to use paint successfully is helped by such knowledge, it is not totally dependent on it, but rather on an understanding of the expressive possibilities of the medium itself, which can only be acquired by actually being involved with the medium and, through this, developing an intimacy with and feeling for it.

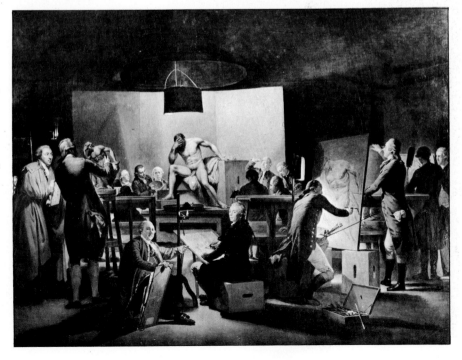

The influence of the academies lasted well into this century. The first academy was established in Florence in 1562, and by 1700 there were over 100 throughout Europe. The number of students allowed to study at the academies was severely restricted. Drawing and painting from plaster casts were major parts of the academy course. The first stage in the academy training was copying drawings, engravings and etchings by famous masters. When the students had attained an appropriate standard, they were allowed to proceed to working from plaster casts. Great emphasis was laid on the accurate representation of anatomical detail, tone and line. The plaster casts were normally posed in attitudes 'from the Antique' as can be seen in this picture of life drawing at the Vienna Academy of Arts *(RIGHT)*.
*Academy by Lamplight (LEFT)* by the English artist Joseph Wright, shows a mid eighteenth century academy class painting from a cast.

As well as plaster casts based on classical poses, students of the academies drew from 'flayed' figures *(RIGHT)*. These figures show the muscles of the body correct anatomically. The painting of the English Royal Academy by the eighteenth century artist Johann Zoffany *(BELOW)* shows rope being positioned to help the model hold his pose. The class is preparing to paint while the models are being changed. The many plaster casts show some of those used at the academy.

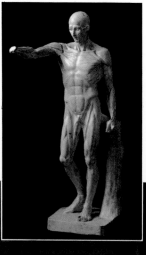

# The academies and their influence

The freedom enjoyed by students in the last two decades or so contrasts markedly with previous systems where the stress was much more on the acquisition of skills under a narrow educational philosophy of training. The art schools of the nineteenth century were concerned with training students for commerce and industry. Then the emphasis was on craftsmanship and designing goods, rather than any interest in the creativ-

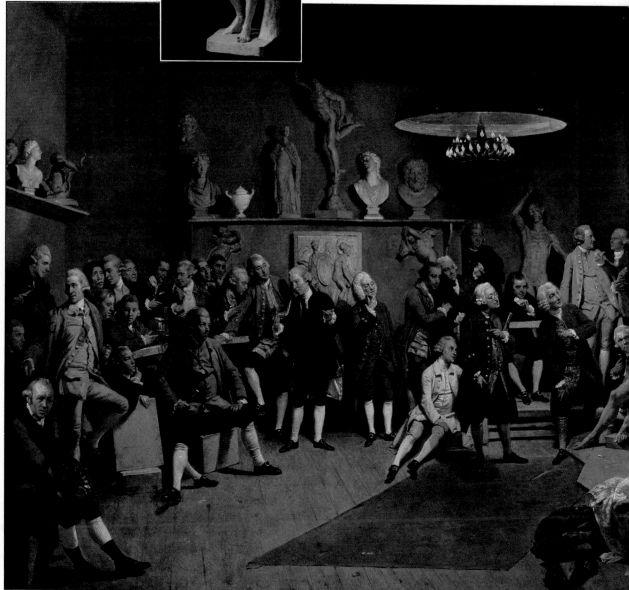

Although the works of women artists has tended to be greatly neglected, there have been many fine female artists. This nineteenth century art school by E. Phillips Fox *(RIGHT)* shows the students' seriousness of approach. Women made great efforts to gain admission to the academies. One early applicant to the Royal Academy schools in London did not specify her first name, was admitted and allowed to remain only when the academy discovered that the statutes did not specifically bar women.

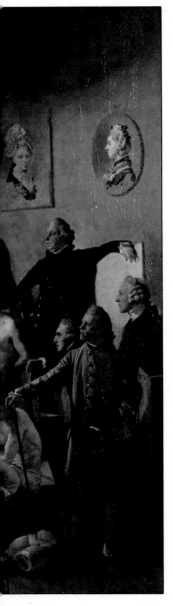

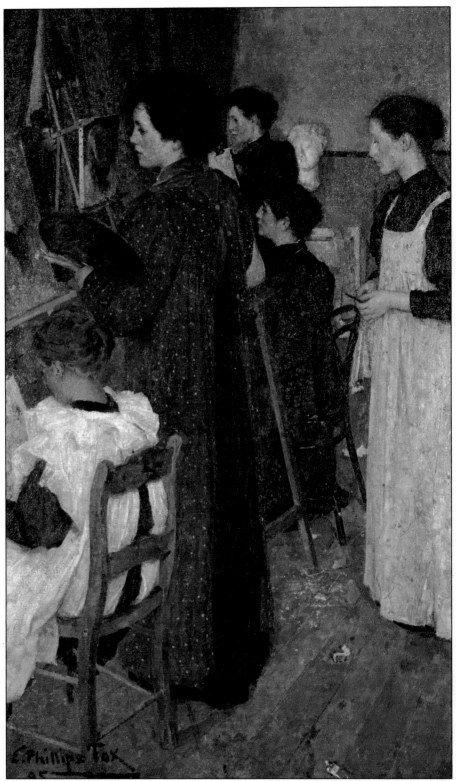

This 1889 etching by the French artist Alexix Le Maistre shows students working for an academy competition. They had to work up paintings from sketches so their work could be judged to see whether they had reached the required standard to continue to the next stage of the curriculum. This approach to art education emphasized the mastery of line and draughtsmanship. The focus of art education has changed radically in the last 20 years or so. Today, much more emphasis is placed on the individual's personal development and self-expression. Although student's work is assessed and, in many instances, given grades, the competitive element is much less important than it was in the days of the traditional academies.

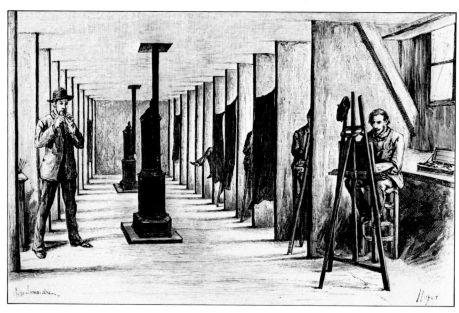

ity of the individual. This vocationalism sprang partly from a belief that art for its own sake was self-indulgent and effete and partly from the desire to harness artistic talent for some practical purpose. Such ideas remained prevalent in many art schools until the middle of this century.

The nineteenth century art schools developed from the academies, which were established in the seventeenth century in France under royal patronage. Numbers of students were severely restricted. In England, the Royal Academy was not established until 1768 and then its student numbers were very restricted. The alternative method of art education was apprenticeship to an established artist. In Europe the gradual development of the academy as an institution was comparatively slow from its inception in 1562 in Florence. The first Academy was organized by the artist and art historian Vasari (1511–1574) and had as its president the great artist Michelangelo (1475–1564). By 1600 there were fewer than 16 in Europe, but, by the beginning of the eighteenth century, the numbers had risen to at least 100 academies. In the medieval period there were no such institutions for then the 'student' was apprenticed to a master, who in turn would have been a member of a guild. In antiquity a similar system prevailed. This approach fostered a mechanical rather than a liberal art, and consequently the horizons set were limited by the functional needs it had to fulfil. This association of art with manual labour which the apprenticeship system produced was only removed during the Renaissance with the appearance of artists of the calibre of Michelangelo and Leonardo. This change in society's

view of the artist led to the development of the academy and, ultimately, began the long road to the freedoms of art education today. Such a record makes a sad contrast to developments in Asia where art was practised by emperors and recognized as a valuable means of expression. Artists had a much higher social status and their qualities were much valued and appreciated.

Even after the great increase in the institutionalization of art education during the nineteenth century, the curriculum in the academies and schools was very traditional and limited. The emphasis was on drawing and until this was mastered the student was not allowed to move on to painting. The student began by copying drawings, etchings, or engravings by famous masters. When a certain proficiency was achieved, the next stage was drawing plaster casts 'from the Antique', which enabled the students to further their skills in drawing and obtain a knowledge of classical art. The ability to draw or paint a plaster cast correctly was highly prized, and set procedures were adhered to in order to achieve this. These included drawing by contours with shading added, so as to obtain the desired three-dimensional effect. After this, the student could then graduate to the study of the human figure, although the competition was severe and the standards set extremely high.

Lecture courses and general instruction in anatomy and perspective were part of the curriculum with the objective of ensuring that the student could represent the human figure based on fundamental understanding of anatomy. The student was expected to be able to formulate the figure with ease from a variety of viewpoints using foreshortening and shading, as well as to simulate movement and the interaction of figures one with another in convincing pictorial space. The aim of the academies was to develop mastery of the human form which was considered essential in solving the problem of depicting objects in the visual environment. There were rigid procedures which began with the student being expected to understand the form of the body as a whole, and then to move on to draw parts of the body such as arms, legs and head. Correction would take the form of the teacher drawing attention to anatomical inaccuracies or wrong positioning. Various phases in this programme were marked by regular competitions after which students whose work was considered of sufficient merit were allowed to pass on to the next stage until their accomplishment was such that they could proceed to the painting studio.

This academic approach was based on a way of drawing from the life model which emphasized line. Coupled with this devotion to draughtmanship particularly characterized by linear modelling was the stereotyped pose of the model. This was so arranged as to evoke associations with the calm grandeur and noble simplicity associated with classical art. This stress on line and classicism implied that art should appeal to the mind rather than to the senses. Truthfulness and authenticity extended to an accurate display of archaeological accessories which were required in finished composition where clarity of action and precise exposition of pictorial features was considered important. The art student aspired to be a chronicler and, although originality was sought, creativity was considered to be a calculated action which would lead to an ennoblement of mind in the viewer. Of course, the finished work would be the result of a complicated process which would be sustained by the desire for expressiveness. The preliminary steps were vastly different from the finished work and the sketches which represented the first stages incorporated movement and lack of finish, but these elements were tempered by reason and deliberation to achieve the polished surface of the completed work. Colour, consequently, served a subordinate role at least in the creative thought in the early stages of the work and, even in the final result, acted more as a support for the form rather than an element in its own right. Form was the vehicle of narrative action, particularly in the depiction of a historical subject.

In contrast to the importance placed on the human figure and its depiction, the student of the academy was also advised and encouraged to sketch daily events in a pocket notebook, a practice stemming back to Leonardo da Vinci. This method was thought to be a relief from the more disciplined techniques and crucial for the student's search for originality and personal viewpoint. Sketches were drawn in a few rapid strokes under the heat of impressions and would be reworked later in the studio. The drawing notes were meant to embody and record immediate observations, stressing immediacy and spontaneity in order to capture a scene's effect.

# The artist today

The type of subject matter depicted by artists of the Renaissance, and indeed later, was partly due to the fact that the majority of works of art were commissioned by the church, the state or wealthy private patrons. The artist was working within a framework acceptable to and making a visual statement largely determined by the patron. This is not so today. It is a pity that more art students do not survive as practising artists after leaving college, partly because of the lack of patrons, public or otherwise, willing to commission or buy works from them. This situation creates both a lack of the financial backing necessary for an artist to continue to work and perhaps also induces a lack of motivation. While at college, the art student today has a relatively short time in which to have free reign and to be fully creative without the pressure to produce the sort of work required and dictated by a patron.

However, because of a lack of patronage, many artists are unable to sell their work or are only rarely given commissions, although some do well. There is a gap which needs to be filled so that art is once more used by society, rather than merely being considered a luxury, easily dispensed with without any great loss. One main way to achieve this is through a more generally widespread art education since, in practice, everyone makes decisions of an artistic nature every day of their lives—such as in their choice of clothes or decor, even if they seldom or never buy original paintings.

*Art School* offers an insight into the methods current in art education. Like art schools and colleges, it presents a framework within which you can develop your own ideas and approaches. As well as encouraging experimentation and imagination, the book, like modern art education, emphasizes throughout the importance of developing a critical awareness of the strengths and weaknesses of your own work. This type of awareness has been crucial for the development of all artists—whether medieval craftsman, Renaissance painter, nineteenth century Impressionist or today's most avant-garde artist.

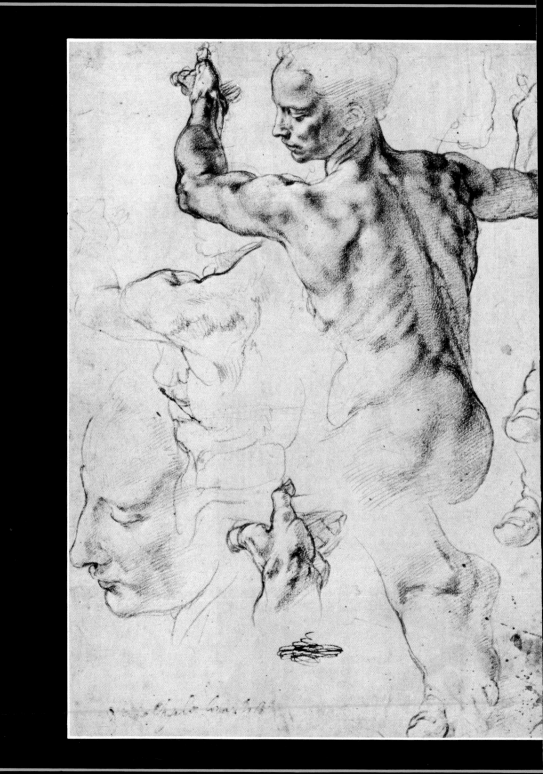

# 2

# FOUNDATION

INTRODUCTION

PERSPECTIVE

MEASURED DRAWING

PROPORTION

DESIGN AND PROPORTION

SHAPE AND FORM

COLOUR

MOVEMENT

SKETCHBOOKS

Michelangelo
*Studies for the Libyan Sybil*

# INTRODUCTION

A student embarking on an art school course usually does so with very little knowledge of the breadth and range of options available. A good first year course in an art school should allow students to develop their potential and awareness of the range of what is on offer to them, so that they can then make an informed choice about how to specialize in their subsequent studies. Thus, the purpose of the first year at an art school is to introduce students to the many disciplines, skills and avenues which are open to them. It should also develop in the student awareness of the attitudes and approaches of professional artists or designers. In one book it is impossible to show the whole range of possible activities at an art school. This book therefore concentrates on the more mainstream activities of drawing and painting. This does not mean that areas such as video or performance are any less valid as subjects of study.

## Self-portraits

Any aspect of drawing or painting involves artists responding to their perceptions of the world. Perhaps the most striking facet of artistic expression is how artists have varied their means and forms of expression so widely through the ages. This series of self-portraits (pp20–23) shows how some of the world's artists have viewed themselves.

Training your perceptions and learning to express your ideas is a crucial aspect of becoming an artist. Look at yourself as objectively as possible – from different angles, in various lights. Your face is a series of hollows and protuberances. How is your character reflected in your face? What are your main features? Examine the rest of your body in the same way. Now look at these self-portraits and work out how the artists have seen themselves, used their media and conveyed their personalities in their work. For instance, Leonardo (3) captured his appearance in a few wispy lines while Léger (23) and Mondrian (22) added atmosphere to their images by applying their medium more heavily. While the faces of Gauguin (19) and Matisse (20) dominate the pictures, Van Eyck (1) allowed the intricate folds of his hat to come over more strongly than his face. Compare and contrast these images in as many ways as possible. Consider, for example, the humour which Bosch (2) and Rubens (7) share, and how this contrasts with the solemnity of Reynolds (9) and Ingres (11). Examine the use of media – the economy of line in Leonardo (3) or Lowry's portrait (24), the spare application of paint by Munch (17) as opposed to Matisse's thick brushstrokes (20).

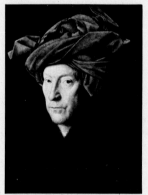

1 Jan van Eyck

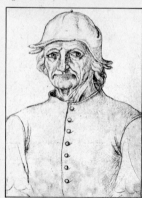

2 Hieronymous Bosch

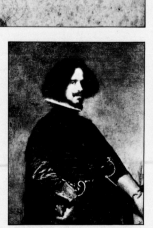

3 Leonardo da Vinci

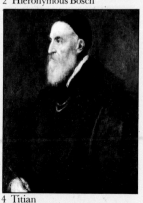

4 Titian

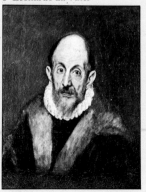

5 El Greco

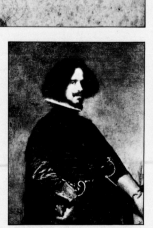

6 Diego Velazquez

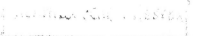

# Starting points

The basic starting point for all students or artists is a visual curiosity about the world. All students of the visual arts must at some point concern themselves with their environment. Many artists make this their sole concern throughout their careers. From a very early age, everyone has to come to terms with the world around them. Look at a child drawing—watch the concentration on the child's face, the activity absorbs their whole attention. Children have a bold and direct approach; the artist in adulthood has to try to recapture this approach. For many people, divesting themselves of assumptions and conventions absorbed over years can be a slow and painful process. Yet, if you take your art seriously, you must constantly re-examine critically what you are doing and how you are doing it.

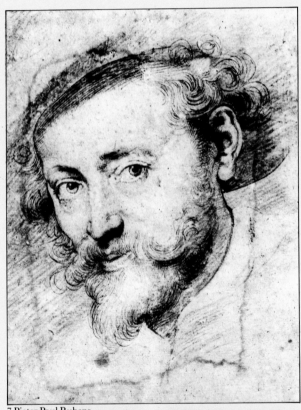

7 Pieter Paul Rubens

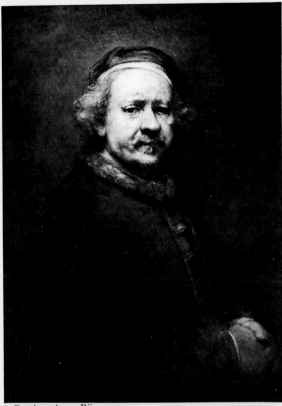

8 Rembrandt van Rijn

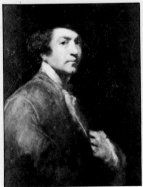

9 Joshua Reynolds

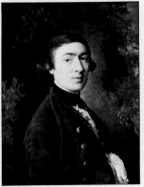

10 Thomas Gainsborough

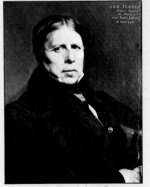

11 Auguste-Dominique Ingres

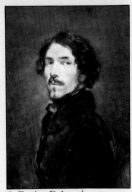

12 Eugène Delacroix

Many art schools give their prospective students one or two projects to do before they arrive at the institution. These projects can vary enormously in content, but many concern themselves with observing and drawing, two basic skills which students should master in their early days at an art school. For instance, a typical project might ask the student to select a landscape, environment or object and to make studies of it in monochrome and in colour, examining its structure and content. Students might be advised to avoid obvious conventions and to use any way of gathering information which seems appropriate.

The purpose of such projects is to test observational skills and to explore use of media. Factors which tutors might look for would include what type of landscape or object was chosen. For example, was a conventional landscape chosen and treated in a conventional way, or did the student look for something a little unusual and

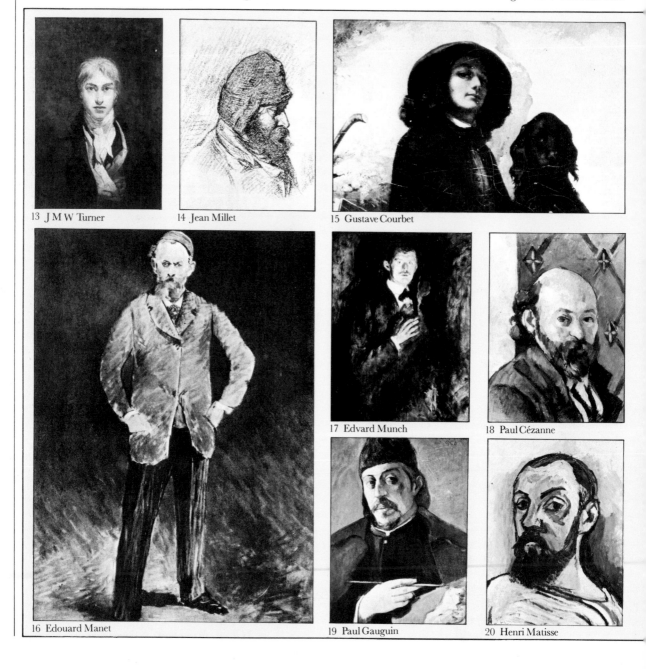

13  J M W Turner

14  Jean Millet

15  Gustave Courbet

17  Edvard Munch

18  Paul Cézanne

16  Edouard Manet

19  Paul Gauguin

20  Henri Matisse

treat it in a personal rather than conventional manner? Your own backyard might well make a more interesting subject than the most famous or dramatic landscape, if you treat it in an interesting way. Never disregard what is immediately around you. Indeed one of the most important functions of the first year at an art school is to encourage you to look around yourself in new and exciting ways. Your own room, house and surroundings may seem familiar and uninteresting, but

they can probably give you rich and varied material for your artistic endeavours.

A second important role of the first year at art school is to encourage students to experiment with techniques and approaches to their work. It is very easy to fall into habits—such as using certain media or treating subjects in certain ways. Are these best for you? What alternatives could you use? When you embark on a piece of work, try to think of different

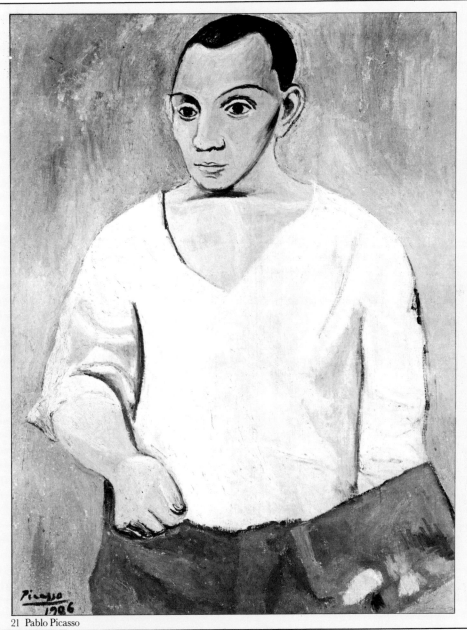

21 Pablo Picasso

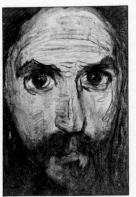

22 Piet Mondrian

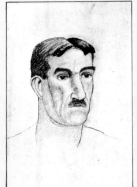

23 Fernand Léger

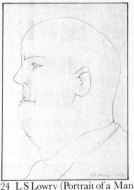

24 L S Lowry (Portrait of a Man)

ways of tackling it. Try some of them out. Do not be afraid to use new media, to experiment with surfaces, techniques and indeed subject matter. If you are automatically tempted to reach for a pencil, try sketching out your ideas in pen or pastels. If you only feel happy working in one medium—such as watercolour or oils—try using coloured pencils, pastels or acrylic paints.

Many students at art school might find it difficult to say what they learned during their first year. Art education today is a process of allowing students great freedoms of choice in the courses they take and the directions they explore. One of the roles of the first year is gradually to break down the assumptions and conventions which students have when they first arrive at art schools and to make them aware of the breadth of materials and media available to them. So the purpose of this section of *Art School* is to help you to examine your previous work, to show some of the possibilities open to you and to encourage you to explore new avenues and processes. However, you should always try to remain critical of your own efforts and you should never be tempted to feel complacent about what you have achieved. Always remember two maxims—never be afraid to experiment, and never stop trying to look critically at your own work.

## LEARNING TO OBSERVE

The ability to observe swiftly and accurately is vital for any artist and you should work to develop your powers of observation. To demonstrate how good or bad your observation is, draw a familiar object from memory. Choose something which you see or use almost every day but which is not actually in front of you. Suggested subjects could include a bicycle, car, typewriter, telephone or washing machine. You should put on the drawing all the details you can remember. When you have completed the drawing, you will probably be surprised how little you have been able to recall even about a familiar object.

## FIRST STEPS

This project is to test and develop your observational skills and the way you use different media. First select a simple object and study it. It would be best to select a subject to which you have easy access – something in your home, for instance. Examine it carefully, pretending that you have never seen it before and noting not only its shape and form, but also think about its texture, colours, areas of light and shade, the space around the object and how the object relates to that space. Look at it from different angles and try placing it in various positions. When you start to work, try to avoid all preconceived ideas and assumptions. Do not draw or paint in a certain way because you feel that it is more 'artistic'. Respond directly to what you see, be curious, explore what you see and experiment with different ways of depicting it and with various media.

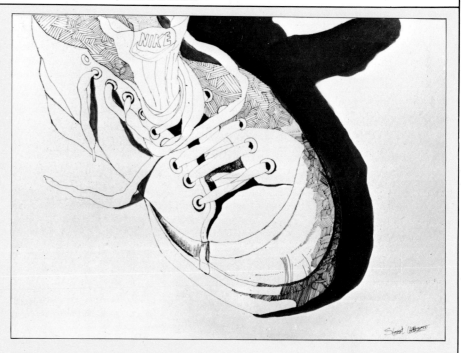

*This pen and ink study shows what can be achieved when you become interested in something for its own sake. The artist is more interested in using the medium (pen and ink) and in placing the object on the surface than simply recording the image. The lively use of line, although rather unsubtle, reveals the artist's enjoyment in what he is doing. This kind of study could form the beginning of further work, but is nevertheless interesting as an enthusiastic starting point.*

## INTRODUCTORY PROJECT

Some art schools ask their prospective students to do some work before they arrive at the college so that the tutors can see the qualities and weaknesses of work produced outside a college context. Such projects usually aim to test out the students' ability to observe and their use of media. As you embark on the course in this book, try a similar exercise yourself and assess your own work afterwards. As an artist, it is important that you make efforts to develop your powers of self-criticism. When you do a piece of work, you should sit back afterwards, perhaps after a few days have passed so that you are not so close to the subject. Look at the composition you have arrived at, think about whether it has served your purposes well or whether a different arrangement would have been better. Consider the medium or media you have used. Could you have perhaps achieved better results with different means? Would a combination of media have been more effective? Do not be afraid to make several attempts at the same subject, exploring different possibilities and approaches. One of the worst things an artist can be is complacent, you should always search after better and more effective ways of depicting your ideas. For this preliminary project, select a landscape and do several studies of it, working towards a final result. Use whatever methods of research seem appropriate.

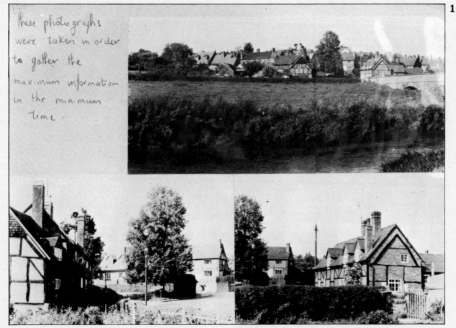

1

*These photographs were taken in order to gather the maximum information in the minimum time.*

*The illustrations on this and the following page show two series of responses to the brief. The first artist has used photographs (1) as a way of researching the scene. This can be an excellent type of reference material and can help speed up the research process. However, in this case, the artist has allowed the photographs to dictate the approach to the whole scene rather too much. The artist could have worked with the photographs rather more. For example, the photograph could have been cut up or drawn on in order to stimulate the artist's imagination and help offer new approaches to the subject. The second artist used another approach by doing quick line sketches (2, 3) of the scene. The first is merely an outline while in the second more details have been filled in. The first establishes important areas such as the spaces occupied by the fields, woods and buildings and their overall relationship to one another.*

2

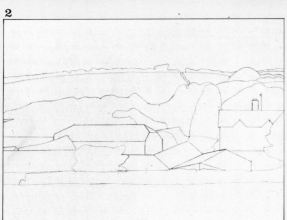

3

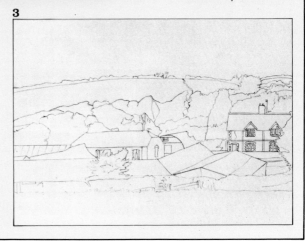

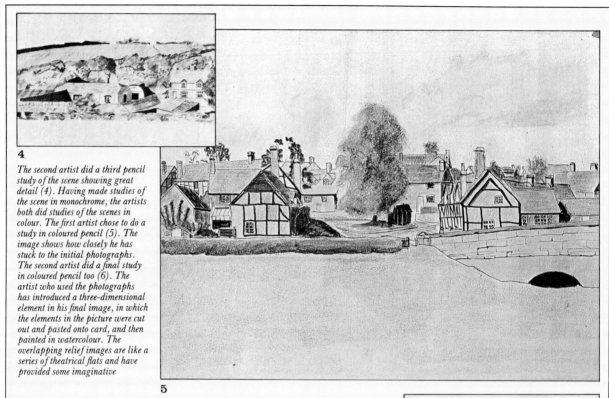

**4**

The second artist did a third pencil study of the scene showing great detail (4). Having made studies of the scene in monochrome, the artists both did studies of the scenes in colour. The first artist chose to do a study in coloured pencil (5). The image shows how closely he has stuck to the initial photographs. The second artist did a final study in coloured pencil too (6). The artist who used the photographs has introduced a three-dimensional element in his final image, in which the elements in the picture were cut out and pasted onto card, and then painted in watercolour. The overlapping relief images are like a series of theatrical flats and have provided some imaginative

**5**

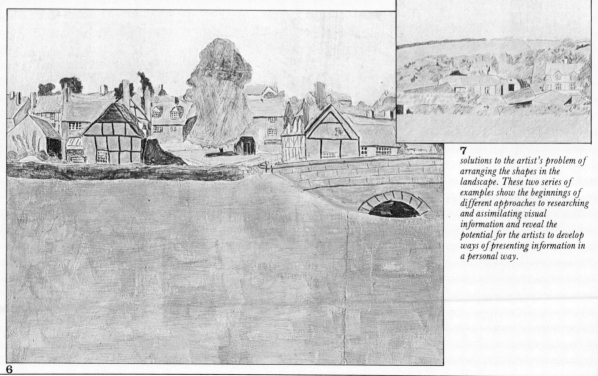

**7**

solutions to the artist's problem of arranging the shapes in the landscape. These two series of examples show the beginnings of different approaches to researching and assimilating visual information and reveal the potential for the artists to develop ways of presenting information in a personal way.

**6**

# Equipment

Art schools supply equipment and materials needed in workshops and specialized study areas, but each student is expected to own a basic range of materials which will enable them to tackle painting, drawing and design projects. Do not use only those materials which you have already mastered. A foundation course is specifically designed to allow you to investigate all the different media and become familiar with the tools of the trade.

However, there is a vast range of products available to the artist and it is as well not to buy too much until you see the demands of the work. It is important to be equipped with suitable painting and drawing materials for all types of work.

**Equipment for basic projects**
Basic equipment should include a good range of materials for developing your drawing skills. Pencils (5) are available in a wide variety of H (hard) and B (soft) grades. Charcoal (4) is a less precise medium useful for free drawing styles and a soft, textured surface. Indian ink (3) used with brush or dip pen gives bold black lines or warm grey washes. A stylo-tip pen may be a more suitable tool for fine work in ink, while a ruling pen (10) can be used with thin paint or ink for linear work in colour. Felt tip pens (1) and markers (20) enable you to draw freely with colour and are particularly useful for rough layouts. A range of sable and hog's hair brushes with flat and rounded ends (2) cover all painting and design work. Gouache (11) is the most versatile type of paint to begin with as it can be applied thickly straight from the tube or watered down. A craft knife (15), scalpel (14) and scissors (13) allow for different types of cutting; and a steel ruler must be used with knives though plastic is adequate for drawing purposes (6). An oilstone (16) is useful for sharpening blades. Compasses (7), set square (8) and T-square (9) are invaluable design aids. A well bound sketchbook (12) enables you to record ideas and rough out designs, but for finished work a good, solid drawing board (21) is essential. Adhesive tape (18), erasers (17) and a palette (19) are also useful.

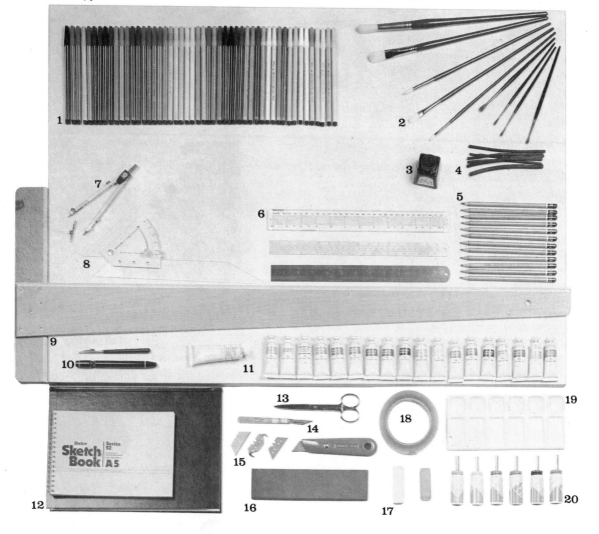

# PERSPECTIVE

When people take up drawing, many of their works reflect their knowledge of drawing in a historical sense. That is to say, they depend on styles which they have seen elsewhere. To some extent, these conventions in drawing are expressions of how people perceive the world. Take, for example, the drawing of the rhinoceros by the German artist Albrecht Dürer (1471–1528). Dürer had not previously seen one of these animals and he produced a drawing from a verbal description or even a written account of a verbal description. Now, despite it becoming possible for later artists to view a rhinoceros at first hand they still tended to portray it in a manner which was more akin to Dürer's armour-plated animal than to what they could have seen with their own eyes. Another convention involved the way in which galloping horses were portrayed. In the seventeenth and eighteenth centuries artists always depicted horses with their four legs extended, and not until photographs taken by Eadweard Muybridge (1830–1904) proved that this was incorrect was the convention dropped.

Both those examples suggest that people learn to read certain conventions in drawings which then become part of their perceptual apparatus. Perception is also governed as much by what people know as by what they see. As a logical extension of this, people tend to draw what they know to be there rather than what they actually see. When drawing, you should attempt to forget both artistic conventions as well as your knowledge of the world. In a sense, drawing is a matter of analyzing and questioning everything that you see around you.

You must also remember that you are developing a language. Perspective is one means by which three-dimensional space is transposed onto a two-dimensional surface.

In many ways drawing is like writing. If you were to sit down, say, in front of a chair and set about describing it in words you would find the task becoming increasingly complex and difficult as you struggled with the language itself and the different categories of information which you had to include. You are translating what you see into language. Descriptive drawing poses the same problems insofar as you are describing what you see, not in words this time, but in lines on a surface. When you begin drawing, you will find yourself in front of the most familiar objects and scenes but you will be confronted with problems of being selective and extracting the visual information which you actually want to depict. You should remember that there is no such thing as an objective interpretation of what you see. Just as people will use different verbal variations to describe what they see, so you will use your own configuration

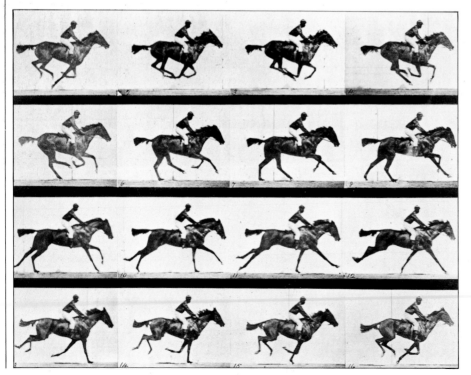

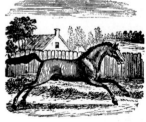

For many years the portrayal of galloping horses involved a convention which was not corrected until after the advent of photography. Until then artists suffered under the misapprehension that, as horses galloped, all four legs were extended. This position came to represent a galloping horse and a woodcut by the English engraver Thomas Bewick (*ABOVE*) dated 1790 shows this clearly  In the nineteenth century, with the use of photographs, however, the pioneer Eadweard Muybridge (*LEFT*) proved otherwise, namely that when off the ground, the horse's legs came together underneath it.

of lines to describe what you see. It is this which makes drawing such a pleasure for it can become an integral part of a detailed investigation of your environment.

# Perceiving space

There are many means by which forms and spatial relationships may be examined through drawing, and you will discover that there are certain rules which pertain to such examinations. There are a number of systems which enable very accurate drawings to be constructed. One example is measured linear perspective drawing. This system will be examined in detail later. Its importance is profound, for although it may be a contrived and somewhat long-winded procedure, it is suitable for all representational drawing. Linear perspective, however, is only one of the many means of examining space and three-dimensional forms, but it can help you to understand fully the extremely complex nature and structural geometry of an object and its surroundings.

There are a number of ways in which people learn to perceive three-dimensional space. Parallel lines appear to converge when viewed obliquely. The distances of single objects become foreshortened—if

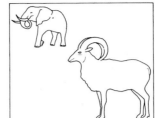
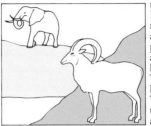
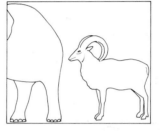

**Perceiving distance**
There are a whole range of visual clues which can help you define distance in your paintings and drawings. In the first picture *(TOP)*, you can assume that the elephant is in the background because it is higher up the picture plane and is considerably smaller than the goat. However, there is no ground, so that the image remains somewhat ambiguous. In the second picture *(CENTRE)* the relative positions of the animals are quite clear. In the third picture *(BOTTOM)* their positions are also clear. The goat is now a little way behind the elephant. This is because it is slightly higher up the picture plane. The proportions of the elephant tell you that it has moved appreciably closer.

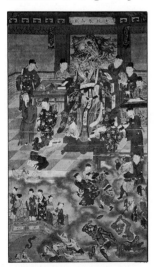

In this drawing *(RIGHT)* the front appears to narrow although, in fact, the lines are parallel. This is because Western conventions of perspective dictate that parallel lines converge in the distance. Therefore, as these lines do not converge, they must be moving wider apart, and so the front seems narrower.

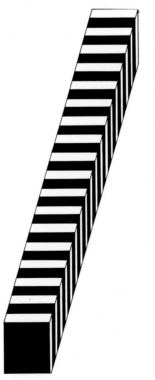

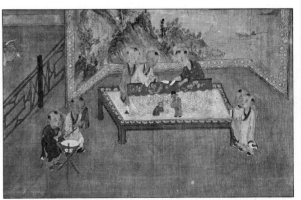

Different cultures reveal the widely differing ways in which artists have, through the centuries, perceived and conveyed space. In Chinese painting, for example, figures of great importance were depicted larger than those around. In this work *(FAR LEFT)* the large figure is Yama, King of the Seventh Hell, who looks on while the much smaller figures of demons and dogs chase souls into the river. The second picture, a scroll painting of children playing with puppets *(ABOVE)* shows

clearly the reversal of Western conventions of perspective, in that the table is wider at the back than the front. This image also shows the use of overlapping to indicate that figures or objects are behind one another. This simple type of depth cue, however, gives little feeling of three-dimensional space to the Western eye.

an arm in a drawing, for instance, is foreshortened drastically then not much more than the hand will be visible. Thirdly, objects of similar size appear to diminish as they recede into the distance. These are the key visual rules. There are other means which together enable us to perceive three-dimensional space more accurately. These devices are also used in drawing. To begin with, the physical act of the eye focusing gives clues to relevant depths. Atmospheric effects are also crucial as tone and colour become greyer or more neutral with an increase in depth. When this phenomenon is applied to drawing it is known as aerial perspective. The shape of cast shadows give clues as to the form and surface nature of the object. Overlapping by foreground objects obscures the view of more distant objects. Finally, texture and pattern appear more detailed when seen closer to than when viewed from a distance.

These factors help the artist to recognize and interpret three-dimensional space and can be applied in drawing, but it is not always necessary to utilize all of these factors in making a representational drawing, indeed, it is usually very uneconomic to do so.

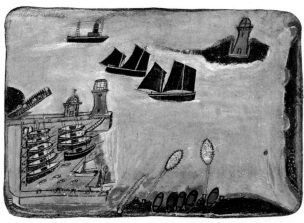

Artists have perceived and portrayed space and perspective in widely varying ways. In *St Ives Harbour (ABOVE)* by the British artist Alfred Wallis, for example, the boats in the foreground are as if seen from above while the sailing ships in the sea are in varying scales. Wallis also used an unusual logic in his painting of sea. He went to the sea, looked at its colour in a jamjar, saw it was not blue but white and so painted it white. In contrast to the rather naive approach of Wallis, is *The Great Day of His Wrath* by John Martin *(BELOW)*. This picture conveys its fantastic image with almost photographic precision. These examples show how one artist applies his own very personal ideas in his work.

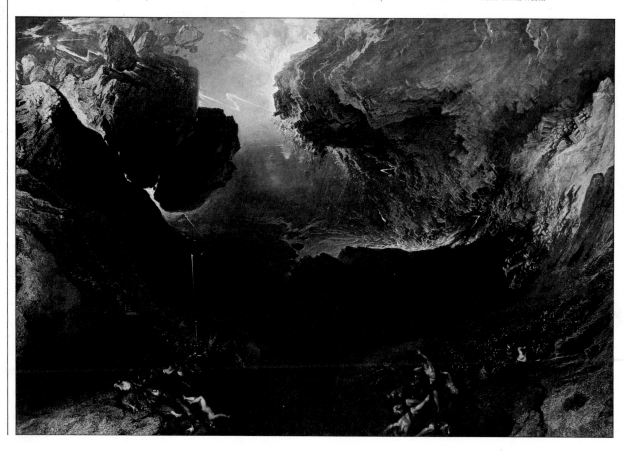

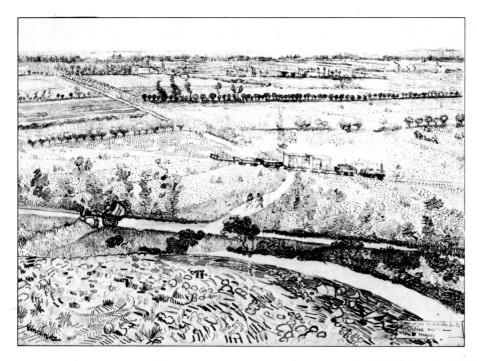

The eighteenth century Venetian artist Canaletto was a draughtsman of great skill. He did many drawings and paintings of Venice which reveal his use of linear perspective. This creates the impression of depth and solidity characteristic of the scenes in Canaletto's work. In *View of Piazza San Marco, facing the Basilica (BOTTOM)* painted between 1730 and 1735, the viewer's eye is drawn into the picture by the lines of buildings on the left and right. In order to give his works increased accuracy, Canaletto often used a camera obscura, a drawing aid which projects the image of a scene or image onto a sheet of paper or glass so that the outlines can be traced. Canaletto probably used a camera obscura for *The North East Corner of Piazza San Marco (BELOW)*. Van Gogh creates an impression of depth in his pen and ink landscape drawing *(LEFT)* by using perspective and scale. Compare van Gogh's approach with Canaletto's, particularly the two artists' use of line and scale.

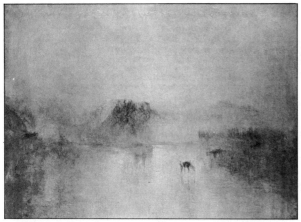

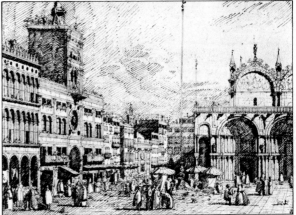

Turner's painting of *Norham Castle* (1799) *(ABOVE)* is one of his first major works and shows the directions in which Turner would subsequently develop. Rather than applying linear ideas of perspective, the impression of distance is conveyed in this work by the increasing saturation of the colours with blue as the eye moves further into the distance. This form of aerial or atmospheric perspective is one which you should consider for your own works. You can work out for yourself how this type of perspective functions. Look around you. The colours of objects close to you will be brighter and more differentiated tonally than those further away. Colours in the distance are less clearly differentiated and tonally more similar. The effects of light on the atmosphere and environment was one of the main preoccupations of the Impressionists, and Turner is frequently regarded as a major forerunner of their work.

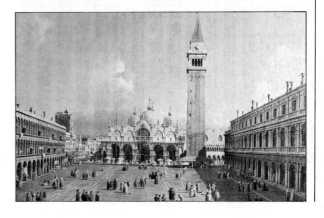

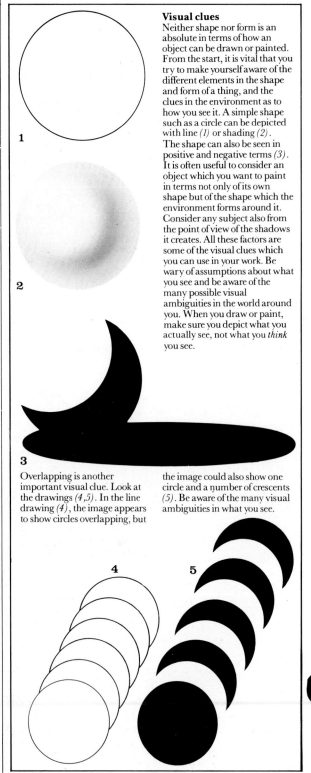

**1**

**2**

**3**

**Visual clues**
Neither shape nor form is an absolute in terms of how an object can be drawn or painted. From the start, it is vital that you try to make yourself aware of the different elements in the shape and form of a thing, and the clues in the environment as to how you see it. A simple shape such as a circle can be depicted with line *(1)* or shading *(2)*. The shape can also be seen in positive and negative terms *(3)*. It is often useful to consider an object which you want to paint in terms not only of its own shape but of the shape which the environment forms around it. Consider any subject also from the point of view of the shadows it creates. All these factors are some of the visual clues which you can use in your work. Be wary of assumptions about what you see and be aware of the many possible visual ambiguities in the world around you. When you draw or paint, make sure you depict what you actually see, not what you *think* you see.

Overlapping is another important visual clue. Look at the drawings *(4,5)*. In the line drawing *(4)*, the image appears to show circles overlapping, but the image could also show one circle and a number of crescents *(5)*. Be aware of the many visual ambiguities in what you see.

**4**

**5**

# Drawing perspective

Perspective refers to any graphic method by which an impression of three-dimensional space is conveyed on a two-dimensional surface or in a space smaller than that being portrayed. It is interesting to make a series of drawings attempting to isolate and utilize the different means of defining three-dimensional space. In practice this is not so easy because these visual clues tend to interact and overlap. A seemingly simple drawing project can become compounded into numerous permutations and alternatives. In this exercise selectivity becomes of prime importance.

**Monocular vision** When drawing perspective you must make your image from a fixed viewpoint and employ monocular vision (vision which uses only one eye). A moving viewpoint and focusable, stereoscopic vision are of great value for day to day use, but, when drawing from life, the situation is very different. It is necessary to use a fixed viewpoint so that the relationships between the various shapes remain constant. Using only one eye, held stationary, reduces the perceived image to two dimensions. Squinting, which makes the objects in front of you go out of focus, can help you to order the tonal values.

Binocular vision                    Monocular vision

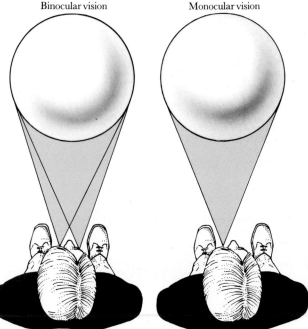

**Monocular vision**
When drawing perspective, you must use a fixed viewpoint. This means that you should use only one eye so that the relationships between the parts of the image remain constant. Stereoscopic vision provides a moving viewpoint which would tend to lead to inaccuracies in your work.

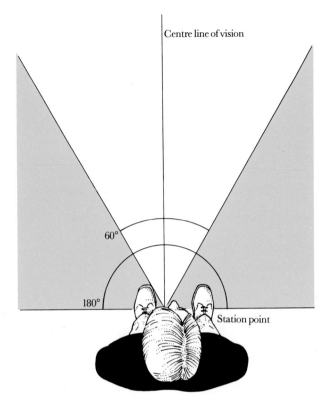

Centre line of vision

60°

180°

Station point

**Range of vision**
An individual's field of vision is 180°, but within that clear vision is only possible within a range of about 60°. Down the centre of that angle runs the centre line of vision which extends from the station point to the object. The name for the narrow area of clear vision is the cone of vision, because it is conical in shape spreading from the station point outwards. For a measured drawing, the station point and cone of vision should cover the whole of the subject you are going to draw. This will, to some extent, dictate where the station point will occur. Thus, if you wish to include tall objects such as buildings, your station point will have to be further from the object than if a smaller object is to be drawn.

When you observe your environment, especially in an enclosed space, you are very much aware of your surroundings without seeing everything in front of you clearly. Your field of vision extends to something greater than 180° yet you only perceive with any degree of clarity within a much smaller range. This narrower field of focus is known as the cone of vision and all that appears outside this range is blurred, although peripheral vision is particularly sensitive to movement. The eye tends to scan and focus over various points, sensing and measuring the space. Drawing within this fixed cone of vision is important because of the fixed station point and the fixed centre line of vision. The cone of vision is usually 15° to 20° either side of the centre line of vision. It is easy to forget these factors and turn your eyes and head freely from side to side, only to become increasingly frustrated by the inaccuracy of your drawing. The measured drawing system requires that the station point and cone of vision be laid out to encompass the parts of the subject matter to be included in the drawing, remembering that you are using a cone of vision and not an angle, and that tall objects must also be accommodated. The cone of vision, therefore, determines the distance of the station point.

## Picture plane

The picture plane is an imaginary vertical plane on which the drawing is plotted. The positioning of the picture plane is a matter of preference and convenience, but it is always perpendicular and at rightangles to the centre line of vision. The further it is away from the objects to be drawn the larger the drawing will be. This distance will also reduce distortion. It is interesting to set up a sheet of glass or clear plastic and do your drawing on this. An accurate drawing can be made of the objects lying behind the picture plane. This will stress the need for a fixed station point because if you move you will see how the objects move around in relation to their images on the picture plane.

## Vanishing points

When parallel lines are viewed obliquely, it is noticeable that they appear to converge. For example, if you look along a railway line the two rails appear to converge as they travel further away from you. Likewise, if you look up at a tall building the sides appear to converge towards the top. The point of convergence of these lines is called the vanishing point. A horizon line in a

Before settling down to your first drawing, you should familiarize yourself with a number of terms and methods. The viewing point or station point is the chosen position from which the object will be drawn. This point should be chosen with care, relative to the nature and size of the object being drawn. A viewing point which is selected too close to the object will result in a dramatic or distorted appearance in the drawing. Choosing the position is a matter of judgement and experience, but is determined mainly by the cone of vision and the size of drawing required. The direct line of sight from the station point to the object is known as the centre line of vision, and it is always taken to extend at eye level and parallel with the ground.

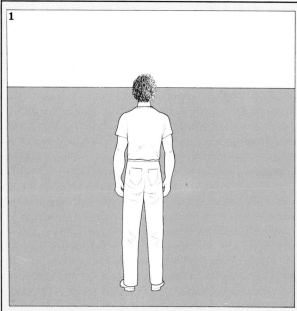

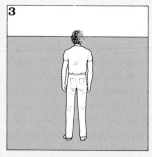

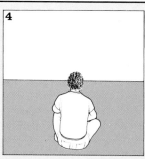

**Changing the horizon line**
The higher up you position yourself, the more of the ground plane you wil be able to see. This is because the higher up you are positioned, the higher up the horizon line is. This means that there is therefore a greater expanse of ground plane between yourself and the horizon line. You can test this by regarding the actual horizon from different positions. First stand (3), then sit (4), and then finally lie down. You will find, that in the last instance, the area of ground which you can see is negligible.

**Ground plane** The ground plane (1) is the extension of the ground on which you are positioned. You must visualize the ground plane as a flat plane extending out from where you stand and having no boundaries.

The ground plane is usually an imaginary plane due to the unevenness of the earth's surface. Only the sea represents a completely flat ground plane.

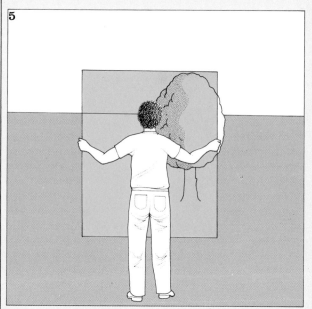

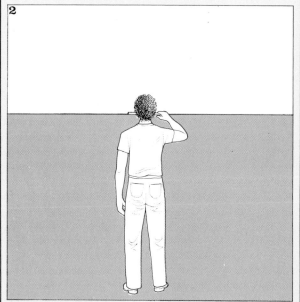

**The horizon** The horizon line (2) occurs at eye level. If you are standing by the sea, you can test this by holding a ruler up at eye-level. You will find that it coincides with the horizon. On land your horizon line, however, will usually be interrupted by objects or undulating ground.

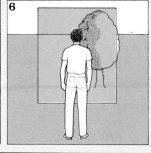

**The picture plane** When you look at an object, imagine that you are holding up a sheet of glass in front of you. This vertical plane is known as the picture plane (5). It is what you see through this plane that you will transpose onto your paper. The first thing which you will draw on the picture will be the horizon line (6).

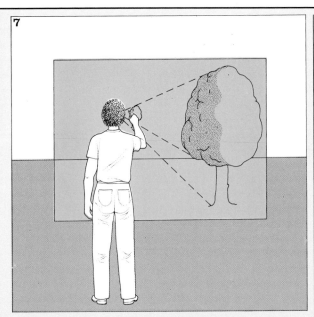

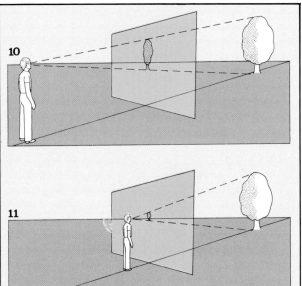

**Drawing on the picture plane**
If you stand at a window, you can use the glass as the picture plane and draw onto it. In this way you will be drawing directly onto the picture plane. You find it easier if you close one eye when you transpose an object onto the plane. By doing this, you will avoid double vision (7).

**Spectator and the picture plane** This diagram (8) shows imaginary lines drawn from the spectator's eye to the object and how they intercept the picture plane. This diagram shows clearly how drastically an object is reduced in size when it is drawn on a picture plane which is located some distance from it.

**Altering your position** You may have noticed when drawing on the window that the closer you came to the picture plane the smaller the representation of the object became. You can test this out by drawing the same object from two different positions, one close to the picture plane (11)another further away (10).

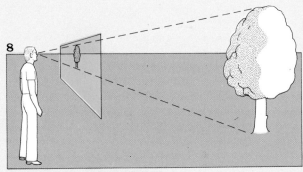

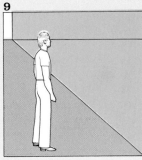

**The relationship between the picture plane and the ground plane** This side view (9) shows that a picture plane is located at right angles to the ground plane. Remember that you will probably not always have your drawing board at right angles, so that the plane on which you are drawing will not always be the same as the picture plane.

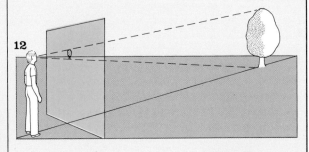

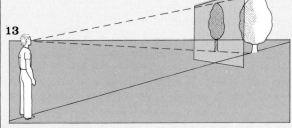

**Positioning the picture plane**
The scale of the representation of the object also depends on its position in relation to the picture plane. The nearer it is to the plane, the larger its representation will be. When you are working out the scale of your drawing, you will have to take into account both your position in relation to the picture plane and the position of the picture plane in relation to the object.

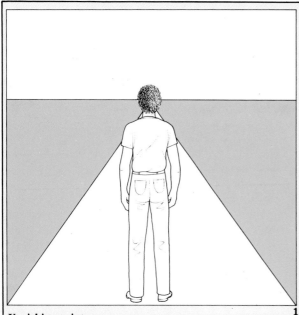

**1**

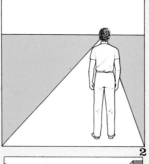

**2**

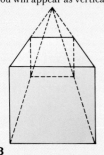

**3**

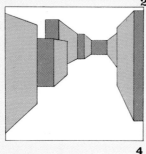

**4**

### Vanishing points

All parallel lines which recede into the distance appear to get closer together until they eventually converge at a point, called the vanishing point *(1)*. Seldom will you actually see this occur unless, perhaps, you find yourself standing on railway lines. The angles at which these lines converge depends upon the spectator's position *(2)*. A line leading directly away from you will appear as vertical.

### One-point perspective

In one-point perspective *(3)* only two faces of the cube are visible. One side is seen straight on, and there is only one vanishing point.

### Invisible vanishing points

Vanishing points are located on the horizon line. However, they will often be obscured by buildings or other objects *(4)*.

When this occurs, it is nevertheless crucial to know where the vanishing points would be located. Although the converging lines will not reach their ultimate destinations, only by locating their vanishing points will you be able to judge the correct angles of the lines.

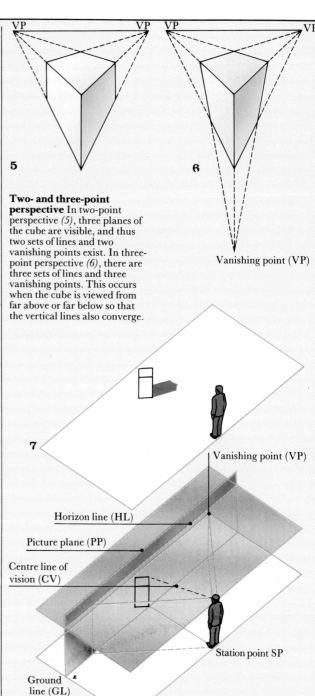

**5**

**6**

Vanishing point (VP)

**Two- and three-point perspective** In two-point perspective *(5)*, three planes of the cube are visible, and thus two sets of lines and two vanishing points exist. In three-point perspective *(6)*, there are three sets of lines and three vanishing points. This occurs when the cube is viewed from far above or far below so that the vertical lines also converge.

**7**

Vanishing point (VP)

Horizon line (HL)

Picture plane (PP)

Centre line of vision (CV)

Station point SP

Ground line (GL)

Ground plane (GP)

### Preparation for drawing

When you have selected an object or series of objects which you intend to draw, you must locate a number of positions in front of you which are necessary for you to draw in perspective *(7)*. The principal ones are the vanishing points, the horizon line, the picture plane and the ground plane.

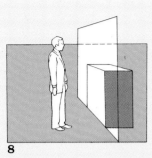

## Convergence

By working out a number of known measurements, it is possible to calculate the convergence of parallel lines. The drawing and the diagram *(8, 9)* depict two different views of the same scene. The object is flush against the picture plane and the shaded area in *(8)* represents the base of the object and its converging sides as seen by the spectator.

**8**

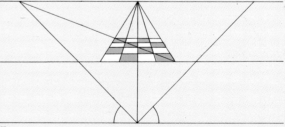

**9**

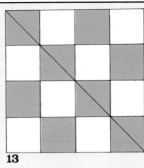

**13**

## Determining the angles of convergence of a grid

Firstly you must measure the width of the grid as well as the width of all the divisions. These distances can be measured out along the ground line (GL) *(13)*.

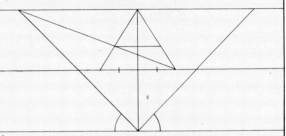

**14**

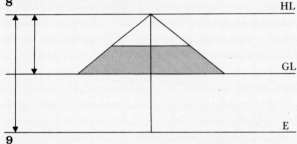

**10**

## Determining convergence

The drawing and the diagram *(10, 11)* depict two different views of the same scene. The object is located some way back from the picture plane. The shaded area in *(11)* represents the base of the object, its converging sides and its position in relation to the picture plane and the spectator.

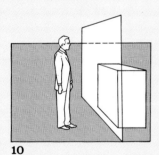

**11**

## Laying out the diagram

First measure the height of your eye above the surface which you are depicting (HL to GL) *(14)*. Then draw in the distance from the picture plane (HL to E). Draw in the centre line (CL). On the line (GL) you will have marked in the measurements of the front face of the grid and the

divisions inside it. From the standing point (SP), draw two lines at 45° to the eye line (E). These extend back to the horizon line (HL). From one of those points a line is drawn forwards to the opposite front corner of the grid.

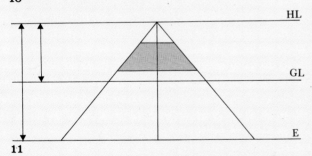

**15**

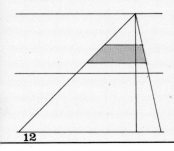

**12**

## Positioning the centre line

The centre line, and therefore the angles of convergence, are also determined by the spectator's position in relation to the front of the object. In *(7)* and *(8)* the spectator is positioned centrally, while in *(12)* he is positioned well to the right. As a result, the angles of convergence are equal.

## Completing the grid

Draw in the sides of the grid and the divisions within it so that they extend back from the ground line (GL) to the vanishing points (VP) *(15)*. The points at which these lines intersect the diagonal which you drew in are where the cross lines of the grid are located.

drawing is determined by where the horizontal line going through the eye meets the picture plane. This line is where the ground plane vanishes. It follows, therefore, that the vanishing points for all lines which are parallel to the line of the ground plane will be located on the horizon line. If you are drawing a box or room, for example, and your centre line of vision meets one of the end planes at right-angles, all the apparently converging lines will meet at the same single vanishing point. All the other lines will be either horizontal or vertical. When drawing this, you would be using one-point perspective. However, viewing this box or room obliquely will present two sets of parallels with which you have to deal. Each set of parallels will have its own

**Drawing curves in perspective** A square grid is constructed in which a circle is drawn *(1)*. In order to draw the circle in perspective, you will first have to draw the grid in perspective. The means of doing this has been explained on the previous page. You can then transpose your circle onto this grid *(2)*.

**Drawing a cylinder in perspective** By changing the height of the horizon line, you can alter the angle of perspective. In this case it has been done in order to extend the circle into a cylinder. As before, you have to use a grid onto which the circle can be drawn in perspective.

vanishing points, and this form of perspective is known as two-point perspective. You should also be aware of the existence of three-point perspective which requires the use of three vanishing points. Its construction is more advanced and is used predominantly in more specialist areas.

# Perspective and projections

If you wish to express ideas in two dimensions you will have to be able to express such ideas through drawing. You will also have to bear in mind that the object being drawn may not actually exist, being merely a visual representation of an idea in the mind. It is also very important that these ideas can be clearly and concisely communicated to a third person, for example if the object was to be manufactured. An accurate, measured perspective drawing will do this but during the developmental stages such visual devices are far too elaborate and uneconomic. Notions of shape and dimension at this early stage can be described by far simpler means. Accurate perspective drawings can be used once the ideas have been finally formalized.

Different techniques can be used for developing visual ideas. Orthographic projections are the most useful as they express all the necessary information relating to the shape, dimensions and arrangement of constituent parts. Such drawings utilize standard conventions so that information is expressed in an unambiguous manner. This would enable a third party to interpret and work accurately from the drawings.

It is often helpful to be able to produce drawings which visualize proposed objects three-dimensionally without the incumbent problems of perspective, and which can be referred to for dimensions and layout. Oblique, planometric, and isometric projections enable this to be done and are the most commonly employed techniques. These drawings are specifically objective and can take on very strange appearances.

Oblique projections are produced from orthographic flat elevations with the addition and construction of parallel sides drawn at convenient angles, usually 30° or 45°. The lengths of the sides are measured and drawn to scale. Planometric projections are produced similarly, using a plan view which is rotated through 45° and has measured verticals constructed to delineate the positions of the vertical sides of the object. All lines are therefore drawn as verticals or at 45°. Isometric projections are produced by selecting and drawing one vertical front edge of the objects to scale. The sides and top views are then constructed to scale from this edge at a convenient angle, usually 30°. Each of these drawings gives particular visual information about the object in terms of shape, form and arrangement together with dimensions. No attempt is made to utilize any form of perspective.

There are many ways by which space and form are perceived and recognized, likewise there are many basic means of attempting to delineate and explain what you see. The methods mentioned earlier are perhaps the more obvious but there are other drawing devices, such as point location or contouring, which in themselves can be treated in a variety of ways and are used in conjunction with notions of perspective. These are all useful tools which help clarify the awareness of space and depth needed by any artist.

Drawing, however, not only involves working in two dimensions, and you should feel free to respond in the way best suited to communicating your ideas. Interesting and quite exciting results can be achieved once it is realized that the picture plane itself can have depth, that you can use several picture planes one behind the other, that the picture plane itself can be dispensed with altogether so that you can simply draw in space three-dimensionally, and that the picture plane or volume of space can be elongated or distorted. Once these ideas move towards actual three-dimensional expression, pencils and crayons no longer suffice and other materials must be found. Metal wires, metal strips, cloth and yarn are a few of the materials which can be used.

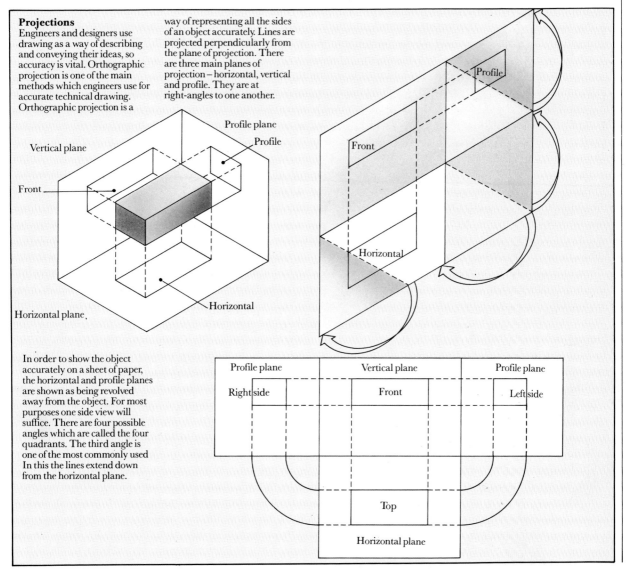

### Projections

Engineers and designers use drawing as a way of describing and conveying their ideas, so accuracy is vital. Orthographic projection is one of the main methods which engineers use for accurate technical drawing. Orthographic projection is a way of representing all the sides of an object accurately. Lines are projected perpendicularly from the plane of projection. There are three main planes of projection – horizontal, vertical and profile. They are at right-angles to one another.

In order to show the object accurately on a sheet of paper, the horizontal and profile planes are shown as being revolved away from the object. For most purposes one side view will suffice. There are four possible angles which are called the four quadrants. The third angle is one of the most commonly used In this the lines extend down from the horizontal plane.

# MEASURED DRAWING

Having begun to understand something of perspective, you can now start to apply those ideas. Measured perspective drawing is a useful way of familiarizing yourself with perspective and developing an accurate way of drawing. Careful re-appraisal of the information on perspective at each stage will help you greatly to understand underlying principles involved in using this drawing system. The method is devised to help you to draw accurately and perceive as objectively as possible. It recognizes the difference between looking and just seeing—perception in this sense is intentional and not passive.

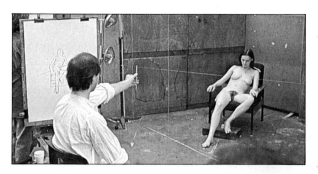

## Techniques

This method of drawing is based on the concept of a picture plane placed between the viewer and the object, a window to the world so to speak, existing at arm's

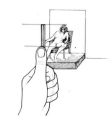

**Measured drawing** By holding a pencil at arm's length and closing one eye so as to avoid double vision, the artist can fix the object he wishes to draw *(ABOVE)*. The thumb is moved up and down the pencil *(LEFT)* so that the proportions of the object can be measured and then drawn to scale.

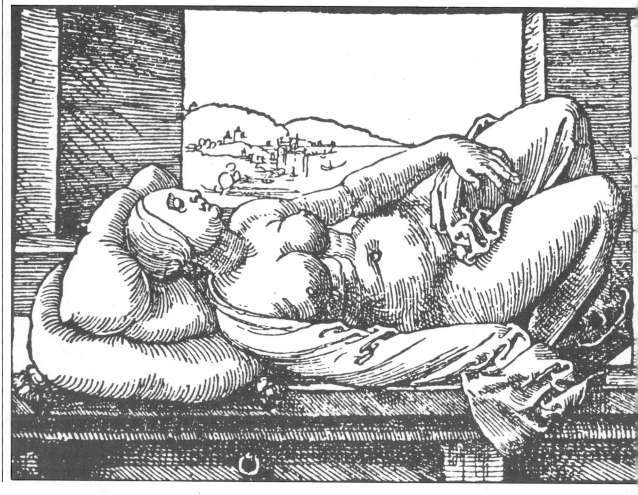

length. The pencil is used as a measuring device. Holding the drawing arm straight out, take vertical and horizontal measurements by sliding the fingers along the pencil and transferring those measurements to the drawing. The measurements are transferred onto the paper in the form of points. Having established a constant set of vertical and horizontal references you can then establish angular relationships. For this type of drawing, you must close one eye in order to take the measurements. If you do not you will see either two pencils and one object or one pencil and two objects. This is why the approach is called 'monocular' drawing. It is vitally important to maintain a fixed position when measuring and to hold your arm fully extended, otherwise serious anomalies will occur in your drawing. This can easily be put to the test.

Take measurements from the same point on the object, firstly with the arm fully extended and then with the elbow flexed. In transferring these two measure-

ments to your paper you will find that the second ones are much smaller. This indicates that if you transcribe the measurements directly to your paper, the drawing will shrink more the further from the object you are. If an object were to intrude between the picture plane and yourself, then the image would be projected larger than the object, in other words larger than lifesize. You should also remember that, as your arm moves in a circle on an axis describing a hemisphere, the picture plane is curved and so small distortions will occur. The obvious answer to this problem would be to draw or

This picture by Albrecht Dürer (*BELOW*) shows a system of measured drawing which involves the use of a grid. Though the system requires considerable care in being set up, it should guarantee considerable accuracy. A vertical frame incorporating a grid is placed between the subject and the artist. This grid represents the picture plane. The artist then draws this grid to scale on the drawing paper. By regarding the subject through the grid, it can be transposed accurately onto the drawing surface.

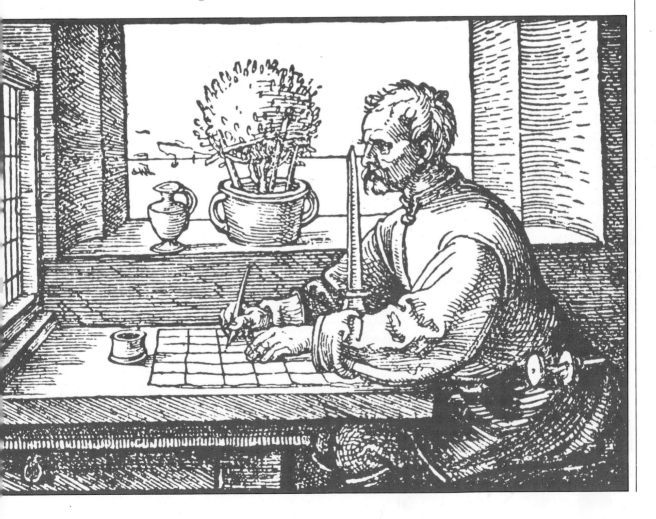

paint on a hemispherical surface to accommodate the distortion. The resulting picture would then have to be observed from a central point with one eye or through a small hole.

It is important for you to realize that measuring is quantifiable, that is to say, under the rules of measured drawing there is a correct answer. Mistakes are inaccuracies which can be corrected by anybody using the same viewpoint with small adjustments to the seating arrangements to accommodate any difference in arm length.

In measured drawing, points are placed to indicate where lines change direction. These lines themselves can denote a wide range of information. They can define the edges of objects, changes of colour or zones of different tone, although these last can be difficult to convey as they often merge through a series of subtle gradations. Strong side lighting or half closing the eyes when viewing the object can help you isolate and note down major areas of tone.

Another useful tool for producing a measured drawing is a grid. You can use transparent grids

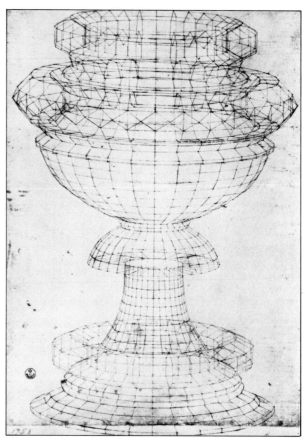

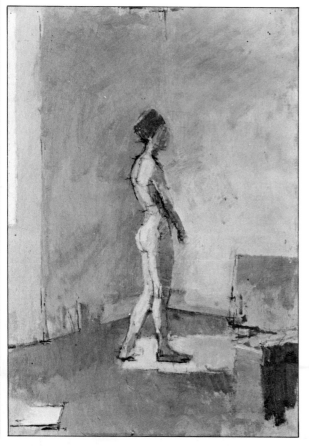

This drawing by Uccello depicting an urn *(ABOVE)* is a good example of a perspective drawing using a grid system. All the surfaces are clearly worked out using the two-dimensional grid. *A Standing Nude* by Uglow *(LEFT)* was sketched during its early stages using the measured drawing system. At various points around the body, it is possible to see the measuring marks describing the contours.

placed in front of the object which you are drawing. When doing this, the vertical plane of the grid represents the picture plane. By producing a grid of the same proportions on drawing paper you can transcribe the image directly through the grid of the picture plane onto the drawing surface. In addition to this you can, by using grids, make formalized enlargements and distortions of the objects in front of you. Grids can be used in many kinds of drawing.

Visual rays can also help you produce accurate silhouettes. If you place an object close to a flat surface and shine a spotlight squarely on it, you can draw around the cast shadow. This will give you a life-size image that reproduces the outer contours of the object. You can even draw directly around the outline of an object.

Observing and measuring silhouettes and spaces between shapes often leads to rather flat drawings so that it is vital to remember that there are other means by which you can perceive and portray three-dimensional space. These visual clues include aerial perspective, texture gradients and blurring.

You may decide eventually that such a drawing system is too rigid for your needs, but you should, nevertheless, get to grips with it at an early stage. It will be easy enough to distort it if you want but it will not be easy to apply it suddenly to some situation if you have never learnt it.

## MEASURED DRAWING

Take a subject, a figure or an object, and position it in some environment so that you have a reasonably complex composition to draw. Using your pencil, start measuring the distances between the various objects in the composition. Begin by noting a configuration of dots, and then start to build up a series of short, tentative lines so that the contours of the objects become better defined. From this stage onwards, you should continue filling in so that the subject emerges clearly from paper. Do not overemphasize the lines because contours do not represent the whole of an object. Later you should define the surfaces inside the contours and describe the play of light over them.

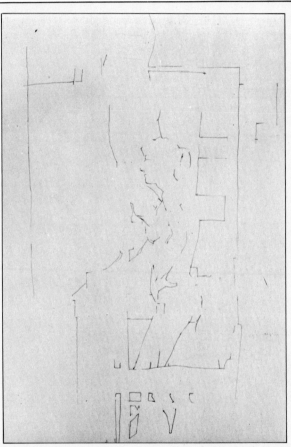

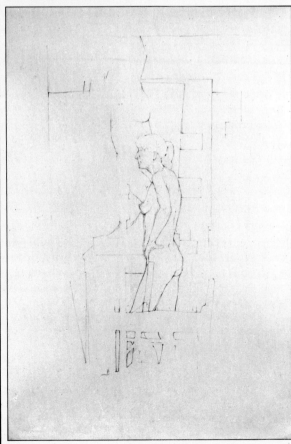

The artist has begun by pin-pointing the extremities of the subject and consolidating the basis of the composition. The position of the figure in relation to the objects around it and its position on the paper itself have been lightly laid in. In the early stages, the artist has not bothered to clarify any of the details or indeed complete any of the contours of the subject. At a later stage more refined detail has been included. The features of the face have been incorporated and more solidity given to the body so that it stands out from its background. The lines which have been used are all short and this has enabled the artist to build up the image steadily and alter the stress of any of the marks, thereby retaining a balance between the various objects.

# DESIGN AND PROPORTION

Proportion is an idea which has preoccupied artists since the ancient Greeks. Artists have felt that notions of proportion and proportional relationships can be founded in mathematics, whereas, the analysis of colour, for instance has often proved more difficult to bring within a scientific discipline. However, the significance of proportion is not just as a series of rules or principles to follow. It has been just as important for artists to reject and do without them as for them to be adhered to slavishly; for, in the final instance, the most important thing for an artist is to achieve whatever they want in the way that seems best, regardless of rules, conventions or principles.

One influential precept of proportion was the 'Golden Mean' and 'Golden Section'. The Golden Mean was first worked out by the Roman architect Vitruvius in his lengthy treatise *De Architecture* in the first century AD. Vitruvius held that the most harmonious relationship between unequal parts of a whole was achieved if the smaller was in the same proportion to the larger as the larger is to the whole.

The proportions of the human body have also occupied artists. Artists such as Leonardo and Dürer have been fascinated with proportion and devoted much effort to working it out. It was felt that the human body divides into eight parts. Using these ideas of proportion and learning to work with them are useful for the beginner. Never use them rigidly if they do not serve the ends you wish to achieve.

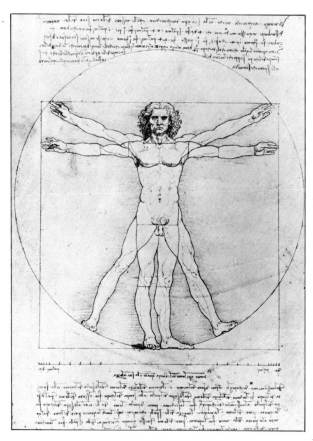

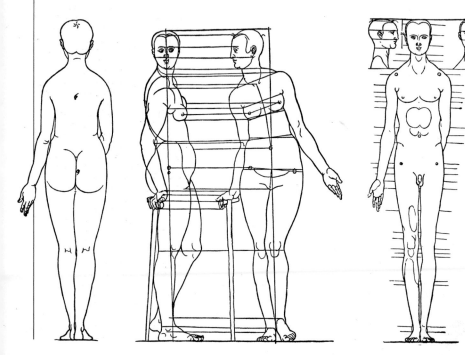

The proportions of the human figure have greatly preoccupied artists, particularly during and since the Renaissance, although earlier artists too has been concerned with the same subjects. This can be seen in Leonardo's *Study of Human Proportions (ABOVE)*, one of the most famous Renaissance attempts to grapple with human proportions, which is, in fact, Leonardo's drawing from a text by Vitruvius, the Roman architect and engineer of the first century AD. Vitruvius held that the navel is in the centre of the body and that a circle drawn from the navel would touch the outstretched fingers and toes of a man lying on his back. He also noticed that the distance between a man's outstretched fingers is about the same as that between the crown of his head and the soles of his feet. This forms a square. Albrecht Dürer also devoted extensive attention to the proportions of the human figure and the relationshps between different parts of the body *(LEFT)*.

**Golden Section** The principle of the Golden Section for long governed the 'ideal' proportions of a triangle and other forms.

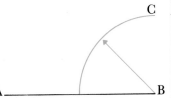

**1.** The line A–B is divided into two equal sections.

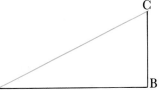

**2.** With the compass on B, draw an arc from the midpoint of the line to C, which is at right-angles to B.

**3.** Join C to A and then B, forming a right-angled triangle.

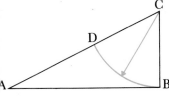

**4.** Put the compass on C and draw an arc from B to cut A–C at point D.

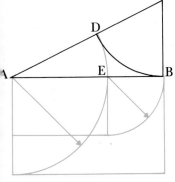

**5.** With the compass on A, draw an arc from B to cut A–B at E. The line E–B is in proportion to A–E as A–E is to A–B. You can now draw a rectangle with the proportions of the Golden Mean.

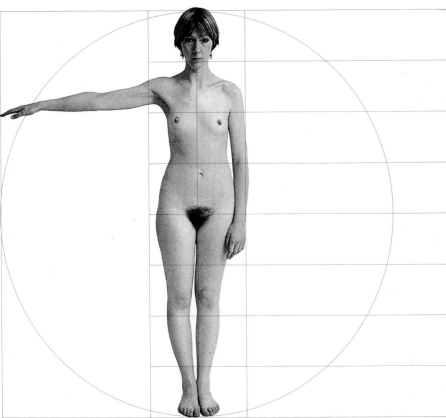

The studies of Leonardo da Vinci and Dürer among others showed that the human body divides into eight equal sections (*ABOVE*). The distance from the crown of the head to the chin is one eighth of the height of the whole body. The navel is about five eighths of the height of the whole body. Similar proportions hold for the horizontal measurements of the body, the distance from the outstretched finger tips of the left hand to those of the right hand is about equal to that from the soles of the feet to the crown of the head. It is possible to divide the figure into even smaller proportions. You should experiment with these proportions, seeing how they can be drawn on paper. Think about how the proportions change if, for example, the body is inclined to one side (*FAR LEFT*). Examine the proportions of a sitting figure. However, it is important for you to realize that no two bodies are exactly the same. The proportions may vary slightly from individual to

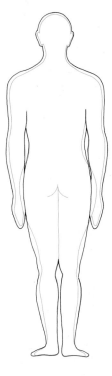

individual, but the general principle that the human body divides into eight equal sections is a good overall guide, especially for the beginner. One of the reasons why the Renaissance artists were particularly concerned with proportion was that the study of anatomy was a subject of detailed investigation at that time. As well as being aware of the overall proportions of the human figure, you should consider how the skeleton forms the frame for the muscles and flesh. There are some differences between the skeletons and figures of men and women (*LEFT*). In general, women tend to have broader pelvises, and the distribution of muscles over the figure differs slightly. The usefulness of guides to the principles of proportion such as this is that they are a guide, and no more. You should always be guided by your own eye and perception, rather than feeling that you have to adhere slavishly to a series of rules.

# DESIGN AND COMPOSITION

The ways in which ideas of proportion and form are applied depend not only on the eye or perception of the artist. An extremely important element is the size and shape of the surface you will be using. Another is the way in which the image is arranged on that surface. If you know what you want to draw or paint, consider at the outset the format of the surface on which you are going to depict it. Should the format be vertical (or portrait), or horizontal (or landscape)? If you are doing some preliminary sketches, experiment with formats to see which suits the subject best.

The next matter to consider is the position of the image on the surface and within the format you have chosen. Do you want the image to occupy a large or small area of the surface? Is the best position for the image in the centre or to one side? Consider in this regard too the areas around the image itself. How important is the background? Do you want it to blend in with the subject? Should the subject dominate or be dominated by its surroundings? If you are drawing a figure, do you simply want to depict the figure? Do you want to show the figure in the context of another figure, some objects or even in an exterior or interior setting? What relationship do you want to establish between the elements in the picture. Placing objects close together can imply some connection between them. On the other hand, objects placed far away from one another can seem distanced. For example, two figures sitting closely together with their heads inclined creates an intimate image, while the same figures standing one at each side of the picture, their backs to one another, may create an impression of distance or alienation. Similarly, a building placed among other larger buildings may seem less significant than the same building standing in splendid isolation in a rolling landscape. These are very important considerations for any artist, and, especially at the beginning, you should try to develop patience when working out the arrangement of the subject.

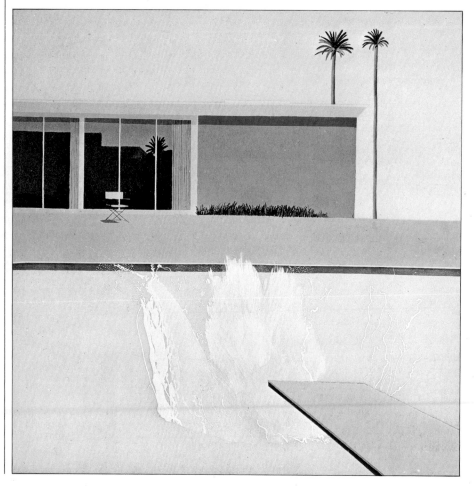

David Hockney, the major contemporary artist, shows an acute awareness of design and composition in his works. The forms in *A Bigger Splash* (LEFT), painted in 1967, contrast sharply. The main subject of the picture was the splash, a momentary explosion of water a split second after the swimmer dived into the water. The swirling lines of the splashing water stand out against the clear colours of the house and setting. Painted in California, the picture gives a very strong impression of the quality of light and clear colours characteristic of the area. Hockney composed his picture using a drawing he had recently done of the building and a photograph taken from a technical manual on swimming pools for the splash. The fact that the figure who has (presumably) just dived into the pool is not actually visible is an important element in the picture. The splash occupies the central position in the picture, the eye being led to it by the diving board. The palm trees, building, carefully positioned chair and the reflection in the window are also vital to the picture's effect. The artist used a roller to apply the acrylic paint. This helped create the smooth tone of the colours.

## POSITIONING THE FIGURE

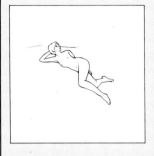 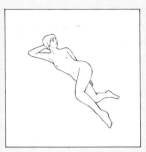 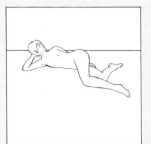 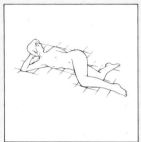

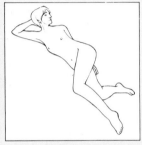 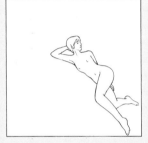 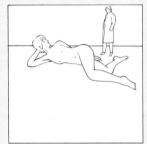 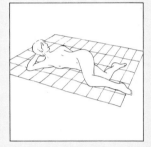

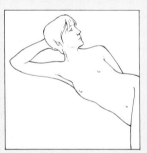 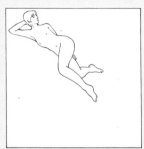 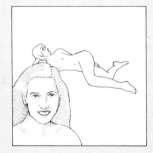 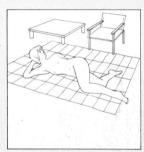

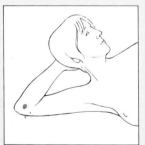 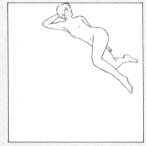 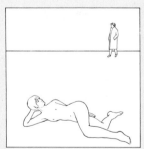 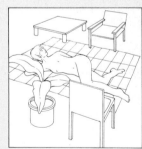

The position of the figure on the surface of your drawing or painting is crucial to the final image. For this project, select a format and do as many studies as you can of a model in one position, placing the figure on the surface in as many different positions as possible. Then combine the model with, for example, another figure or some objects. Look at what you have achieved and assess the advantages and disadvantages of each pose. Factors which you could examine individually include size, position, scale, and background. Repeating this exercise several times with different figures and formats will give you valuable insights into the way design and composition affect the picture you make. This project is also a good lead-in to the use of sketchbooks as a way of working out ideas by experimenting with different approaches before you embark on your actual drawing or painting.

# SHAPE AND FORM

Shape and form are vital elements in the organization of any work of art. Neither shape nor form, however, is an absolute. As with so much in art, a lot depends firstly on the perception and skill of the artist, and his or her ability to convey ideas, and, on the other, on the eye of the spectator and how the image is perceived. Any shape can represent many different forms depending on whether it is, for instance, drawn in line alone or has tone or shadow added. When considering a drawing or painting, you should always think about the forms you want to depict.

Think of them not just as positive shapes against a background, consider also the shape of the background and the relationships between the different parts of the background. Shapes can be positive or negative and the relationship between the two is extremely important for conveying an impression of solidity or three-dimensionality in your work. It is a useful exercise to experiment with drawing one image in as many different ways as possible. Some suggestions are to draw the image as line, line with tone, as shadow alone, as tone alone. Try out different ways of showing tone—one-directional line, cross-hatching, blended charcoal tones, lines in hard pencil or heavily applied soft pencil.

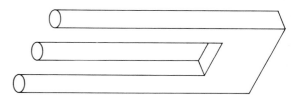

**Line and form** It is difficult to give the impression of solidity using line alone. Indeed, a highly deceptive image can be created (*ABOVE*). Artists such as the Dutch painter Maurits Escher have deliberately exploited such possibilities in their work. The addition of shading and tone can help you to avoid such ambiguity. Another important type of potential visual ambiguity of which you should be aware in your work as an artist is the balance between positive and negative shapes. The image (*RIGHT*) can be either two profiles facing one another or a candle stick, depending on the way you look at it. If you are thinking about painting or drawing a scene, it is a good idea to look at it in terms of both the positive and negative shapes and the

relationship between them. These two types of ambiguity show that neither shape nor form is an absolute, the impression of both depends on the eye and skill of the artist as well as on the perception of the viewer.

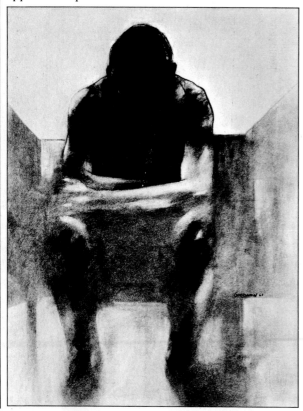

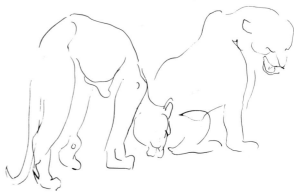

There are many different approaches to conveying form in drawing, two widely varied ones are illustrated here. In Sydney Goodman's *Man Waiting* (*LEFT*), the artist has used the expressive possibilities offered by his medium, charcoal, to create a powerful study of the man's figure. The clear outline of the man's bowed head and shoulders contrasts with the heavy shading applied to the upper part of the body. The shading becomes much lighter in the lower half of the body. Highlights on the arms add to

the impression of solidity created. A very different approach is seen in *Lionesses* by the French artist and sculptor Henri Gaudier-Brzeska (*ABOVE*). The great potential of simple line work is shown in the impression of fluidity and movement created in this powerful study of feline forms.

**Form and shape** The impression of solidity which many artists seek in their work is created normally by a combination of lines which give shape to what otherwise might be merely a line of series of lines. There are many ways of creating an impression of solidity with a basic shape such as a circle. This series of shapes *(RIGHT)* is based on a simple circle *(1)*. With the addition of shading and tone the circle can become a disc *(2)*, hole *(4)* or sphere *(5)*. The same circle can be converted into a cylinder *(3)* by adding another circle, two lines and some shading. You will need to practice and experiment to enable you to be able to convey three-dimensional form and shape on a two-dimensional surface. Take a simple shape and try out as many ways of adding shape and form to it as possible. As well as the ones shown here, use different types of line, solid shading and highlights. Look at the effects of light and shade on the environment around you.

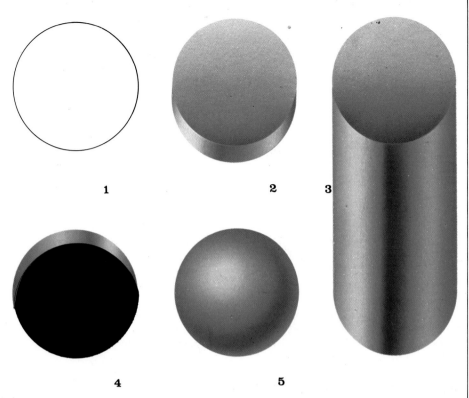

1    2    3

4    5

## EXPRESSING FORM

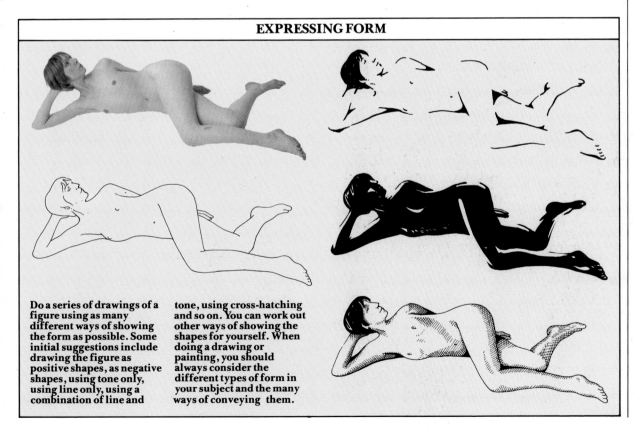

Do a series of drawings of a figure using as many different ways of showing the form as possible. Some initial suggestions include drawing the figure as positive shapes, as negative shapes, using tone only, using line only, using a combination of line and tone, using cross-hatching and so on. You can work out other ways of showing the shapes for yourself. When doing a drawing or painting, you should always consider the different types of form in your subject and the many ways of conveying them.

# COLOUR

For artists at all levels, the study of colour is both exacting and rewarding. Colour is important in all the arts—from painting to films, photography, sculpture, design and printing. The history and traditions of colour in art are extremely rich and varied, ranging from the first mark made by cave dwellers with coloured earth or ash to today's high technology of laser colour. There is also a wide range of theories about the use of colour in art, but these need not concern you at this stage. Similarly, the science of colour is also difficult to approach for those new to the study of colour. Colour systems and science, however, seem remote from the artist alone with his or her ideas and paints. Nonetheless, it is most important for the artist, however inexperienced, to experiment with different coloured paints and papers. It is virtually impossible to be objective about colour, constant experiment and analysis of what you have achieved are essential for you to acquire and develop knowledge of and skill with colour. When beginning to study colour, many artists discover aspects of colour which then last them throughout their careers.

## Colour—types and properties

One of the most influential experiments with colour was the splitting of white light into its constituent spectrum of colours using a triangular prism by the English scientist Sir Isaac Newton (1642–1727) in the mid 1660s. Newton named seven divisions of colour—red, orange, yellow, green, blue, indigo and violet, the colours of the rainbow. The artist's colour wheel, a popular traditional colour aid for artists, is similar to the Newtonian divisions, except it only has six divisions—red, orange, yellow, green, blue and violet.

The study of colour has long been preoccupied with the idea that all colours can be made from a smaller group of fundamental colours, called 'primary' colours. The primary colours derived from the spectrum are red, yellow and blue. 'Secondary' colours—or those made by combining primary colours—are orange, green and violet. Three pairs of colours can be made when each primary is paired with a secondary. On the colour wheel these form a series of diametrical pairs, called 'complementary pairs'. Yellow and violet form one pair, red and green another, and blue and orange the third.

However, this neat grouping of colours has its problems for the artist. It is based entirely on the visible spectrum of light, and does not transfer well into terms of pigments, because the spectrum relies on the absolute purity of the primary colours. This is difficult to achieve in pigments. This means that, if you mix yellow and

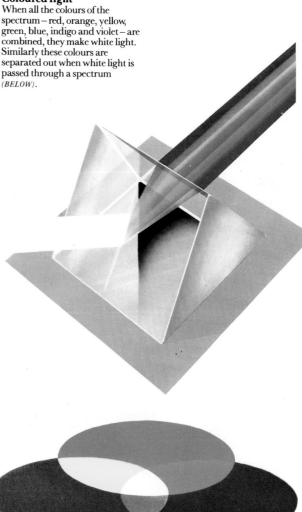

**Coloured light**
When all the colours of the spectrum – red, orange, yellow, green, blue, indigo and violet – are combined, they make white light. Similarly these colours are separated out when white light is passed through a spectrum *(BELOW)*.

**Additive primaries**
Red, green and blue are the additive primaries. When all three are combined they create white light. The secondary colours which they make are yellow, magenta and cyan.

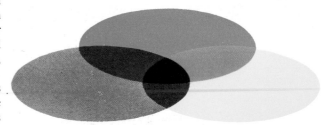

**Subtractive primaries**
Cyan, magenta and yellow are the subtractive primaries. When they are combined they make black. The secondary colours which they make are red, violet and green.

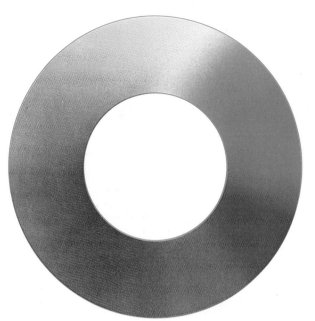

### Complementary colours
The complementary colours are those which are at opposite sides of the colour wheel. Complementary colours contain no common primary colours. The three sets of complementaries are orange and blue, yellow and violet and red and green.

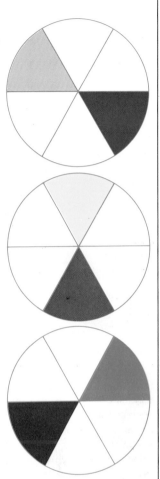

**Colour wheel** The colour wheel shows the colours and the main gradations between them. The three primary colours *(RIGHT)* when mixed together create the secondary colours of green, violet and orange *(BELOW)*.

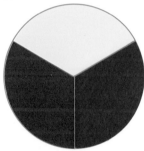

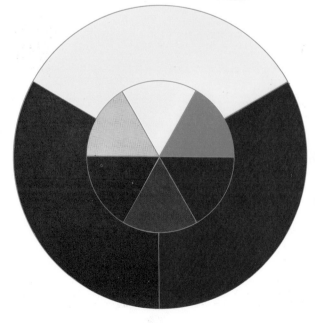

### Mixing pigments
The primary colours in painting are red, blue and yellow. Combining red and yellow produces orange; a mixture of blue and yellow makes green. Mixing red and blue does not create the expected violet but a nondescript brown.

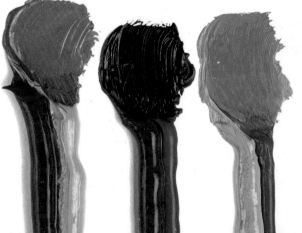

blue light, green will result, but if you mix yellow and blue paint, the rather muddy result might be termed 'green', but bears little relationship to green pigment. Similarly, blue pigment mixed with red does not produce purple pigment. Bear this in mind when working with colours. You can make a spectral colour wheel with your paints. When you have made the basic version, try to expand it, finding new subtleties of colour between each segment in a systematic way.

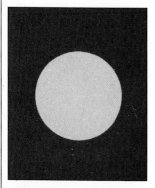

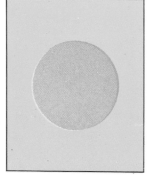

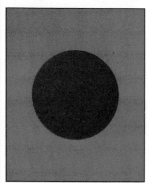

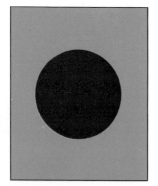

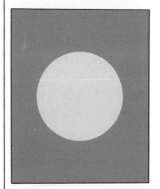

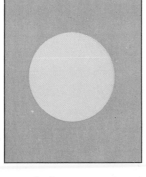

**Colour perception**
The individual's perception of colour is affected by the colour of the background on which the main colour is seen. In these examples *(ABOVE)* a light grey, dark grey and pale green are seen against different backgrounds. Examine how the middle colour appears to change, although it in fact remains the same.

# Experiments with colour

So much about colour is taken for granted. Even the artist is often blind to the vast storehouse of limitless colours and colour relationships which are all around. You should be wary of assumptions which you may—even unconsciously—have about colour. These may limit your openness to new possibilities in colour and new combinations of colours. Your own continuing observations of the real world should form the basis of your use of colour in your drawing or painting. To help you find out more about colours and their properties, keep a colour notebook. Include in it any interesting colours you come across. Over a period of time, this will build up into a document showing the almost infinite range of possible colours you can use.

Another useful experiment is to try to put down on a sheet of paper divided into squares as many variations on one colour as possible. In addition to pigments—singly and in combination—use papers and a variety of other coloured objects.

These ideas will help you understand the potential of your paints. Mixing different pigments and adding new colours will deepen your knowledge of colours and how they work. This may seem a rather unsystematic approach, but there is no substitute for knowledge about colour gained from personal observation.

# Colours in combination

Using colours together skilfully enables the artist to exploit the language of colour to the full. Although it has often been thought that there were rules about combining different colours, there are no intrinsically 'right' or 'wrong' colour combinations. Most cultures and times have their own assumptions about which colours may be combined and which are associated with particular groups of people. In Western cultures, for example, black is usually associated with death and mourning, whereas historically white has the same function in China.

Today, however, people are surrounded by colour in all aspects of their daily lives—not just the colours of the natural world, but new developments such as dayglo, neon and laser colours. All around, colours combine and interact in a wide variety of ways and you should try to become aware of the ways in which this occurs.

The appearance of a colour often depends on its context. Yellow on a white background will appear very different from the same yellow on a black background. Identical blues on a red, yellow and green background

## COLOUR WHEEL

Draw a circle and divide it into 12 equal segments. Now paint in the three primary (red, yellow and blue) and three secondary colours (orange, green and violet) in the positions indicated on the diagram. When this has been done, you can mix the adjacent pairs and fill in the gaps in between with the resultant mix. How would you describe the colours produced? This exercise will enable you to make your own – albeit simple – colour wheel.

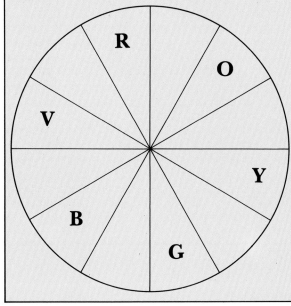

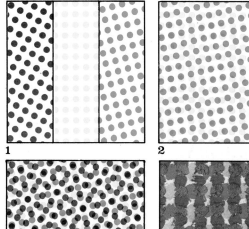

1

2

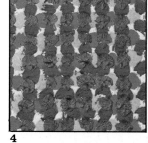

3

4

**Process colours**
In printing, the full colour spectrum is made up from numerous dots of the three colours known as the process colours. These colours are cyan, yellow and magenta *(1)*. When combined in varying proportions, most colours can be produced. For example, cyan and yellow combine to produce green *(2)*. When printed colours are magnified, the combinations of dots can be seen *(3)*. You can see the dots on some large advertisements if you look closely. The phenomenon of colours combining in the viewer's eye has been used by artists, especially the nineteenth century Pointillists who used dots of pigment to create apparently solid colours as well as subtle tonal variations *(4)*.

## PAINT TEXTURE

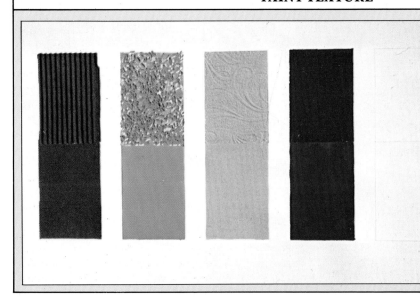

The colours on the left have been textured and you will notice that the areas which have been so affected appear darker in tone. This is because of the shadows which are thrown over the surface. Lay down some strips of colour and try this out for yourself, experimenting with different types of texture. Use a variety of media as well as a number of texture-producing materials. Possible choices include textured papers, sticking rice to the surface and so on. Texture is an aspect of the perception of colour which has been exploited by artists throughout the ages.

## OPTICAL MIXING OF COLOUR

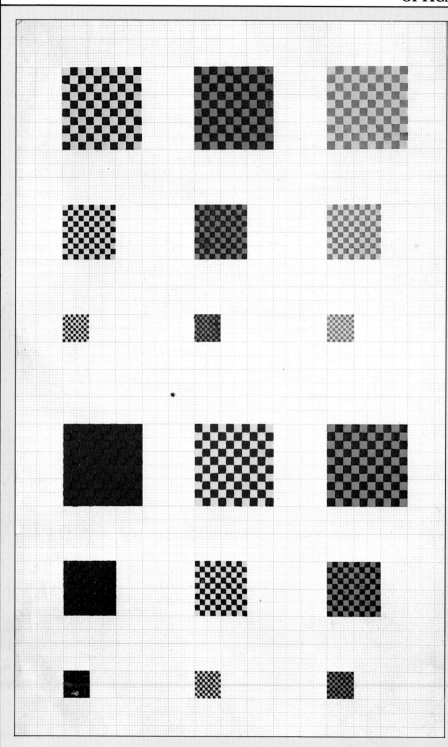

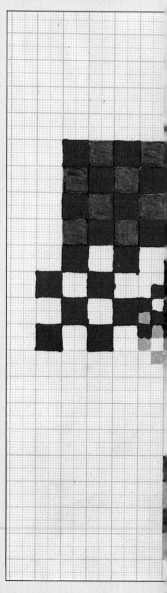

**Take a sheet of graph paper.** On this you can build up organized grids of colour, combining first the primary colours and then the secondary colours. You will see how in the first instance optical fusion results in secondary colours being formed and how in the second you make broken or tertiary colours. There is no reason though to stick rigidly to these arrangements. Experiment with mixing secondary and primary colours together and then try mixing more than two colours. Leave some squares blank or add some black squares so as to change the tonal values.

*In the first of these two examples (LEFT), the artist has varied the* scale of the patterns and in doing so has altered the manner in which the colours fuse. The smaller the squares, the smoother the resultant colour appears to be. In the second sheet (BELOW), the artist has placed colour combinations adjacent to each other. By doing this, double fusion has been achieved. That is to say, the individual colours fuse together and then the areas fuse with those next to them.

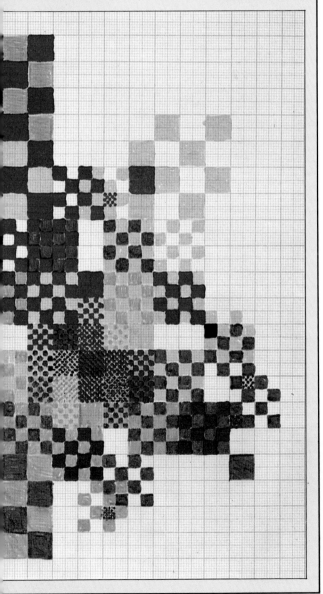

will again differ in appearance. Making colours on your palette forms new colours, but colours can also be mixed optically, or in the viewer's eye. This was the reason why the nineteenth century Impressionist painters particularly used broken colour on their canvases. What seems to be an area of a single colour on an Impressionist painting will often consist of many small fragments of separate colours. For example, a violet area may be made from quite separate brushmarks of red and blue pigment. The violet colour results from the red and blue combining in the viewer's eye and brain. The small scale and large number of the different marks makes it impossible for the eye and brain to identify individually, so the combination presents the viewer with the impression of violet. Blue and yellow can be used in the same way to create green. One of the great masters of this use of colour was the French artist Georges Seurat (1859–1891).

Since the early nineteenth century, industry has produced many completely new colours and has greatly improved the quality of colours which had hitherto been difficult to produce as pigments for painting. Until the nineteenth century, artists must have seen and known many colours which could not be included in art because they could not be manufactured. Industrial development has helped by making traditional colours more readily available. Ready prepared colours in pots or tubes are also much more convenient to use and have an extremely high degree of permanence and durability.

Today, colours are being produced which were undreamed of even 30 years ago. Metallic paints, fluorescent and laser colours are only some of the colours and colour qualities familiar today. In addition, most of these new colours are readily available to anyone from art stores, decorator's shops or printers. This proliferation of new colours has had a profound effect on the use of colour in art and design. It has also influenced artists' ideas about colour. The colour wheel of six hues derived from the spectrum, divided into three primary colours and three secondary colours seems less important than it did formerly. All these new colours have found or will find their way into painting, sculpture and design. They can all be used by the artist. Investigate some of these materials; they may provide you with new ideas and inspiration.

The projects in this section show you some of the ways in which colours can be combined. Try these ideas out, but also always try to work out your own ways of using colour and creating new and different colour effects. Whatever medium and surface you use, an awareness of and willingness to explore colour are vital for you as an artist.

## RANDOM COLOUR COMBINATIONS

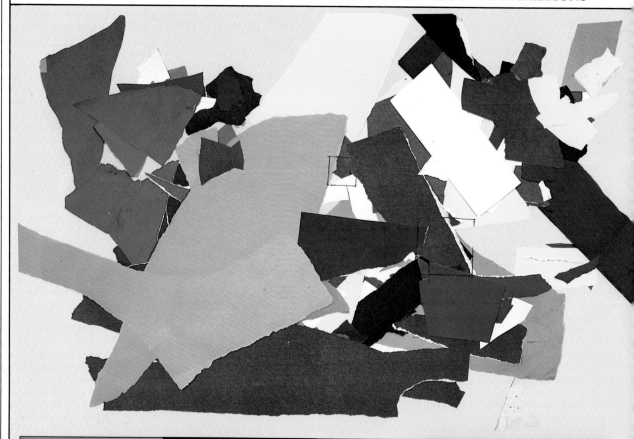

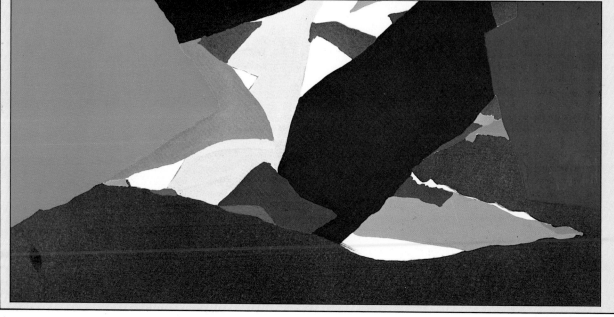

Take sheets of coloured paper and cut these into arbitrary and irregular shapes. Drop these onto a sheet of white paper so that they arrange themselves in a completely accidental fashion. After this, stick them down to the paper in the same manner as they fell. Select a small area and endeavour to recreate the colour arrangements using paint. You will find this a useful exercise in perception which you will be able to repeat many times.

## SYMMETRICAL COLOUR PATTERNS

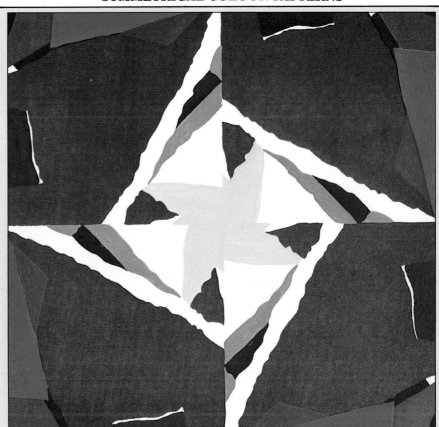

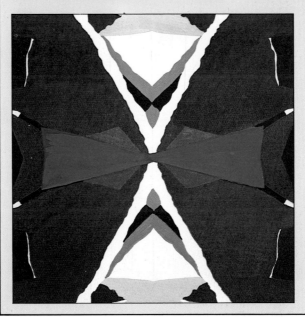

*From the area of random colour (ABOVE LEFT), the student selected an area in the centre and painted it in gouache. As the original consisted of coloured papers, the colour had to be matched exactly. In this example (LEFT) the main colours are green and blue with some red. Orange, yellow and purple are less important. Look at the area you have chosen and work out the relationships between the colours. How does the painted sample area differ in appearance and impact when it is isolated from its surrounding colour sequence? Repeat this exercise with other areas of the same sheet, or do the same with different colour combinations. This exercise is valuable for making you familiar with how colours work in combination and for questioning any assumptions you may have about colour by showing unusual combinations.*

Isolate a square area from the chance sheet. Draw out a square grid of four squares each one the size of the square you selected. Now paint in the original square into the grid four times but each time have the different side of the original square uppermost.

*This exercise shows how you can use chance configurations to create a symmetrical pattern. Look at what you have done and assess the balance of the pattern. How do the colours work together? Which is the main colour? Both the examples illustrated have a predominance of red. Examine how this colour interacts with the other colours. This exercise is an example of how you can create shape out of apparently random conjunctions of colours. Using your sheet of random colour, repeat the exercise several times using different areas of the sheet as examples.*

## COLOUR IN

The study of colour in nature is very important for the artist. For this project, you should select a plant or other natural object and make several studies of it in different media. Think of the subject in terms of its colour, how the colours change in different lights, how the colours relate to the textures of the surfaces, how the colours are affected by the shape of the object. How can you best convey the three-dimensionality of the subject on a two-dimensional surface? Combine the media you choose with different techniques. For instance, try rendering the subject in pen and ink using various types of line or cross-hatching to convey the surfaces and textures. Rarely does nature present you with a flat surface with no variations of colour. Try to work out the minute changes across the surface of a leaf, for example, look at the tiny indentations and veins or where one leaf overlaps with another. Depth is another factor which you should consider. Think about the shadows, undulations and hollows on the surfaces. If the plant you select is relatively simple, repeat the exercise with a more complex series of colours and forms, such as a flowering plant or collection of leaves or mosses. Before you start to draw or paint, do not forget to look at your subject from varying angles and viewpoints.

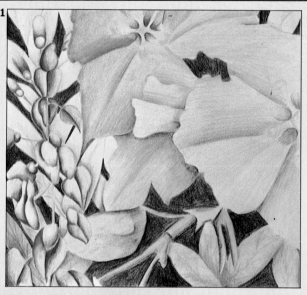

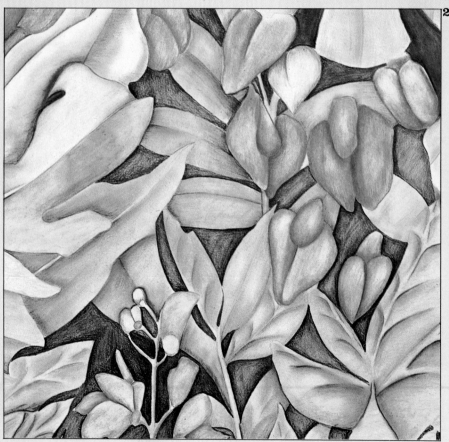

*For this project the artist selected a lobelia as the subject of her study. This plant offers a combination of variegated colour and differing textures which the student has tried to research and depict in various ways. The first studies (1,2,3) were done in coloured pencil to different scales. Doing a drawing on a large scale will allow you to explore the tiny variations in colour more extensively than is possible on a smaller format. Look at the different blues and greens used in these studies. As the next step in her examination of the colour in the plants, the student decided to use graph paper on which to stick pieces of coloured paper (5). It would also be possible to try the same approach with coloured pencils (6), using a slightly different colour for as many of the squares as possible. Using graph paper helped the student concentrate on the colours rather than the forms. The end result is therefore somewhat two-dimensional. The purpose of making studies such as these is to explore the subject from as many different aspects as you can. Therefore, you should not hesitate to experiment, no matter how unlikely your ideas might seem at first.*

## NATURE

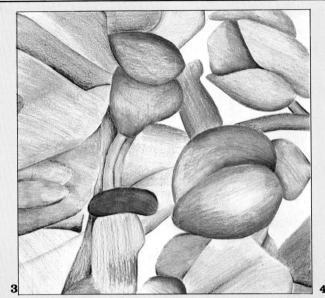

3

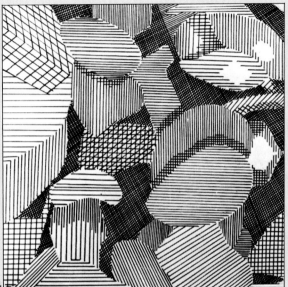

4

5

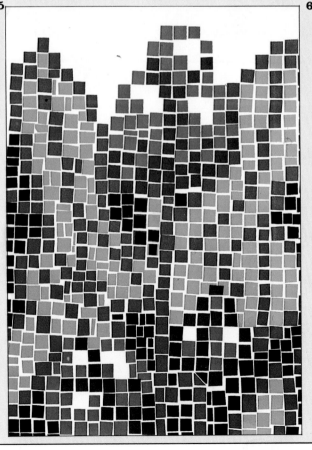

6

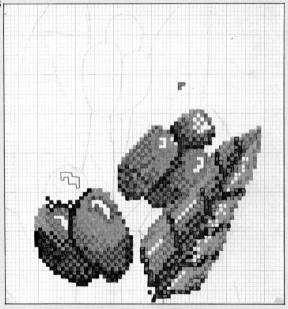

It is useful to do sketches of the subject in different media. For instance the artist here used pen and ink to do a black and white study (4). She has used different weights and configurations of line. This is an effective way of exploring the texture of the surfaces, as opposed to their colour. In some respects, this example is the counterpart to the colour examination with graph paper. The artist who did these studies is a textile designer, and so she continued her examination of the lobelia into textiles which showed the striations and textures of the plant very effectively. Do not feel that you have to restrict your interests just to drawing or painting.

For this project, try to see the whole environment around you in terms of colour. If possible, set up a corner in your studio or the room in which you paint and fill it with as many different colours as you can. Include stripes, flat colours, patterns, plants, rugs, in short anything which has a strong colour. The exact way in which you combine these elements is less important than juxtaposing as many different colours as you can. This will stimulate your imagination and help you see new facets in the widely varied world of colour. When you have set up the colour studio, take some tissue paper and portray your colour environment on paper, using only the tissue paper. This type of collage work is particularly effective with tissue paper because the paper is translucent, and so it can be stuck down in layers to show subtle colour modulations.

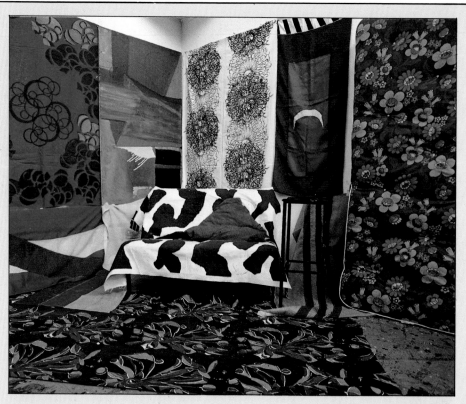

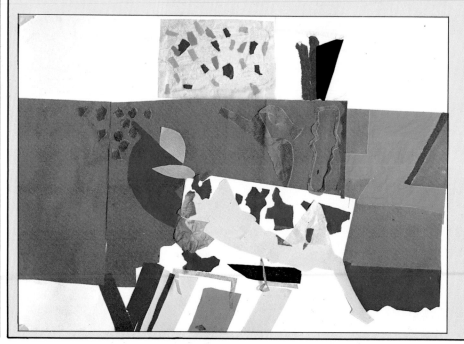

In the colour studio setting (ABOVE), you can see how many different colours have been combined to give a vibrant environment of colour. Note especially how bright floral patterns have been juxtaposed with stripes and more solid areas of colour. Using tissue paper, it would obviously be difficult to render all the detail exactly, so these examples show how the students have tried to convey the atmosphere and overall impression of the studio in their pictures. Also you will notice that these pictures do not reflect exactly the colours in the studio. This is because the students have become interested in colour for its own sake and have begun to concentrate on the impact of colour within the work rather than as a reflection of reality. This is something which this project should encourage you to do. The basic setting should stimulate your your responses to and awareness of colour. The main colour in the first example (LEFT) is orange with some emphasis on its complementary blue.

**▶LLAGE**

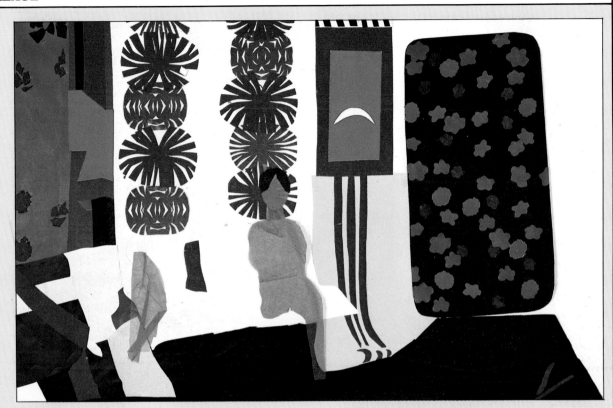

This image (ABOVE) shows an attempt to depict the studio in a fairly naturalistic way. The shapes of the red and orange wall-hanging have been cut out and stuck down. Similarly, the blue flowers and patterns on the righthand side of the picture were cut out from different colours of tissue paper. The artist has made good use of the translucency of coloured paper, on the figure for example. When working with tissue paper, keep the shapes you cut out simple until you develop confidence in dealing with the material. More complicated shapes can be difficult to stick down.

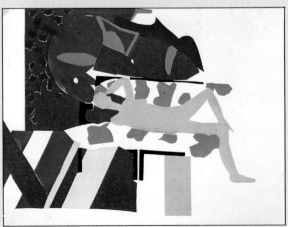

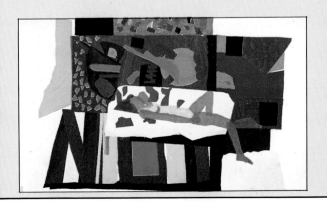

These two images show the figure in almost identical poses, but the subject has been treated differently. In the first (ABOVE) the figure is a much paler colour than in the second (LEFT). The cover on which the model is lying has also been depicted differently, being a lighter blue in the first and darker in the second. Both examples, however, show the artists concentrating on the qualities of the colour rather than on the figure.

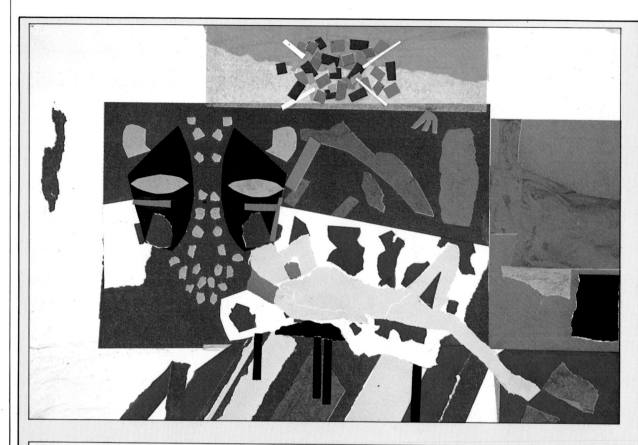

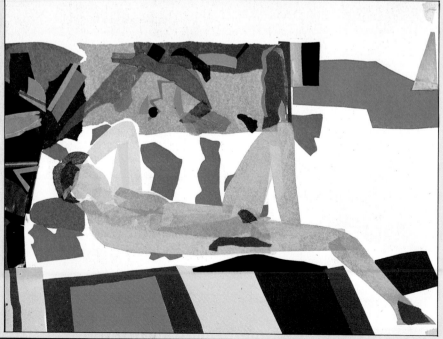

These larger illustrations show in more detail how the layers of tissue paper have been overlapped. To depict the flesh tones, several layers of different coloured paper have been placed over one another (*LEFT, RIGHT*). The areas of highlight are rendered with lighter paper, and the shadows, such as under the leg, with darker paper. The artists have also repeated the colours of the figure in the background. For instance, the yellow of the figure (*ABOVE*) is taken up in the floor covering and the orange flesh tones (*RIGHT*) reappear in the two wall hangings. It is important in this exercise that the figure is seen as part of the setting and not as an element on which the viewer's attention should focus.

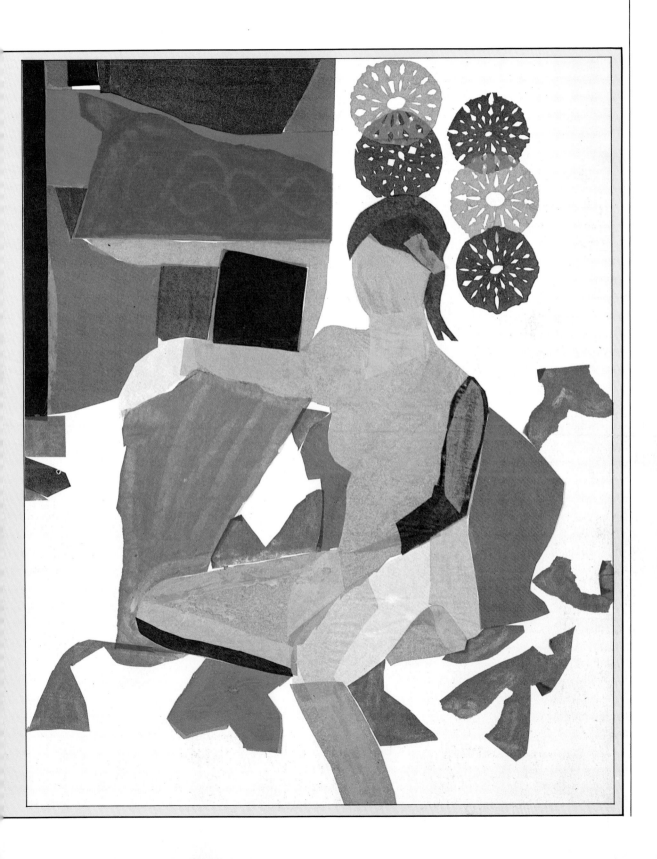

# MOVEMENT

Although a drawing or painting shows a static scene, there are many ways of giving an impression of movement, and this often contributes greatly to the effectiveness of the image you create.

The moment in the movement which you choose to portray is a major factor in this. For instance, an apparently small change in angle of the body can add to the vitality of the image. It is often more effective to show not the extreme point of a movement, but rather, the instant before, for example, the arm raising a hammer is at its highest point. You should bear in mind that movement will probably affect the whole of the figure, even if only slightly. When you place one leg in front of the other, you will tend to change the position of your torso. Train yourself to observe what happens to people's bodies when they move and make a mental note of possible poses. Practise drawing quickly and try to have someone pose for you for short times to enable you to develop speed and accuracy of observation. Do not despair if it takes some time to achieve proficiency, great patience is needed.

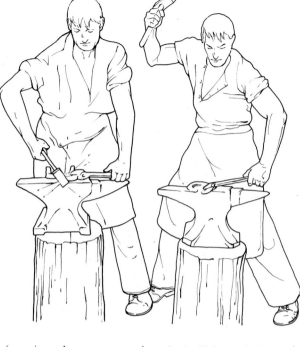

**Movement** An impression of movement can be conveyed in a picture in many ways. For instance, the change in pose *(BELOW)* shows how the increased diagonal line in the second figure *(RIGHT)* greatly enhances the vitality of the image in comparison with the more static pose *(LEFT)*. When depicting a scene in which movement is an important element, work out which instant in the movement will convey your ideas best. For instance, which of these pictures of a blacksmith at work *(ABOVE)* reveals most energy and movement? The first image *(LEFT)* shows the impact of the hammer, while the second *(RIGHT)* shows the tension in the whole figure, particularly the two arms, as the hammer is being moved. It is noteworthy that in this image the hammer arm is not fully extended. Rembrandt achieves a more lyrical impression of movement in his sensitive painting *Woman Bathing in a Stream (RIGHT)*.

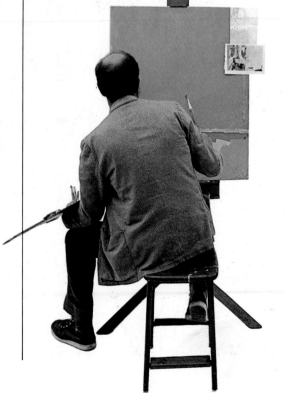

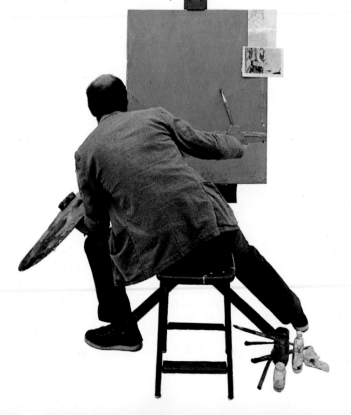

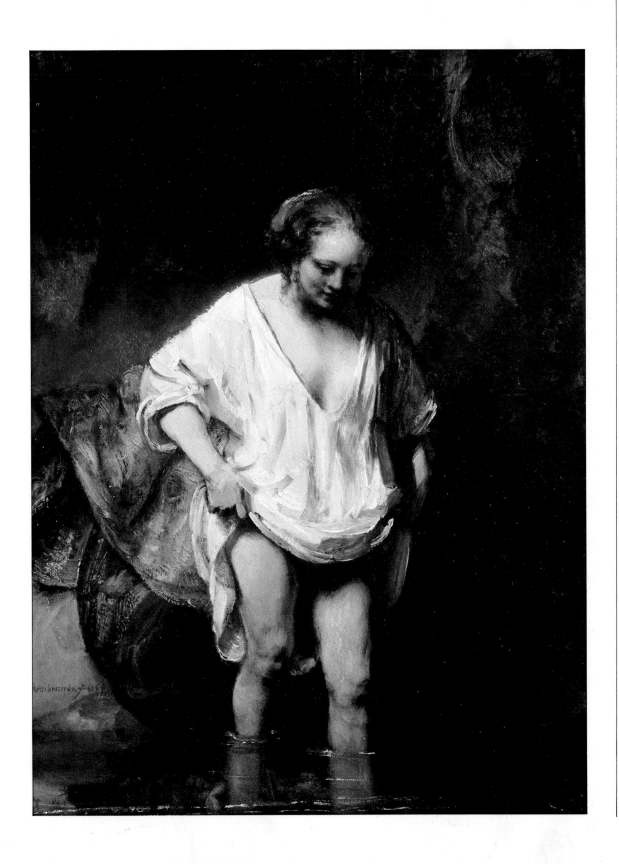

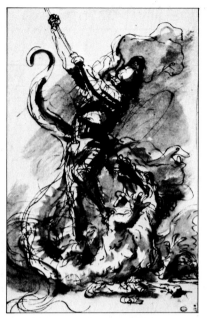

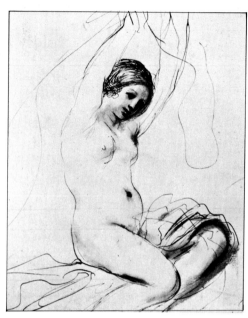

Drawing media offer different possibilities for portraying movement and lending vitality to an image. For example, the bold and vigorous pen strokes of the seventeenth century Italian artist Salvator Rosa shows how effective a combination of free, swirling pen lines with wash can be. In *St George and the Dragon (FAR LEFT)* the energy of the sweeping drawing strokes is more important in the image than the realistic depiction of detail. *The Woman Bathing* by Guercino *(LEFT)* shows a less strident kind of movement. The langourous *Study for a Pink Nude* by Henri Matisse *(BELOW)* conveys the curves of the pose using charcoal and smudging to soften the contours of the body. The torso has been highlighted using putty rubber or bread as an eraser. Vigorous pencil strokes *(BELOW RIGHT)* can also be used to create a lively image of a static subject.

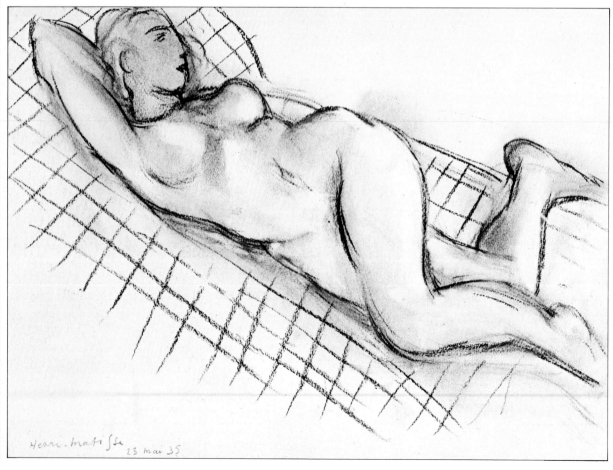

## RAPID DRAWING

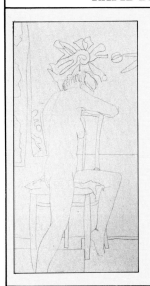

**Pose a model and draw the figure quickly. The model should stay in position for no more than four or five minutes. The purpose of this exercise is to train you to observe and draw quickly.**

*This drawing, done in about four minutes, shows good coordination of hand and eye, and accuracy of observation. Coordination and accuracy are vital for drawing movement. The speed which you will develop in this exercise will also be useful for other aspects of your drawing, even when you can take longer over the exercise. In this type of rapid drawing it is vital to locate the figure firmly in its context.*

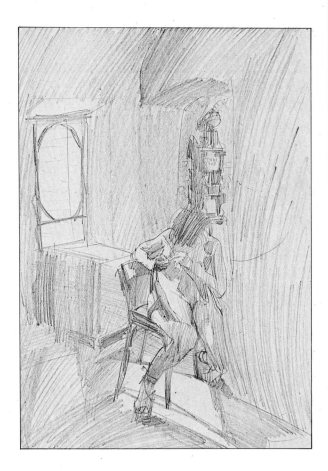

## DRAWING MOVEMENT

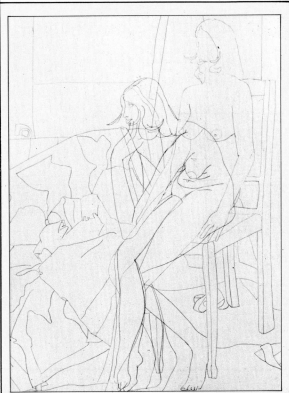

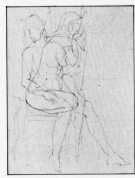

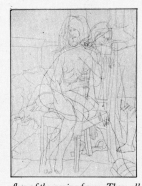

**When you have built up some expertise at drawing a model quickly, you should attempt to draw the model actually moving. Have the model make a small series of movements which can be easily repeated. Pay special attention to locating the model and to showing the model's position clearly.**

*This series of pictures shows three artists' approaches to drawing movement. The poses are drawn on the same piece of paper to show the* flow of the moving figure. These all show the importance of clearly depicting the context of the drawing. The movement is clearest where the surroundings have been well worked out. This exercise is extremely important as a way of training your eye and your drawing hand, but it will probably take some practice before you develop real competence at it. If you have difficulty drawing a whole moving figure, go back to drawing a posed figure as rapidly as possible and work on from there.

# SKETCHBOOKS

The sketchbook is an invaluable tool for artists as a device for formulating and recording ideas and indeed for stimulating the imagination to produce imagery spontaneously. Sketchbooks—also called scrapbooks or notebooks—are an important facet of work in art schools. One particular drawback to the word 'sketch' is that it implies a drawing process which is transitory, somewhat vague and a little inconsequential. These implications tend to detract from the real usefulness of the sketchbook.

## Sketchbooks—uses and formats

The sketchbook is used primarily for collecting, collating and analyzing information. The merit of any particular page obviously varies from what may be the germ of a masterpiece to a simple 'doodle'. A sketchbook drawing may have taken days or a matter of seconds to do. The main point is that each drawing should be as clear and precise as possible. Clarity is important for processing thoughts and ideas. Even if the sketchbook is being used simply as a 'memo' book, then it is important to ensure the purpose of the sketch is clear, otherwise when you go back to the book for reference, it is frustrating if you cannot recall why you did the drawing in the first place. So the sketchbook can contain drawings in all the mark-making media, colour work, collage, montage, photographs, notes about textures and so on. Above all, the sketchbook is a working

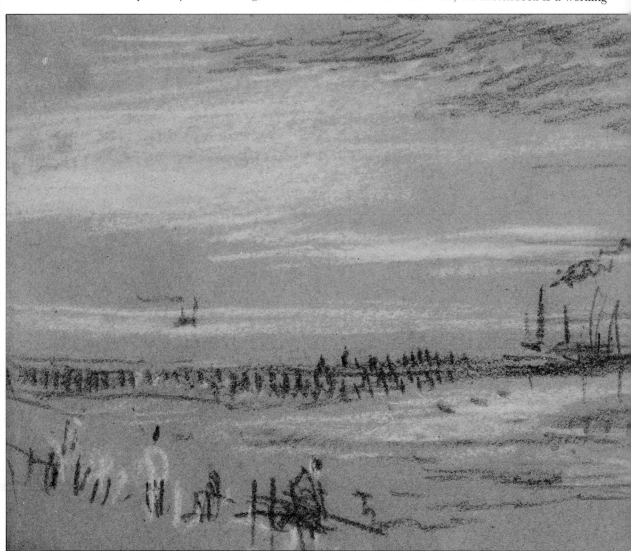

In this sketch *Jetty* by Turner *(BELOW)*, only three colours have been used: black, white and red chalk. The strokes have been simply sketched in and the forms barely hinted at. This is particularly true of the figure in the foreground and the ships moored at the end of the pier. The whole effect is light and ethereal. The sketch by Michelangelo *(RIGHT)* is very different. Through the use of strong cross-hatching, the figures have acquired a powerful solidity. There is little use of contour, most of the forms being defined through light and dark.

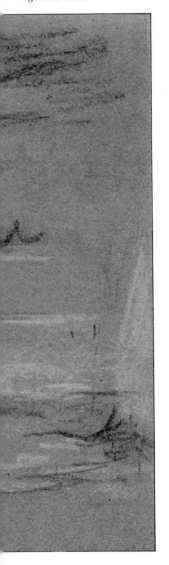

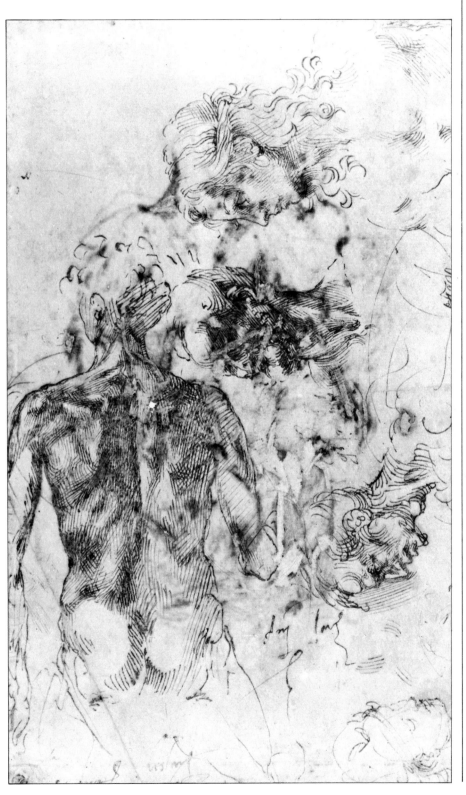

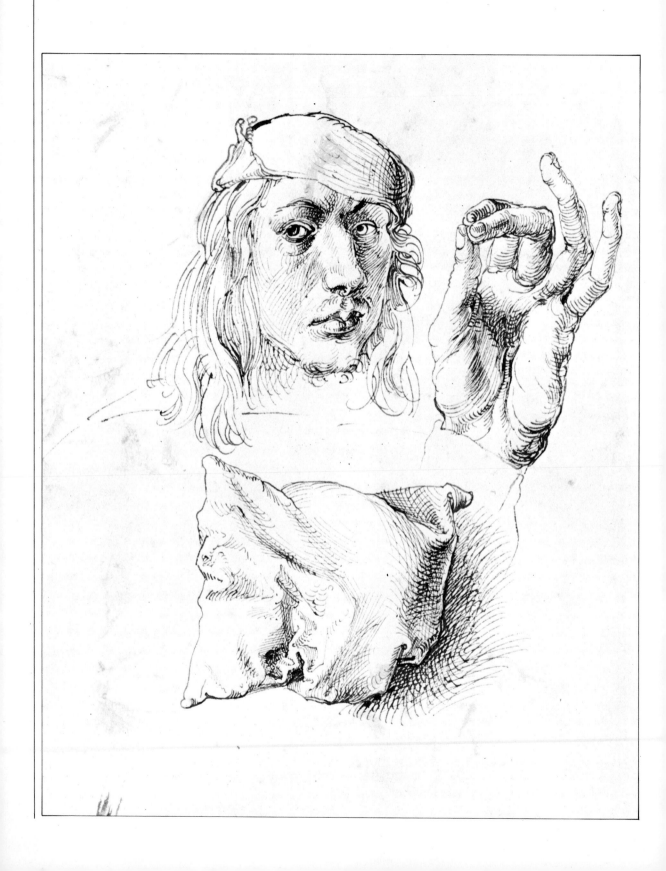

tool—there is nothing precious about the sketchbook other than the work it contains.

As books are available in small as well as large sizes, they are invaluable to artists as a place in which they can begin some simple mark-making experiments. These can range from a simple index of marks made with different tools or equipment to some more subjective exercises in varying media, exploring abstract images or variations on a theme, for example. Sketchbooks can even serve as repositories for written notes and texts, externalizing ideas or simply recording points of research or related material. All of this helps artists to widen their ideas and understanding, enabling them to define and clarify their particular concerns.

Preparatory drawings, basic working drawings, whether technical or otherwise, can all be initially laid out in the sketchbook together with collected reference material of all descriptions. This type of information collecting is especially important where research is necessary in order to carry out a detailed study of a subject or theme. Being able to look at your thoughts recorded over a period of time can suggest new directions for your research in a very economic way. New ideas arise through grouping, association and constantly watching for connections. For example, if you are working out the best approach to a landscape drawing, you could move rapidly from monochrome drawings to taking notes in colour. Accidents in applying colour could lead you to a formal study of striated colour bands across a surface. Irregular application of pigment could lead you into an investigation of surface texture which could, in turn, soon give rise to a study of pattern. All of this could occur in an afternoon and could be done most economically—in terms of time and space—in the sketchbook format.

Detailed study of a subject is essential for any artist. The sketchbook should develop into a serious analytical document with major and minor themes and an underlying structure. It perhaps begins with a layout of all information relevant to the project in hand. This information is sorted and sifted until a major theme evolves. This in turn becomes more and more refined until it becomes the preparation for a finished work. By using the sketchbook as a way of working out ideas, the artist can approach, say, a canvas with much of the work prepared and can at once begin to concentrate on the painting itself.

However you choose to use a sketchbook, there are certain points to bear in mind. The real advantage of the sketchbook lies in the simple fact that it is a bound collection of sheets of paper available in a range of sizes and surfaces that can be easily transported and used in a large number of locations and in a variety of ways. It is, therefore, worth bearing in mind how you mean to use your sketchbook before buying one. For instance, it would be inconvenient to take a large loose-bound book on a cycling trip, while it would be equally difficult to use a small hard-bound book for large-scale painting. There is no real reason for you to be restricted to commercially available artist's sketch pads. Any sturdy book with unlined paper could be used, or you could easily make your own made-to-measure book. There are many ways of binding sheets of paper yourself, your local library should have the information.

All of this can be left to your own discretion, the important thing to realize is that the organized use of sketchbooks is one factor which separates the dilettante from the more serious artist. Sketchbooks provide a format which can be highly personal without being pretentious and may even prove of more value than the finished works of art.

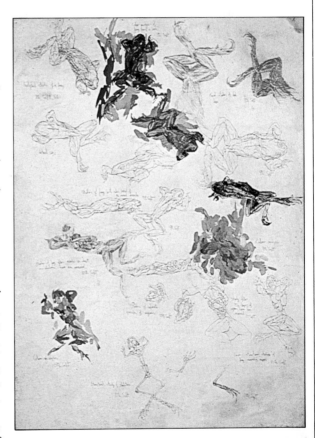

On this sheet from one of Dürer's sketchbooks (*LEFT*) there are three studies: a self portrait, a hand and a small pillow. In all three Dürer has used cross-hatching to define the surfaces.

On this page (*ABOVE*) a student has made a series of studies of a toad. As well as drawing it from different angles, he has experimented with black and white washes and colour greys.

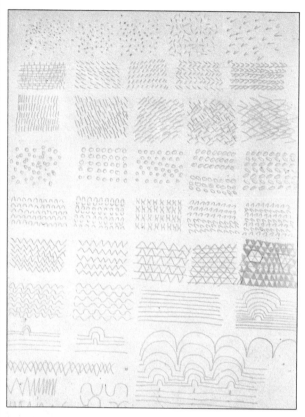

### Sketchbooks

This student has experimented with various lines and marks and different configurations of mark as well as with patterns *(LEFT)*. You will find this a useful exercise as it will make you aware of the wide range of marks which you will be able to use when you begin to make more finished sketches. Broaden the experiment by using a variety of pens, pencils and crayons. Although this study of the roots of a tree *(BELOW)* is a straightforward line drawing, it has been enlivened by the varying quality of the line. Sometimes just a delicate wisp of grey has been applied, while in other parts the artist has used powerful black lines. The two pages from a sketchbook *(BOTTOM)* show a collection of images of a single subject. You should use your sketchbook to explore the enormous range of shapes, textures and colours which exist in the natural world. This will help you develop images and ideas for your own work.

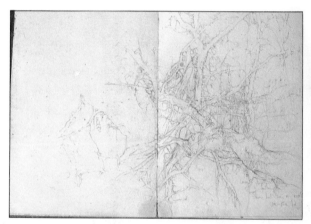

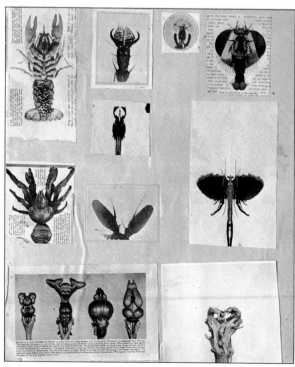

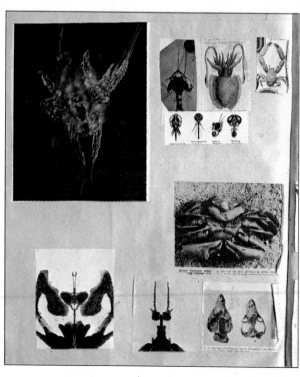

## EXPLORING AN OBJECT

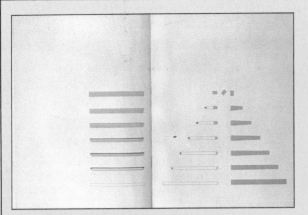

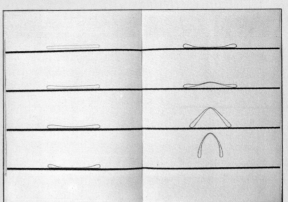

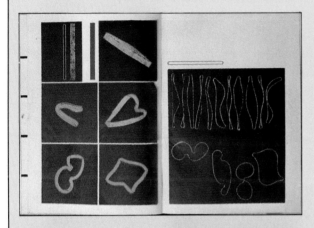

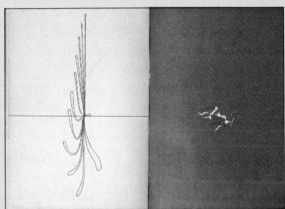

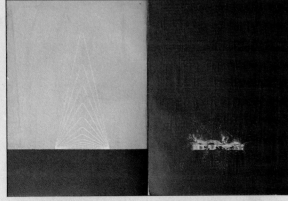

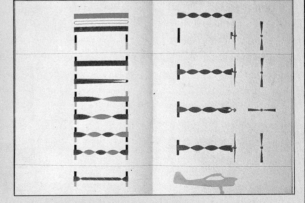

Take any small, common object such as a pencil or fork and describe its shape, scale and function, as well as any special qualities of its own which you can think of. You must not use any words or symbols, nor should you limit yourself to any number of drawings. The purpose of this is to give as full a description as possible of an object solely in visual terms.

*In this project the student chose to illustrate and explain an elastic band in purely visual terms. He has used a whole range of media such as paint, ink and pencil and has tried to illustrate all the properties of an elastic band such as its flexibility and elasticity. Its shape and scale have also been explained, while the last drawing illustrates one of its uses.*

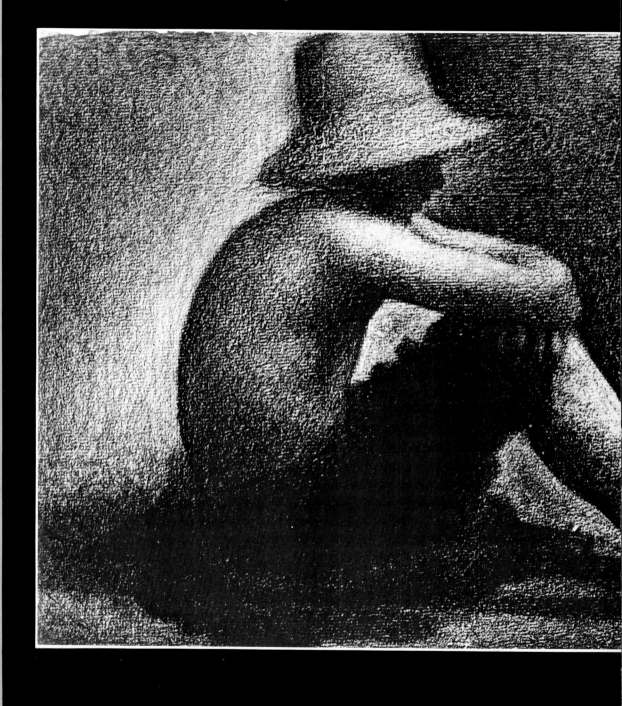

# DRAWING

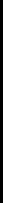

Georges Seurat
*Seated Boy with Straw Hat*

# INTRODUCTION

Drawing is the most immediate way of conveying an idea or feeling in pictorial terms. It requires only one simple mark-making instrument and a relatively plain surface. A few lines, carefully chosen or made spontaneously in response to perceptions, can produce a complex symbol or represent a natural form. By means of drawing, thoughts can be given visual form, while forms and structures embodying a whole range of concepts and intuitions can be invented and developed. Drawing is the most fundamental activity of the visual artist.

## The Renaissance and its legacy

The naturalistic style which is the legacy of the Renaissance is still, generally speaking, the most powerful influence in the appreciation of drawing. Other traditions of drawing have become important influences on artists in the last hundred years or so. These have affected the manner in which artists perceive and portray space, but many have still retained a preoccupation with the representation of space in terms of three dimensions, regarding their pictures, to some degree, as windows onto the world.

The most important feature of the Renaissance was the movement away from the medieval concept of God and the church as the omnipotent centre of life towards an absorbing preoccupation with humanity and the natural world. Leonardo da Vinci (1452–1519), whose interests ranged from anatomy to engineering and from botany to painting, is representative of the searching outlook of the Renaissance. The art of medieval Christendom was dedicated to the glory of God and the power of the church. Its iconography, its systems of symbols, was prescribed and utilized stylized forms in what was largely a conceptual art form. The Renaissance which swept across Europe in the fifteenth century, shifted the focus of attention to man and, supported by developments in philosophy and science, brought a new analytical and perceptual discipline to bear on the representation of form and space.

The artists who were inspired by the new ferment of ideas began to break away from the more stylized concepts of medieval art and strove to bring an increased naturalism into their treatment of religious themes. Figures acquired a greater sense of volume and plasticity and were placed in settings where three-dimensional space was defined increasingly clearly. Working directly from human models and the environment in which they lived, artists began to transcribe what they perceived rather than relying on handed-down conventions. The study of anatomy and perspec-

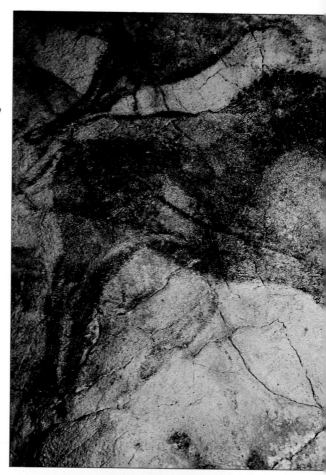

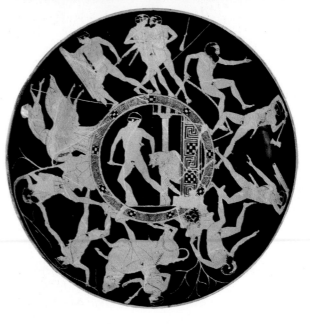

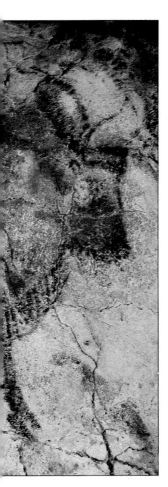

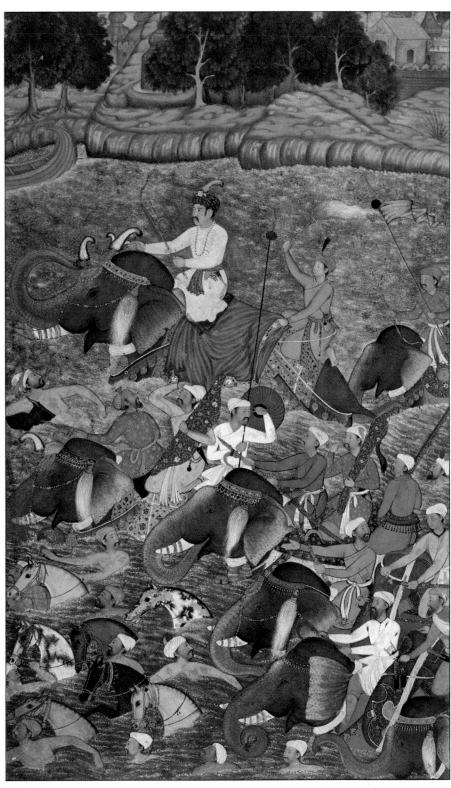

The cave drawings at Altamira in Spain reveal early man's innate ability to draw. This powerful image of a bison *(ABOVE)* captures the strength and vitality of the animal. It was drawn in natural earth pigments. By the time of the ancient Greeks, linear drawing linked to a sophisticated stylization of the figure *(LEFT)* had developed. The forms of the figures are composed with great elegance and rhythm. The lines are drawn on clay with a fine brush. The conventions of Eastern art differ starkly from those of Western art. For example, space and distance are expressed by arranging the forms according to the principle that figures nearest the top of the picture are furthest away and those at the bottom are nearest. In *Crossing the Ganges (RIGHT)* by the Persian artist Akbar, the figures are drawn with delicacy and refinement.

tive became part of artists' repertoires enabling them to produce accurate representations of what they saw.

Although the Renaissance covered many European countries and cultures and took on different forms and characteristics, all had one thing in common: the use of drawing as a means of investigating nature, experimenting with geometry, perspective, proportion, composition, perceptual aids, and the free expression of the imagination. Never before had drawing demonstrated such a variety of functions. This legacy of the Renaissance dominated Western art and art education until the great surge of modernism at the end of the nineteenth century, associated mainly with the Impressionists and the Post-Impressionists.

## Alternative traditions

It is easy to forget about other artistic traditions for the simple reason that they have never enjoyed the prestige which, over the centuries, has been lent to Western art, and in particular that of the Renaissance. The traditions of non-Western art are, however, increasingly important for anyone interested in drawing and draughtsmanship for the simple reason that so many traditions have been exploited and incorporated into the work of so many nineteenth and twentieth century artists. In the great early civilizations of Sumeria and Egypt, drawing was used primarily as a preparation for sculpture and painting. Forms were invented which embodied the religious ideas and practices of the community. The images were then drawn out for the sculptors, painters, goldsmiths and ceramicists to follow when doing their final work. Drawing in its own right is only seen in papyrus rolls or inscribed on various materials.

Drawing did, however, help Egyptian craftsmen to evolve and define the relationship of various parts of the human figure in a way which is now considered typical of Egyptian art. The special feature of the Egyptian manner of treating the figure is the interesting fashion in which different viewpoints of the main parts of the body were taken and then reassembled in such a way as to give maximum emphasis to the most characteristic and recognizable aspect of each part. In this way, the side view of the head clearly showing the features in profile is combined with the front view of the torso. In a female torso, one breast is usually shown in profile. The lower torso is shown in profile, the legs in side view, and the feet also in side view indicating their length and right-angled connection with the ankle. A front view of an eye is combined with the side view of the head.

## Eastern art

In Islamic art and various Eastern and Far Eastern artistic traditions, drawing was primarily the first stage

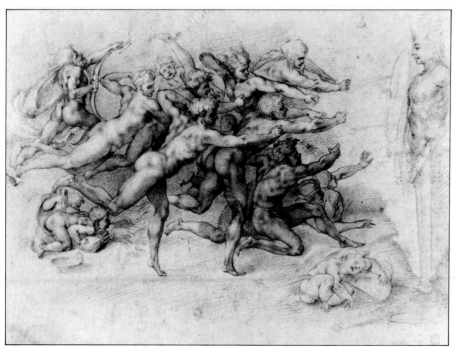

Michelangelo Buonarotti was one of the greatest artists of the Renaissance. His drawing, *Archers shooting at a Mark (LEFT)*, shows great draughtmanship. The drawing was done in red chalk, and Michelangelo used the medium with a light and sensitive touch to reveal the intricacies of anatomical structure. The rhythmic movement of the composition is echoed in each individual figure. This shows the physical and spiritual energy for which Michelangelo is renowned. The artist paid little attention to the background which is no more than indicated. This helps focus the viewer's attention on the figures. Natural chalks (red, black and white) were an important drawing medium especially until the eighteenth century. Conté crayons are today the nearest equivalent to natural chalks. They are less easily broken than natural chalks, and are available in a small range of colours.

in producing a painting. It was the means of delineating the various forms of a composition and establishing the relationships between them. Drawing also played a fundamental role in the development of a stylized method of depicting human figures, animals, architecture or landscape, and formed the basis for certain accepted artistic conventions. The perspective which was developed in the Renaissance has never been used in Islamic art, and spatial relationships were indicated by other means. Forms seen nearest to the viewer were placed at the bottom of the picture. The middle distance and the forms furthest away were placed higher up. There was often no variation in scale and this convention is usually complicated by the fact that figures which have special importance, such as gods, saints, mythical heroes, kings or queens, were made larger than the other figures. Another simple means of describing recession was done by having one form partially covered by another. The partly hidden form was thus easily recognized as being farther away despite its relative size in the composition.

In China and Japan other principles were used. The close relationship between calligraphy and drawing and painting, which was a feature of Islamic and Indian art, was even closer in Japan and China. Although commonly referred to as painting, a large proportion of Chinese and Japanese art is more accurately described as drawing. Working with one colour—black—and often using only one brush, artists produced marvellously sensitive images of figures, animals, flowers, landscapes and other natural forms. Line was sometimes used, often varying in thickness, to express different qualities of the subject. Perhaps the most impressive works are those in which a single brushstroke conveys a leaf, a branch of bamboo, a petal of a flower, a fruit or the body of a bird. Not only does the single stroke of a brush describe the shape of the object, but it can also express qualities such as movement, variations of light, modulations of edge, changes of spatial direction, vitality, passivity, softness or hardness.

## Modern art

The term 'modern art' has become a label for almost any type of non-traditional art practised since the late nineteenth century. This complex period is full of contrasting styles and philosophies. Just as all present-day artists, amateur or professional, are exposed to a bewildering range of images illustrating the whole history of world art from cave paintings to the most recent and often bizarre activities of performance artists, so the revolutionary changes in art that came

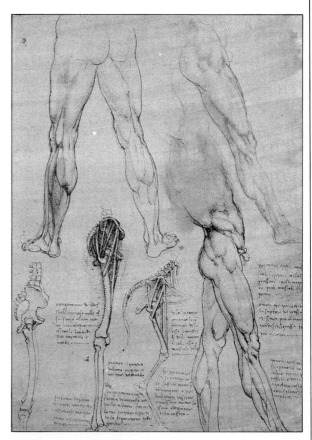

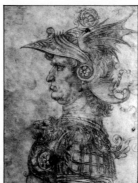

Leonardo da Vinci's interest in science was reflected in his drawings. The anatomical structure in this study *(ABOVE)* is treated with great precision. An interest in the human form was one of the characteristics of the Renaissance. For some of his figure drawings, Leonardo used silverpoint *(LEFT)*. This is seldom used today because it requires a surface specially prepared with a chalk ground which can then be drawn on. This produces a fine, delicate line, but sureness of handling is essential because erasing is extremely difficult.

about at the turn of the century also, in part, resulted from a relatively sudden exposure to artistic conventions from different periods of world art. Artists opened their eyes and minds to new influences and saw that European conventions were but a tiny part of what was possible and legitimate to express the creative imagination. Casting aside the accumulated effect of the Renaissance, artists began to explore alternative means of expression and evolve new philosophies.

With the Impressionists came a new concept relating

to the physical nature of a painting. From the Renaissance until the nineteenth century, the picture plane was regarded as a window through which to view the world. In other words, there was an attempt to deny the physical quality of the picture plane so that the illusion of real space could be created. The Impressionists, while making representations of the real world, accepted the two-dimensional quality of the picture plane, but used both linear and aerial perspective. Also they gave new emphasis to brushstrokes. Indeed, such artists almost made a virtue of the abstract patterns created by the paint. This was the first step which released art from the bonds of figurative expression. From this date onwards artists no longer felt constrained to use those pictorial devices which were developed centuries earlier during the Renaissance.

One result of this new outlook was that it encouraged artists to study alternative artistic traditions. In his drawings which were done during his last years in the south of France, Vincent van Gogh (1853–1890) made considerable use of the Japanese drawing style and using pen and ink built up his images in a similar way with series of dots and lines. In *Les Demoiselles d'Avignon* (1907), Pablo Picasso (1881–1973) turned to traditions far removed from European ones. The stylized faces in this painting were based closely on African masks while the portrayal of the face in profile with its single eye staring out at the spectator recalls Egyptian stylistic traditions. With Georges Braque (1882–1963) a year later, Picasso carried these experiments further. Drawing objects from different viewpoints and incorporating these views in single paintings, these artists developed a style of painting which was called Cubism. In carrying out these experiments, they were drawing to a great extent on the hitherto neglected traditions of Egyptian art and primitive cultures.

Drawings, often in colour, became the predominant tool for experiment. Often starting with drawings from

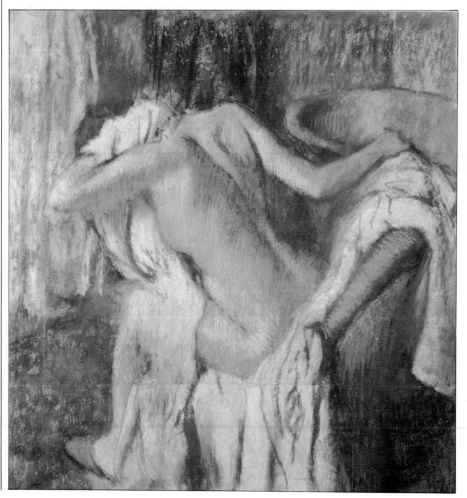

*After the Bath, Woman Drying Herself (LEFT)* drawn in 1880, is a fine example of the draughtmanship of the French Impressionist artist Edgar Degas. The forms are treated with considerable breadth, but contain subtleties of modelling which reveal his extensive practice and deep knowledge of the human figure. Charcoal was used to establish the outlines and areas of shading on the torso. Degas used a variety of pastel strokes — short and pressured for the carpet with dark zig-zags on top, long, sweeping purple strokes for the shadows on the towel, while the bluish reflection on the white fabric is produced by softer, slurred strokes. The repetition of colour across the picture encourages the eye to move across the surface. The pose of the woman, in which her back is parallel to the picture plane contributes to the geometry of the composition. This drawing was done on cream-coloured paper which gives the overall impression of warmth, while the paper's texture helps create the flecked surface of the picture. Degas experimented with many types of fixative, as pastels always need fixing to stop the surface being damaged. Today many varieties are available commercially.

natural forms or invented compositions in a free figurative style, artists like Wassily Kandinsky (1866–1944), Piet Mondrian (1872–1944) and Paul Klee (1879–1940), would use a sequence of drawings to push their original conceptions further and further towards abstraction. Later, the founders of Dada and Surrealism renounced more than artistic conventions. They challenged the accepted notions of reality, claiming that the irrational fantasy world of the subconscious was more real than the external world of sense perception. Believing that people were trapped into a very circumscribed view of what was real, the Surrealists aimed to shock the spectators of their works out of their conditioning and thus to initiate them into a world of the unrestrained psyche which was capable of producing bizarre and unlikely images.

Through these and other experiments by different groups, modern art has moved a long way from the naturalism of the nineteenth century. Artists today have an enormous range of techniques and traditions on which to draw. All these traditions reflect, at least to some degree, contemporary life and its multiplicity of influences—from the earliest of the world's art to cinema, television and all the popular imagery with which everyone is bombarded day after day.

When embarking on your own drawings or paintings, you should be aware of the traditions and conventions which have preceded you. Make yourself open to the many and varied images from the world of art which are readily available today. However, it is vital that you do not let yourself become intimidated by the richness and variety of these images. The most important thing is for you to work in the way you want to. As a beginner, you may not be able always to achieve the effects you desire. However, constant practice and experimentation with different media, surfaces, and subject matters will help you to gain proficiency and develop your own style.

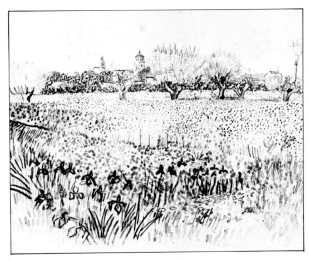

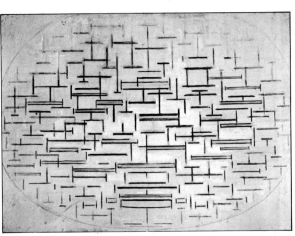

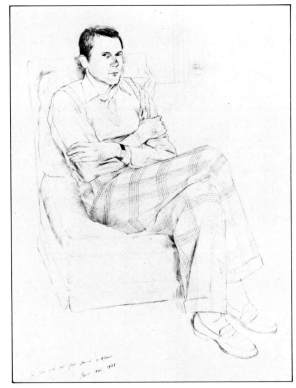

Among the attractions of drawing are its immediacy and versatility. Van Gogh's reed-pen drawing of a landscape *(TOP LEFT)* portrays light and shade very effectively. Another Dutch artist, Piet Mondrian responded to nature very differently. For his drawing of the sea *(LEFT)* he moved towards an abstract image combining horizontals and verticals. The contemporary British artist David Hockney drew Jean Léger *(ABOVE)* with great economy. The lines on the trousers both depict the check pattern and show the figure's cross-sections.

# MEDIA AND SURFACES

## Drawing media

Anything that makes a mark and any surface that will receive it are the basic essentials of drawing media. There is a great range of drawing materials available, and artists have always been tempted to try out different methods. You should remember that personal discovery through experiment is the best way to become familiar with the properties, qualities and potential of the various drawing media. Moreover, while it is useful to learn the traditional methods of handling media, it is also a function of the creative imagination to extend these methods and explore new possibilities in the search for qualities that best express your own outlook.

Art stores stock a bewildering range of materials. The number of common graphite pencils, for example, is considerable and they range from hard (light) to soft (dark). If the hardest was given a very sharp point, it could practically cut through cheap paper if reasonable pressure was applied. A pencil like this is for delicate, precise work and is more suited to mechanical drawing than, say, landscape sketching. The softest which is available gives a rich, dark tone with a polished look and a velvety line. As with all really soft pencils, it wears down quickly and the graphite is shattered easily within the wooden body if it is dropped on the floor.

Charcoal pencils, in both medium and soft grades, are an alternative. They are more gritty and less smooth to use They work best on rough surfaced paper and produce a deep matt black. Various coloured pencils are available in a wide range of hues including black, white and various shades of grey. Some of them are soluble in water and, after being applied to the paper, can be brushed with water to produce blended tints and washes. Chinagraph pencils in black and white are specially manufactured for drawing on smooth or polished surfaces.

Charcoal is an excellent material for bold work and is much softer than a charcoal pencil. It can provide a subtle range of tones up to a deep intense black both in line and in tone. There are, however, hazards in using it. It dusts off very easily and some good work can be erased by the inside edge of the drawing hand brushing over parts of the drawing. It also snaps easily if used vigorously, which can be frustrating for the impassioned artist. The best results are produced on a textured surface because charcoal slides ineffectually over smooth paper. All charcoal drawings should be sprayed with fixative.

Conté crayons, in black, red or sepia, are an alternative to charcoal. Manufactured in different grades from

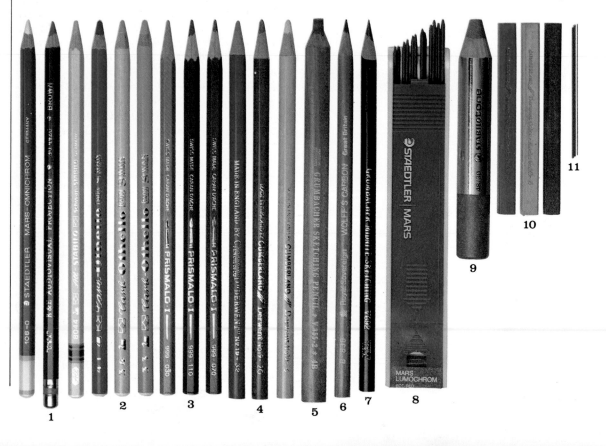

medium to extra soft, they lack the crisp freshness of charcoal but do not dust off and adhere to most types of paper. Pastel represents yet another medium. These sticks are produced in an enormous range of colours and tints. They are extremely soft and powdery, and can break up very easily if handled roughly. The art of using pastels is often referred to as pastel painting. In this case the colours are blended and merged on the paper in the same way as paint on canvas. They are best used on toned paper with a lightly textured surface. Oil pastels are an excellent alternative to soft pastels. They do not rub off; they can be worked over with turpentine, scratched into and blended together.

For pen and ink work, a wide range of nibs is available. Generally speaking, an ordinary writing nib is as good as any, although mapping pen nibs are best for fine work. Inks are usually waterproof, brilliantly coloured, and should be diluted with distilled water for wash effects. A good blue-black writing ink can be diluted with tap water and is a very good medium for pen and wash.

Watercolour is one of the best media for wash drawings as its consistency and transparency is designed for this very purpose. Mixed strongly, watercolour can be used with a pen by applying the paint to the back of the nib with a loaded brush.

### Pencils

While it is possible to draw with any instrument which will make a mark on a surface, pencils are one of the most popular drawing media and come in an extremely wide variety of types and styles. Coloured pencils (2,3,4) are available in widely ranging colours. They cannot always be erased completely. Graphite pencils (14) come in up to 19 degrees of hardness, ranging from EE, EB, 6B to B, HB, F, and H to 9H. Carbon pencils (6,12) range from BBB to HH. Interesting effects can be created with colour blocks (10), litho crayon (15), wax pencil (9) and other pencils for writing on film and plastic surfaces (1). Sketching pencils (7) can also have flat leads (5). Clutch pencils (17) need sharpening less frequently than ordinary pencils, and replacement leads are available in graphite (11,18) and coloured (8) forms. Conté drawing pencils (13) are made in black, brown, red and white. A pencil holder (16) is also useful.

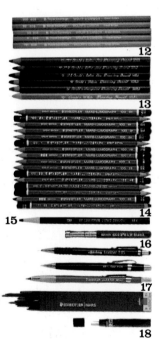

## Drawing surfaces

The most universally used paper is cartridge paper. It comes in various sizes and weights, in separate sheets and made up into sketchbooks. Rolls are also available up to 5 feet (1.5 m) wide. Perhaps the most important thing to remember when choosing paper is texture. Generally speaking, smooth, hard paper is used for pen and hard pencil work, rougher surface paper for charcoal, crayons and soft pencils. For quick studies, notations, working drawings and sketches, a cheap, light-weight poster paper with one side lightly textured is both economical and practical.

Watercolour paper is the obvious choice for watercolour work. Hot press, not and rough are the three surfaces which are available. Hot press is a smooth surface and best for fine detail. Rough, as the word suggests, is the most heavily textured. Not is somewhere in between. A variety of hand-made water colour paper is available. These are usually rough textured but free from the sometimes mechanical texture which mould-made paper has. Watercolour paper is an excellent surface for all drawing media.

An enormous variety of coloured and toned papers is available. Which sort you select is a matter of personal taste. The cheaper range may prove too soft for vigorous work and too absorbent for wash drawings. Ingres paper is an excellent lightly textured paper. Made in a number of tones and colours, it is ideal for pencil and crayon work.

Boards for drawing on are available in shops but they are very expensive and, unless you have something special in mind, they are simply not worth the money. Except for drawings done for their own sake, it is quite unnecessary to spend money on high quality papers. Indeed, expensive papers can be inhibiting for the sketcher. Unlike painting, where the permanent results are important, technical risks can be taken with drawing. This is particularly so as enquiry and visual curiosity are the principal aims. It does not matter too much if some drawings eventually fade or even disintegrate, provided some new insights have been gained and some new skills developed. For these reasons, unconventional methods and materials should be explored for their special qualities.

Coffee, shoe polish, varnish, soot and many other unusual materials have been used in drawing. The same can be said for the manner in which they have been applied. Splattering, blotting, sponging, scratching, scraping, tearing, burning and other means have all been used to telling effect. Experiment on wood, canvas, hardboard or any other surface which appeals to you.

# FIGURE DRAWING

This approach to figure drawing uses an analytical method which also includes expressiveness and free interpretation. Its main aim is to further understanding of the form and structure of the human figure and encourage you to give expression to this understanding using a series of concepts which relate to the particular structural features of the figure. This helps to train your mind and eye to respond to perceptions in an organized way and to search for accuracy and truth in formal and spatial relationships. This will help you convey the organic and rhythmic unity of the figure, its general structure and volumetric or three-dimensional qualities. The expressive and interpretative aspects of the approach also explore ways of communicating the knowledge which is gained by analysis, and also include experiments with 'free' expression where criteria of accuracy give way to intuitive and emotional responses. This involves experiments with scale, media and mark-making and consideration of how to relate the figure to the space it occupies.

## The volumes of the figure

The human figure is a single volume existing in space. It subdivides into seven main related volumes—head, neck, torso, two arms and two legs. The arms in turn subdivide into upper and lower arms, hands and fingers, the legs divide into thighs, lower legs, feet and toes, and the head into eyes, ears, nose and mouth. Each of these divisions has its own volumetric characteristics. When drawing, your first task is to work out the volumetric characteristics of each part of the figure.

**Axes and directional lines** In simple terms, the larger volumes of the figure are basically cylindrical, each part having a central axis. These axes are an important aid to analyzing the figure. The first stage of the analytical process is to determine the direction in space of these axes, and thus of the volumes that contain them.

However, other features of the figure do not lend themselves so readily to this type of analysis, partly as they are not always cylindrical in shape. The idea of directional lines helps to deal with these. To establish the figure's directional lines, you should ask yourself in which direction the parts of the figure move in space and to what degree they incline in relationship to each other. In combination, these concepts can be used to establish the position of a volume in space.

**Cross-sections** The next step in coming to terms with the problem of representing volumes on a two-dimensional surface is to consider the cross-sections of

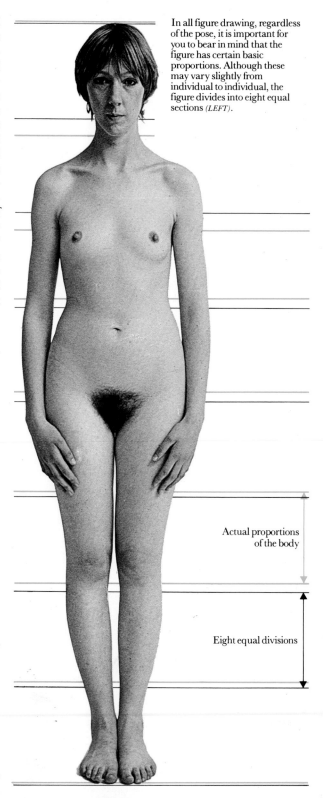

In all figure drawing, regardless of the pose, it is important for you to bear in mind that the figure has certain basic proportions. Although these may vary slightly from individual to individual, the figure divides into eight equal sections *(LEFT)*.

Actual proportions of the body

Eight equal divisions

**Axes and directional lines**
An important step in analyzing the figure or part of the figure and their direction in space *(BELOW)*. Having established the axes, consider next the figure's directional lines. To work these out, ask yourself in which direction the parts of the figure move and how they incline in relationship to one another *(BOTTOM)*. Two main directional lines are between the shoulders and between the pelvic crests. In combination, the axes and directional lines help establish the position of a volume in space.

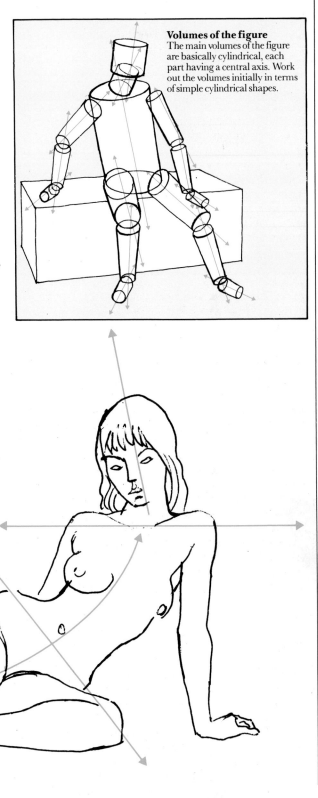

**Volumes of the figure**
The main volumes of the figure are basically cylindrical, each part having a central axis. Work out the volumes initially in terms of simple cylindrical shapes.

the figure. The basic cylinder shows that in order to represent volume, lines indicating circumference must be added to the lines denoting length and direction. Volume—the figure's three-dimensional quality—is indicated on a two-dimensional surface by the cross-section in conjunction with the other lines. Complex forms require a greater number and variety of cross-sections to establish their volumetric characteristics.

In drawing the figure, you require an awareness of cross-sections, and an appreciation of their value and importance in determining the structural features of whatever part of the figure is being drawn. It is obvious that most drawings of the figure are not covered with drawn cross-sections, like an explanatory diagram. However, using cross-sections in a diagrammatic way to explore the structural features of the figure helps greatly to establish an understanding of it as a volume, rather than a surface to be imitated.

**Torso and spine** The torso is the largest volume of the figure. It is formed from two sub-volumes—the upper part, determined by the thorax, and the lower determined by the pelvis. These are connected by the spine, a flexible rod allowing hips and chest a variety of movements relative to each other—forwards, backwards, sideways and rotational. In naturally assumed standing poses, the relationships between these movements working around a centre of gravity largely determine the disposition of head, neck, and legs.

In drawing the figure, it is always important to establish the relationship of thorax to hips. For example, if the weight of the body is taken mainly on one leg, this pushes the hip upwards on this side and the shoulder drops towards the hip to compensate. This compresses the forms on this side of the torso and produces a complementary stretching on the other side. The spine curves to allow for this, and the neck continues the line of curvature. To counterbalance this movement, the head tilts slightly in the opposite direction. The leg is not taking much weight, so it is relaxed and the knee flexes accordingly. These contraposture movements, as they are known, demonstrate the natural poise and rhythmic relationship of volumes which delighted artists of the Renaissance.

**Cross-references—visual scanning** As all objective drawing involves making a visual assessment of proportions and formal relationships, the concept of visual cross-references can be used to help establish these relationships as accurately as possible without relying on elaborate measuring devices. The best way to think of cross-references is to imagine the eye travelling on a great many straight lines connecting various parts of the figure in a form of visual scanning. Some of these lines will travel across areas of the

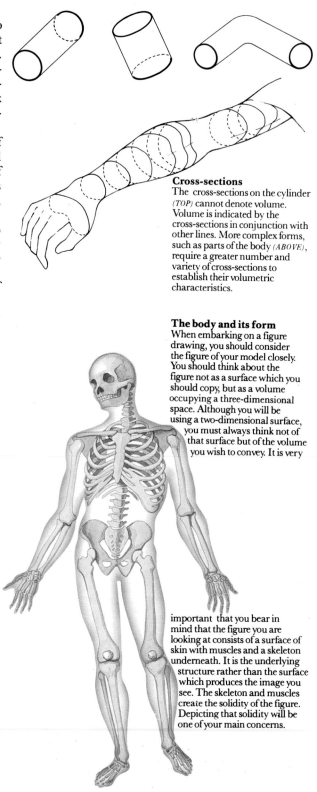

**Cross-sections**
The cross-sections on the cylinder *(TOP)* cannot denote volume. Volume is indicated by the cross-sections in conjunction with other lines. More complex forms, such as parts of the body *(ABOVE)*, require a greater number and variety of cross-sections to establish their volumetric characteristics.

**The body and its form**
When embarking on a figure drawing, you should consider the figure of your model closely. You should think about the figure not as a surface which you should copy, but as a volume occupying a three-dimensional space. Although you will be using a two-dimensional surface, you must always think not of that surface but of the volume you wish to convey. It is very important that you bear in mind that the figure you are looking at consists of a surface of skin with muscles and a skeleton underneath. It is the underlying structure rather than the surface which produces the image you see. The skeleton and muscles create the solidity of the figure. Depicting that solidity will be one of your main concerns.

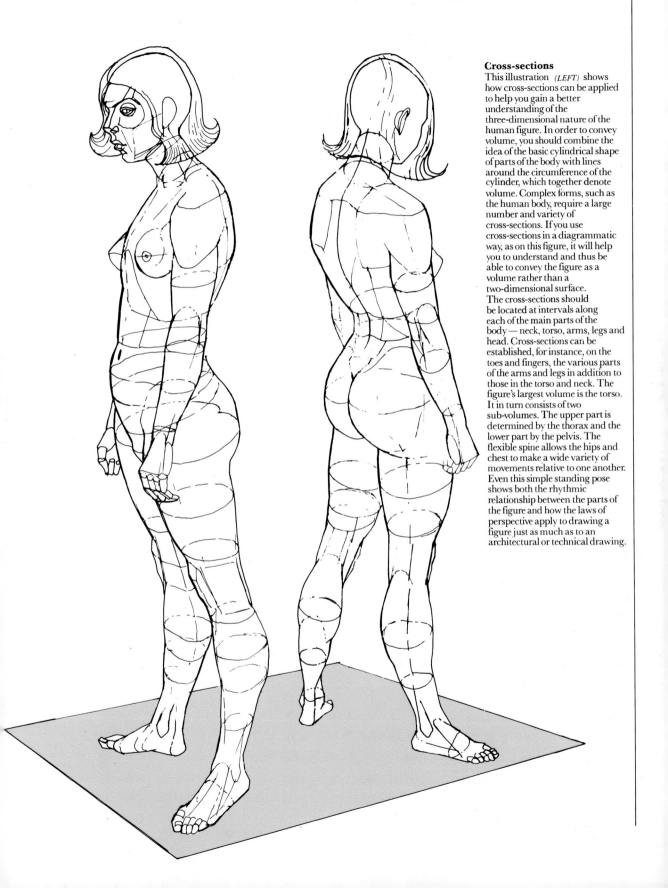

### Cross-sections

This illustration *(LEFT)* shows how cross-sections can be applied to help you gain a better understanding of the three-dimensional nature of the human figure. In order to convey volume, you should combine the idea of the basic cylindrical shape of parts of the body with lines around the circumference of the cylinder, which together denote volume. Complex forms, such as the human body, require a large number and variety of cross-sections. If you use cross-sections in a diagrammatic way, as on this figure, it will help you to understand and thus be able to convey the figure as a volume rather than a two-dimensional surface.

The cross-sections should be located at intervals along each of the main parts of the body — neck, torso, arms, legs and head. Cross-sections can be established, for instance, on the toes and fingers, the various parts of the arms and legs in addition to those in the torso and neck. The figure's largest volume is the torso. It in turn consists of two sub-volumes. The upper part is determined by the thorax and the lower part by the pelvis. The flexible spine allows the hips and chest to make a wide variety of movements relative to one another. Even this simple standing pose shows both the rhythmic relationship between the parts of the figure and how the laws of perspective apply to drawing a figure just as much as to an architectural or technical drawing.

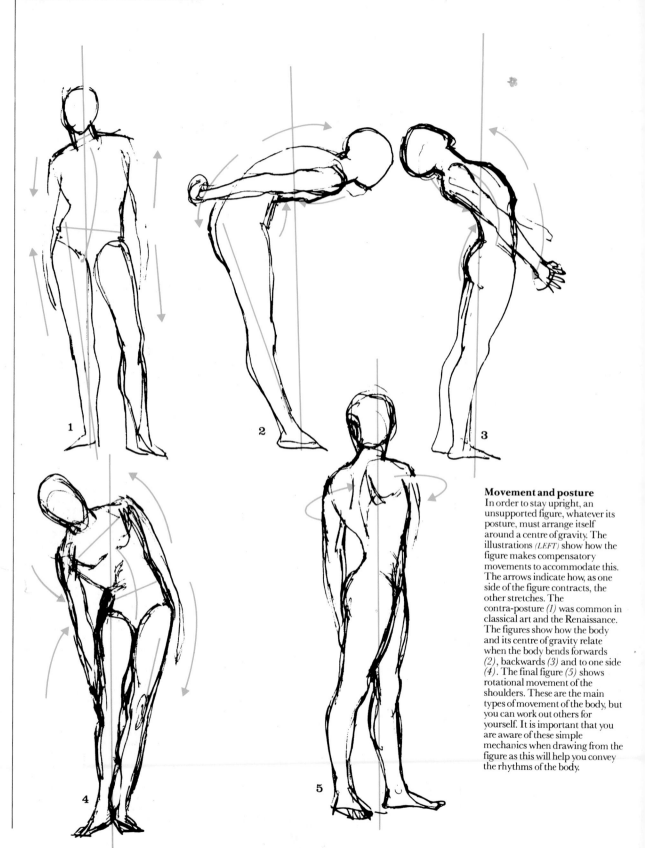

**Movement and posture**
In order to stay upright, an
unsupported figure, whatever its
posture, must arrange itself
around a centre of gravity. The
illustrations *(LEFT)* show how the
figure makes compensatory
movements to accommodate this.
The arrows indicate how, as one
side of the figure contracts, the
other stretches. The
contra-posture *(1)* was common in
classical art and the Renaissance.
The figures show how the body
and its centre of gravity relate
when the body bends forwards
*(2)*, backwards *(3)* and to one side
*(4)*. The final figure *(5)* shows
rotational movement of the
shoulders. These are the main
types of movement of the body, but
you can work out others for
yourself. It is important that you
are aware of these simple
mechanics when drawing from the
figure as this will help you convey
the rhythms of the body.

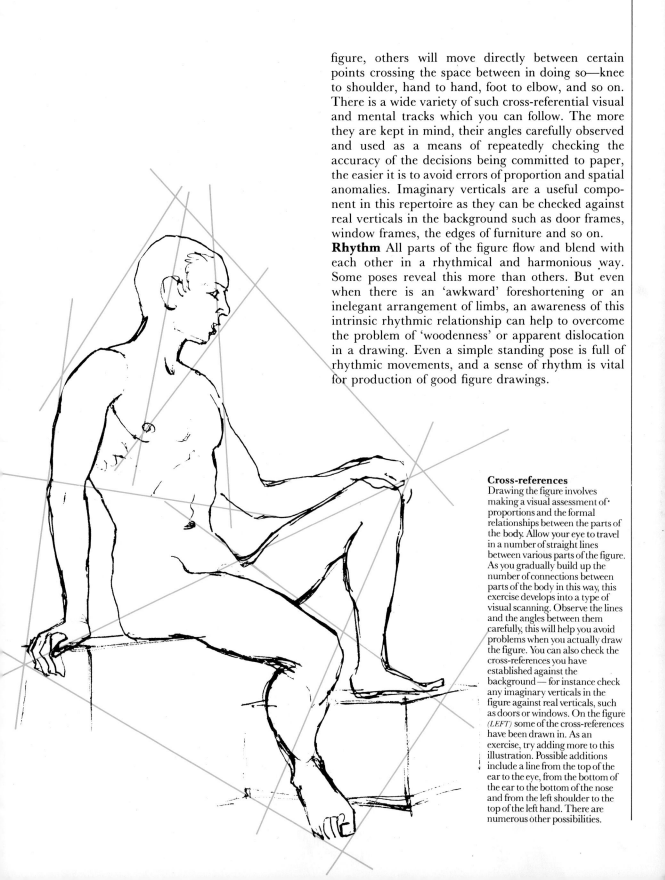

figure, others will move directly between certain points crossing the space between in doing so—knee to shoulder, hand to hand, foot to elbow, and so on. There is a wide variety of such cross-referential visual and mental tracks which you can follow. The more they are kept in mind, their angles carefully observed and used as a means of repeatedly checking the accuracy of the decisions being committed to paper, the easier it is to avoid errors of proportion and spatial anomalies. Imaginary verticals are a useful component in this repertoire as they can be checked against real verticals in the background such as door frames, window frames, the edges of furniture and so on.

**Rhythm** All parts of the figure flow and blend with each other in a rhythmical and harmonious way. Some poses reveal this more than others. But even when there is an 'awkward' foreshortening or an inelegant arrangement of limbs, an awareness of this intrinsic rhythmic relationship can help to overcome the problem of 'woodenness' or apparent dislocation in a drawing. Even a simple standing pose is full of rhythmic movements, and a sense of rhythm is vital for production of good figure drawings.

**Cross-references**
Drawing the figure involves making a visual assessment of proportions and the formal relationships between the parts of the body. Allow your eye to travel in a number of straight lines between various parts of the figure. As you gradually build up the number of connections between parts of the body in this way, this exercise develops into a type of visual scanning. Observe the lines and the angles between them carefully, this will help you avoid problems when you actually draw the figure. You can also check the cross-references you have established against the background — for instance check any imaginary verticals in the figure against real verticals, such as doors or windows. On the figure (LEFT) some of the cross-references have been drawn in. As an exercise, try adding more to this illustration. Possible additions include a line from the top of the ear to the eye, from the bottom of the ear to the bottom of the nose and from the left shoulder to the top of the left hand. There are numerous other possibilities.

# Posing the model

Painting and drawing from life is one of the best established traditions of fine art and remains so for sound reasons. A nude figure provides a great variety of shapes and angles through which the artist can learn to understand three-dimensional form. Part of the value of a life model is that the pose changes minutely all the time, and the play of light over the form can be studied at length. Some artists, with a good knowledge of form and volume, prefer to use photographs as reference, but a flat image is lifeless and gives only part of the information to be gained from the real subject.

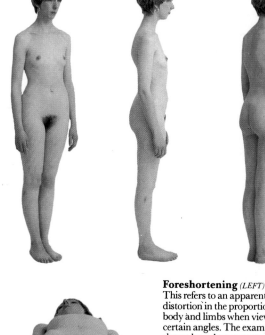

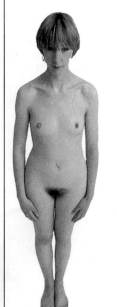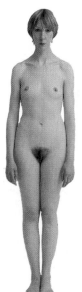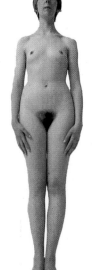

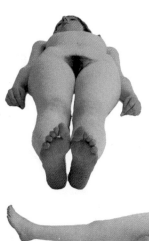

**Foreshortening** *(LEFT)*
This refers to an apparent distortion in the proportions of body and limbs when viewed from certain angles. The example shown here demonstrates how the body appears 'telescoped' when viewed straight on. Note how the legs seem short and broad while the torso recedes. Very little of the upper half of the body remains visible at all. It is important to learn to measure by eye, or with the aid of a pencil held out at arm's length, and to discard preconceived knowledge in favour of the evidence before your eyes.

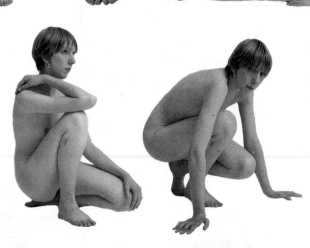

**Viewing from above, below or straight on** *(ABOVE)*.
These three poses show the importance of your angle of vision in relation to the model. Seen from a high viewpoint *(LEFT)*, the legs appear short and the body broad and disproportionate. The opposite effect is gained from a low angled viewpoint *(RIGHT)*, since the figure is still distorted, but now elongated and thin. A more central viewpoint close to the model's own eye level and at sufficient distance to see the whole figure clearly *(MIDDLE)* gives a truer impression of the form.

**Similar poses**
These two poses show the variety of form caused by shifting the model's position, although the basic structure of each is similar. The folded arm *(FAR LEFT)* gives the impression of compactness and linear coherence, while the outstretched arms in the other pose *(LEFT)* spread the weight of the figure in a quite different way, while preserving the flow of the outline. The light falls more evenly on the figure with the upright emphasis, but where the body is curved over the legs, dark shadows define the forms.

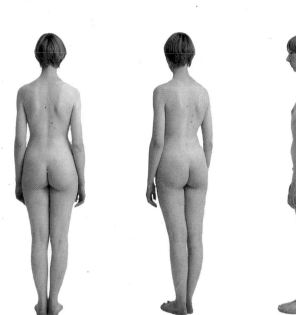

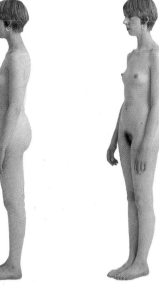

## Choosing a viewpoint *(LEFT)*
The seven poses shown here demonstrate a complete rotation of the model through all the angles of the pose. A different silhouette and illumination of the form occur at each angle. It is therefore of great importance to walk around the posing model before you start work to discover which aspect interests you most. In a busy college studio it is not always possible to take the exact position which you would like, but there is no need simply to start work wherever you happen to be. Choosing the viewpoint, and if possible the pose and environment too, are as much part of the work of life drawing as handling the drawing materials and should be taken as seriously. Take a little time before you start.

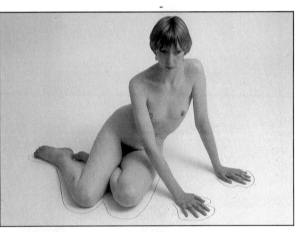

## Marking the model *(LEFT)*
A model will need frequent rests, as posing in a fixed position is very tiring. In order to reconstruct the pose correctly, draw round the model on the floor, chair or bed at the start of the pose so that you both have a definite guide.

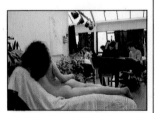

## The model in an environment *(ABOVE)*
Although it may sometimes be better to isolate the model for close study of the human form, you should always be aware of the effect of the surroundings, whether as a specially created environment or in terms of the general activity in the studio.

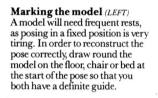

## Different poses *(LEFT)*
The fluid articulation of the human body means that an infinite number of poses are available, since even a slight change in pose may considerably alter the overall effect. With the addition of simple props even more changes can be made. Wherever possible construct the pose in a way that interests you and try to explain quite clearly to the model what you would like to see. You may wish to illustrate a particular mood, recreate a classical pose, or you may be looking for something quite simple to provide a basic drawing exercise. Remember that in a tiring pose the model may need more frequent rests and your working sequence will be less consistent.

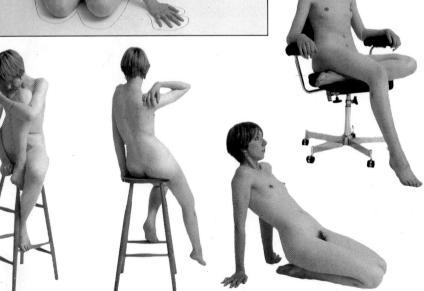

# The drawing process

**Using simple shapes** As a first exercise, you should try to apply the ideas discussed above by drawing the figure as a set of simplified volumes. The value of this exercise is that if it is done paying maximum attention to the ideas already outlined, it will help you acquire a valuable understanding of the basic structure of the figure. This understanding of the rhythmic relationship of volumes in the figure is important because, without it, drawings can only too easily look inarticulate and flat. The eye will cling to the edges of the figure or flit from one shadowed area to the next without comprehending the volumes that produce them. In addition, the study of anatomy which can be very useful if related to this understanding of volumetric structure might otherwise never proceed beyond a sort of map-making.

The aim of the exercise is to try and determine what are the most characteristic features of each sub-division of the figure using only geometric solids to express them. Apply this principle to head, neck, chest, upper arms, lower arms, 'body' of the hand, fingers and thumb, the abdominal area, hips, thighs, knees, lower legs, the 'body' of the foot and toes. The geometric solids should be based on and variants of the cube or rectangular solid, sphere or ovoid, cylinder and cone. These basic forms can be sliced, truncated or made to interpenetrate and link up as required.

This exercise need not literally represent the figure in terms of cubes, cylinders and cones, but these forms should be borne constantly in mind as a basis for simplifying and interpreting the volumes of the figure.

These basic volumes are a permanent feature of the figure in so far as they are related to the rigid structure of the skeleton, but naturally the human figure is subjected to gravity and other forces depending on whatever posture it adopts. This affects the shape of the basic forms, producing flattenings, stretchings, or compressions, in their exterior 'coverings', but not in any way changing their essential structure. The appearance of these basic volumes changes dramatically however, depending on eye-level and viewing point. For example a leg seen in a normal standing pose is a totally different shape to a foreshortened view when the model is reclining. This is why it is important to apply all you know about perspective and cross-sections to sorting out problems of foreshortening and unusual eye-levels.

Two of the most important points relating to drawing from the figure have still to be made. First, before you become involved in an analysis of the parts

## USING SIMPLE SHAPES

Draw a figure as a series of cylinders. Looking at the figure in this way will help you see the basic structure of the figure more clearly, as you will not be distracted by its surface appearance. Practise this several times with the figure in different positions.

of the figure, you should have responded to it as a whole. The old axiom 'the whole is more than the sum of its parts' certainly applies to figure drawing, so it is vital that you give primary consideration to summing up the pose as a whole—establishing the movement and rhythm, the orientation of the figure in space and its position relative to your eye-level. Only after this will further investigation of its structure have any meaning. The mind and eye are all too easily drawn towards detail, they must be disciplined to respond to the larger issues, and so it is important to recheck the disposition of the whole figure frequently. Inventiveness and an imaginative response to the exercise are essential. You should allow yourself freedom to interpret your task in a personal way, and you should give thought to the potential for aesthetic exploration in the way the forms are drawn.

**Expression and intuition** Intuition and imagination are vital even when trying to make an accurate analytical drawing from the figure. This is the 'creative' aspect of the work. Without it even the most careful and precise drawing, correct in all its details is no more than a fine example of craft skills.

In order to produce good figure drawings, it is important that you try to develop an understanding and appreciation of the figure as a series of rhythmically related volumes existing in the three dimensions of space, and a spontaneous, intuitive response to perceptions in order to capture the vitality and 'life' of the figure, while also pursuing an aesthetic concern with the figure itself and the media being used. Eventually you should be able to make a synthesis of these factors which will suit your own ability and interests.

Unlike the analytical aspects of figure drawing where accuracy of observations and a developing familiarity with structure are vital, accuracy of proportions is not so relevant when you are trying to

---

## EXPLORING STRUCTURE

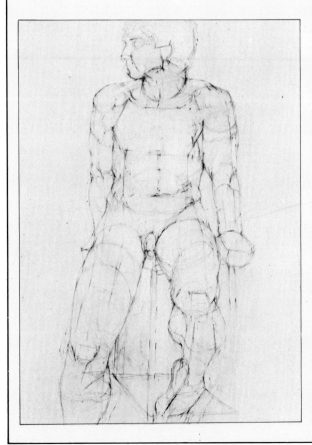

Draw a seated figure using basic volumes as a way of understanding and exploring the figure's structure, and conveying its three-dimensionality. First apply the information about sections discussed on pp 84 to 93 by doing a drawing in pencil showing the sections. Then try to convey the same information about the figure using tones. Charcoal or chalk might be suitable media for this.

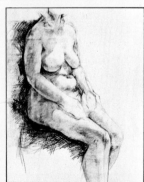

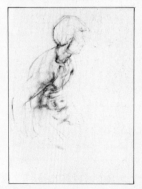

*The pencil drawing of a seated male nude (LEFT) uses sections to establish the figure's basic volumes as a way of understanding its structure. The three-dimensionality of a figure occupying space is quite well expressed, although some of the rhythmic quality of the figure has been lost. The tonal study of a seated female nude (ABOVE) done in black and white chalk, uses the tones to give the fullest possible expression to volume. It succeeds reasonably, and is well observed, except for the legs which are large and disproportionate. This was due to a relaxation of concentration and a failure to see the figure constantly as a whole. In the third example (ABOVE), the unity of the whole figure has not been forgotten. The drawing in charcoal and pencil lays the foundation for further development. For the detail in the collar bone area, the artist did not 'copy', but used the visual clues available to express the structure and articulate light and shade.*

## RAPID DRAWING

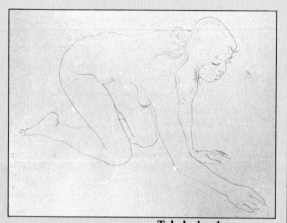

**To help develop your powers of concentration, do a series of rapid drawings in pencil. Take no more than four minutes and try gradually to build up more speed. You will need to maintain your concentration throughout.**
*The standing figure (LEFT) was drawn in only 90 seconds. The attempt to capture impressions as immediately as possible is intuitive rather than analytical. Abbreviations and anomalies of detail are unimportant, providing the vitality of the whole figure is conveyed. The longer time of four minutes taken over the kneeling figure (ABOVE) allowed for greater accuracy and detail.*

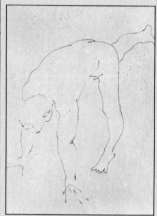

**Having built up some confidence at rapid drawing, draw a figure in motion. Ask the model to carry out a small sequence of motions, holding each stage of the sequence for about 10 seconds, and then repeat the sequence. Concentration and the quick assessment of pose are vital in this.**
*In rapid drawing, it is important not to let the eye be distracted by nonessential detail. Absolute concentration is crucial so that you can quickly assess the pose, its areas of tension and relaxation, rhythms, movements and position in space. As the model repeats the series of movements, store the images in your mind while trying to record them on paper. If your first attempts are unsatisfactory, persevere and always make yourself concentrate as hard as possible For this drawing (RIGHT) the model performed the final position*

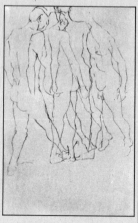

*of each for several seconds. The sequence was repeated a number of times. The drawing conveys the different stages clearly and economically, avoiding a jumble of overlaid lines.*

catch the immediacy of spontaneous reactions. Detailed analysis is not called for. Concentration, however, is even more important. Assessments of pose—its rhythmic movement, spatial disposition, areas of tension and relaxation—have to be carried out at high speeds. It is important to work quickly, not allowing time for the eye to be seduced by interesting detail, in order to develop spontaneous responses and intuitive abilities.

To develop this facility, you should pose the model for only short periods. Start with a maximum of 10 minutes and working gradually to poses of only one minute. Moving poses can be useful for forcing the mind to concentrate and retain visual impressions. Perceptions have to be recorded while the figure is actually performing a set of movements—walking, kneeling, crouching, twisting and so on. The same

## SELF PORTRAIT

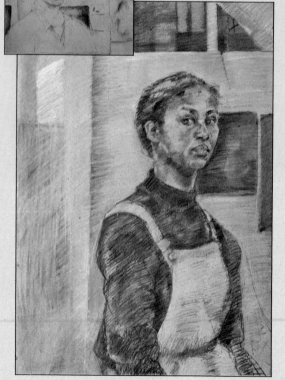

**Draw a self-portrait using coloured pencils and wash.**
*This drawing (LEFT) is rather tentative and lacks careful observation. The second (BELOW) shows more confidence and expresses the volumes well. The free use of colour produces a flickering multi-coloured surface.*

movements should be repeated a number of times to allow the mind time to 'store' the image, and only when a perception has been reinforced a number of times should an attempt be made to record it on paper.

Another exercise, excellent for developing concentration, is to draw the figure without looking at the paper. Line is the best method to use, and the 'rules' can be relaxed at points on the figure where lines cross—so as to express the overlap of limbs, for example. The line should attempt mainly to follow the outer contour of the figure and give expression to movement and volume in an abbreviated and direct way. To aid this process, imagine the point of the pencil actually moving around the edges of the real model. Also try and retain an impression of how fast the point is travelling, otherwise one side of the figure might be drawn slowly, and then without being aware of it, as the line moves on, it begins to do so at greater speed, producing startlingly obvious mismatches of contour. Although following the contour has been advocated for this exercise, no real impulse should be inhibited, and, if you are prompted to move the lines inside the edge, you should feel free to do so.

The results will look very bizarre at first, but with plenty of practice and no relaxation of concentration, some lively and interesting results can occur. Major distortions and dislocations will be less evident and the drawing will have the virtue of spontaneity and capture the rhythm, movement, and unity of the pose. This is a method Rodin followed at times and it would be useful to study his line and wash drawings.

The value of any form of rapid drawing is that if any worthwhile results are to be achieved they can only be produced as a result of intense concentration. The mind really must focus its attention sharply and maintain this throughout the drawing. Also the feelings can be given a free rein, so the excitement and energy created by stimulating perceptions can be communicated through the drawing. A very fine balance is necessary between the iron control of the will exercised in concentrating and the 'leaping horse' of the feelings.

It is important for all rapid drawing done in this context to make a statement about the whole pose. Dealing only with a section of the figure defeats the purpose. You should experiment with different media and try to allow the intrinsic qualities of whatever medium is being used to predominate—the fluidity and transparency of watercolour, the depth and richness of Conté crayon or pastel, the clarity and sharpness of a pen line, the crisp tonal qualities of charcoal, and so on. These are not rules. As stated

before, there are no rules. You should use the media as your own aesthetic sense dictates and the nature of the task suggests.

**Distortion and experiment** The type of analytical approach discussed earlier is designed to give familiarity with some basic facts about the figure and to train the mind and eye in observation. It is a form of discipline that sharpens the perceptual faculties. Once the facts have been assimilated, a response to them becomes virtually automatic and they can form a basis for meaningful exploration of other qualities. Over a period, patient study together with the freedom acquired through rapid drawing should have been brought into a synthesis and thereby produced a genuine feeling for homogeneity among the parts of the figure, the value of rhythm and the need for 'expressiveness'. This can then become the model for

## KEEPING A SKETCHBOOK

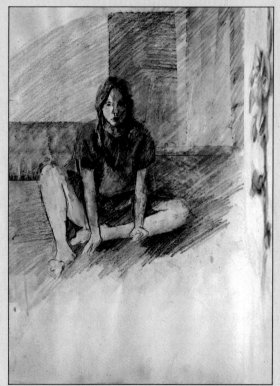

Keep a sketchbook and try out ideas for figure drawing in it. A sketchbook is one of the most important tools of an artist. You can jot ideas or thoughts down quickly or take time to develop some of your thoughts.

*For this sketch, the artist sat on the floor in front of a mirror. She has used coloured pencils and wash. The energetic strokes of the pencil build up the forms boldly. The subject is generally well handled. This is a good example of how sketchbooks can be used to develop confidence in handling media.*

experiment. Nonetheless, whatever distortions are explored and freedom of expression indulged in, the whole drawing should obey an inner logic that is the equivalent of but not a strict representation of the forms seen in nature.

This principle is clearly seen at work in the drawings of many modern artists who use distortion and dislocation to communicate their vision and personal preoccupations. The power of the imagination, based on an appreciation of this unity in both nature and art, is the catalyst required for giving it expression. Each artist 'sees' the figure in different ways and uses distortions for different ends. In this context it is useful to study in detail the work of great draughtsmen like Picasso, Matisse, Giacometti and Schiele among others.

**The figure and its background** It is a personal decision whether or not to include the background in a figure drawing. If your aim is simply to study the forms of the figure, the surrounding area is not so important. However, you can usefully extend the analyses of structure and space into the containing environment. The Swiss artist, Alberto Giacometti (1901–1966) is an excellent example of an artist seeing the figure and its containing space as a single motif. The figure becomes one unit in a range of components that go to make up the whole image. If you wish to make an objective analysis, then the conceptual tools described in the first part of this section should be used. The problem of establishing accurate formal and spatial relationships is greater, but so, too, is the potential for exciting image making.

In the same way that distortions can be exploited in working from the figure, the environment can also be treated as a jumping off point for imaginative interpretation. Interesting possibilities open up by situating 'props' between the viewer and the figure, interposing open frames or 'false' windows, for example. Large mirrors produce fascinating extensions of space and offer a real challenge to sorting out the complexities thereby created. These 'props' are typical of art school life-drawing studios, but you can create much the same effect at home.

This type of study can be applied to drawing the figure in any environment. A studio environment is necessarily artificial and its environmental potential is limited. Therefore you should make the most of any possibility for doing figure studies in a variety of natural surroundings. A sketchbook is an essential requirement and should be taken wherever there is the chance of recording new or familiar situations involving the human figure.

**Anatomy** A knowledge of anatomy can be very useful as an aid to a study of the subtle complexities of the nude figure. It is perhaps essential if your main aim is outright objectivity. There are a number of quite good books on anatomy for artists and you should study these if possible.

However, diagrams and drawings of the arrangements of muscles in such manuals are often presented without being related to the three-dimensional aspects of the figure. The intricacy that the depiction of each individual muscle reveals is often a hindrance rather than a help. What is important is that you observe the way muscles form blocks or units on the figure, an example being the way the pectoral muscles in the male figure form a broad plane across the front of the chest. Particularly important are the areas of the figure where bones lie just under the surface, for example the collar bones, part of the rib cage, the vertebrae (particularly at the base of the neck), elbow, wrists, ankles, pelvic crests, most of the skull, hands and feet, knees and shins. At these points, the skeleton influences the forms markedly, and offers a series of stable features that reveal the inner rigid structure of the figure. These are valuable as cross-reference points. Also important are the areas where tendons appear just under the skin, giving a special character to the form. These areas include the wrists, back of the hand, front of the ankle and the massive Achilles tendon that links the calf muscle to the heel, the top of the foot, the back of the knee, and the front of the neck where a hollow is formed between inner ends of collar bones. These areas should be closely studied and their structural significance noted.

The best way to learn the value of anatomy is to examine the figure carefully with a good set of anatomical illustrations to hand. The model can then be asked to tense and relax different parts and you can try to trace the more important muscle divisions. A sinewy male model is best for this purpose.

Figure drawing is a tough discipline, calling for the maximum possible attention, sensitivity and discrimination. To excel, you should be like a concert instrumentalist and practise every day. If a life model is not available, use yourself. Draw your own hands and feet, do self-portraits try using a full-length mirror. Failing this, draw any object that is lying around, arrange still-life groups, but whatever you are drawing, you should apply the concepts that were discussed at some length in this section. The ideas and applications discussed here can also be applied to drawings which are not of the human figure. Try some of the exercises using objects, make still-life groups using the same ideas of observation, analysis, rhythm, intuition and inventiveness.

This discussion of figure drawing did not go beyond describing the figure as a series of geometricized volumes. This was to concentrate attention on the organization of the figure in relatively basic terms. However, when these forms and the awareness of rhythm and vitality, spontaneity and freedom of expression have been absorbed, this provides a foundation for a more careful study of the subtleties of the figure. When this knowledge has become second nature, you can turn your attention to surface modulations and try to carry analysis and expression to a more refined level.

**The human body**
The study of anatomy used to play an important part in art education. Today, although it is less frequently a formal part of the curriculum, artists still need to develop a knowledge of the body and its anatomical structure. The bones of the skeleton *(BELOW LEFT)* form the frame for the muscles *(BELOW)*. You may find a good set of anatomical illustrations useful, these will show the muscles and bones. If you study these while looking at a figure, you will be able to see more clearly how the body is structured beneath its surface. Ask your model to tense and relax different sets of muscles so that you can see how they work. Look at the model in different poses and work out how the positions of the muscles have altered. Note how the muscles tense and relax in pairs. When you have become familiar with the structure of the body, look at how the skin sits on the muscles in different ways. On a young person, the skin will be tauter than on an older person.

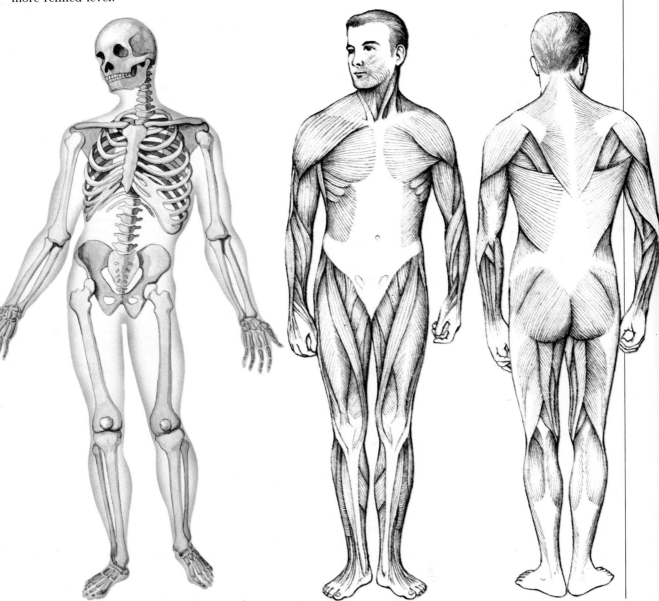

# DRAWING AS ENQUIRY

One very important function of drawing is as a method of enquiry and exploration. Enquiry refers to a use of drawing as a means of gathering and recording visual information, a long established practice for becoming familiar with and understanding the characteristics of the world of the perceptions. This is primarily objective and involves attempting to record impressions and study the visual properties of objects. Secondly, enquiry is a use of drawing as a way of searching for effective aesthetic images, a process of exploration with the aim of discovering meaningful configurations of forms, whether figurative or abstract. This activity is primarily subjective and involves a personal attempt to make value judgements about the quality of the images produced. Both aspects frequently work together in the act of drawing. Indeed it is difficult to imagine work by an established artist in which these factors do not combine to some degree. Technical skills develop through the exercise of these principles, because the clearer you 'see' what you wish to achieve the more likely you are to evolve the means of achieving it. Of course, the more your drawing involves a genuine search for truth in either an objective or subjective way, the more your critical faculties will develop.

## Drawing from the natural world

One form of visual recording is often referred to as sketching, and sketchbooks are primary pieces of equipment for any artist, amateur or professional. However, the word 'sketch' can have unfortunate connotations, as it is often associated with quick notations done hastily and without any real concentration. Hence the word 'sketchily' is often used to denote slightness and lack of real observation or attention.

The first lesson to be learned is that no valid drawing can be done without the involvement of thought, feeling and judgement. In this context, thought is a process of focussing attention on what is being drawn, whether figurative or abstract, and the ability to reflect on what you are doing. By the term feeling is meant the involvement of emotions, the excitement and sensations in looking at the object, in evolving images, and in the

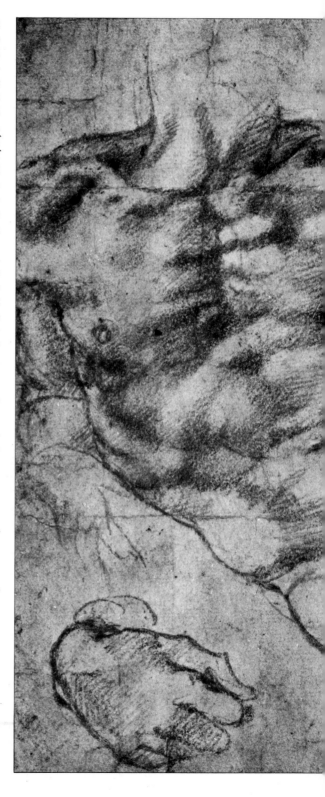

One of the main ways in which artists have used drawings over the centuries is as a way of evolving images which are then finally depicted in a different medium. Michelangelo's study for the creation of Adam *(RIGHT)* on the roof of the Sistine Chapel shows the artist's profound knowledge of anatomy. The major volumes of the figure are powerfully stated, and this is carried over into the muscles of the figure, culminating in a monumental and almost superhuman effect.

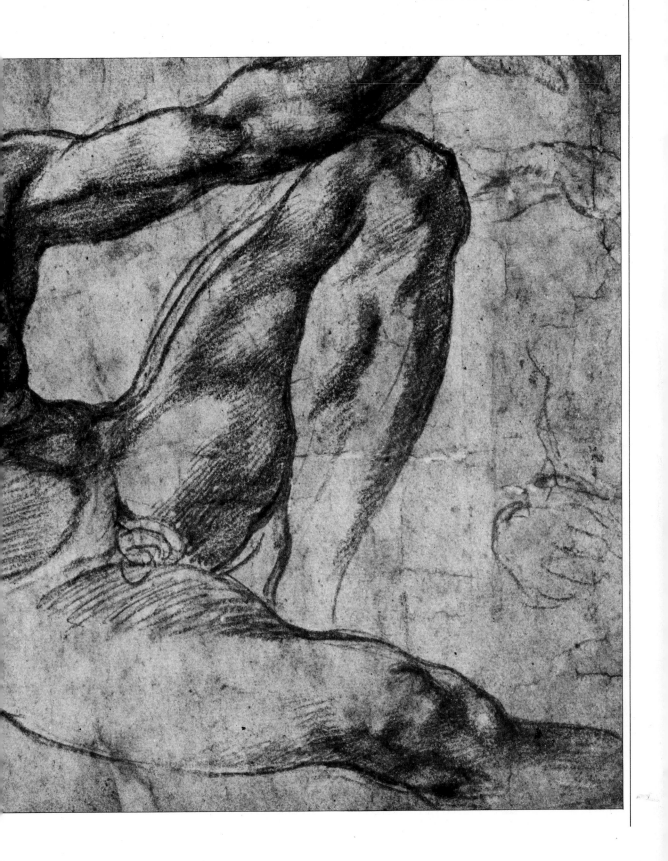

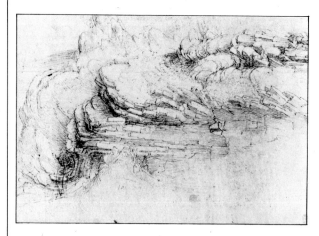

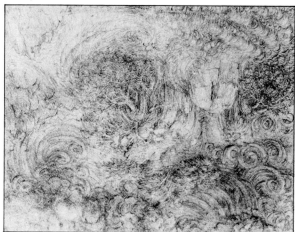

act of drawing itself. Judgement is what is brought to bear on the problem of evaluating what you are doing—both as a continuous process while drawing, and as a way of applying critical analysis to what is produced.

For example, if you are interested in landscape, what sorts of drawing should you be doing? There are no general prescriptions, it all depends on your particular interests and aims. If you are interested in the forms and structure of landscape, its hidden architecture, so to speak, then an analytical approach would be relevant, in order to try to reveal its underlying geometry and formal relationships. Try bearing in mind the dictum of the French artist Paul Cézanne (1839–1906): 'nature can be reduced to the cube, cylinder, and cone'. You could take this as a specific aim in order to construct a

For the landscape artist, working out of doors is often essential. The British artist John Constable attached great importance to working in this way. For this, his sketchbook was particularly useful as it allowed him to note down impressions. This study of the village of Dedham *(BELOW)* is a fine example of wash drawing. Constable has captured the drama of contrasting light and shade. The impression of spontaneity conveyed by the picture is achieved with great economy of means. When doing a landscape drawing, or for that matter a drawing of any kind, you should not be led astray by the desire to convey atmosphere. You should rather try to use light, shade and texture to reveal form and structure rather than to denote a mood or feeling. Try to delineate the relationships between parts of the composition.

The drawings and notebooks of Leonardo da Vinci are one of the most interesting examples of how drawing as enquiry can be used in many different contexts. Leonardo's scientific interests were revealed in his anatomical drawings, which were done with great precision. The sketch of rock stratification *(TOP)* indicates Leonardo's interest in the world of nature. One characteristic of the Renaissance was an interest in man as a subject of study, another was an increased curiosity about the natural world. Sketches like those of Leonardo were one way in which artists expressed this curiosity. The movements of water — rivers, streams, the sea — have proved of perennial interest to artists both contemporary and historical. In his drawing *Deluge (ABOVE)*, Leonardo has used fine strokes to convey the surging water. These drawings show Leonardo's awareness of the shaping process of natural forces,

an element common to both his anatomical and natural studies. When embarking on a landscape drawing, it is important that you ask yourself a series of questions about your aims.

What general approach do you wish to adopt? For example, do you wish to depict the forms naturalistically or do you want to try to show the underlying relationships between them? Do you wish to focus on a large section of the landscape, or a small portion, as in these Leonardo drawings? Do you wish, like Leonardo to concentrate on individual objects — such as rocks, trees and their leaves, or plants? Do you, on the other hand, want to show the broad sweep of the landscape — hills and valleys, for example? If your interests are in the larger scope, you may find it useful to do initial sketches of the different components of the picture before embarking on the general image.

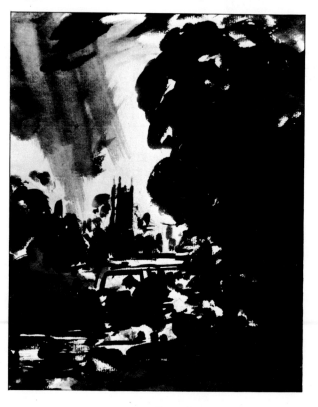

geometric analogy to the forms in nature, or simply keep it in mind as an aid to structuring your visual perceptions. In the first instance, you should try hard to examine the forms of the landscape as objectively as possible, avoiding the impulse to jot something down in haste without examining its formal qualities closely. You should try to express precise relationships between the various parts and respond to the interplay of horizontals, verticals, diagonals, rhythmic movements, swellings and hollows, hard and soft forms, and so on, without being led astray by atmospheric effects. Light and shade, texture and colour should be used to reveal form and structure rather than to express a particular mood.

You must decide whether to study a large expanse or just a small section of landscape. If the latter, should it be in the foreground, the middle distance or even the distance? Should there be a concentration on particular objects such as trees, bushes, rocks, hedges? Should the drawing include figures, animals or vehicles? If you decide to show a narrow spread of interest and to treat the forms realistically, you may need to make detailed drawings of the various components of the subject, depicting their formal qualities and surface features. This is not only a means of gathering information about the superficial aspects of each object under scrutiny, but also a way of understanding their particular characteristics, the way in which they differ structurally from each other. The drawings and notebooks of artists such as the German artist

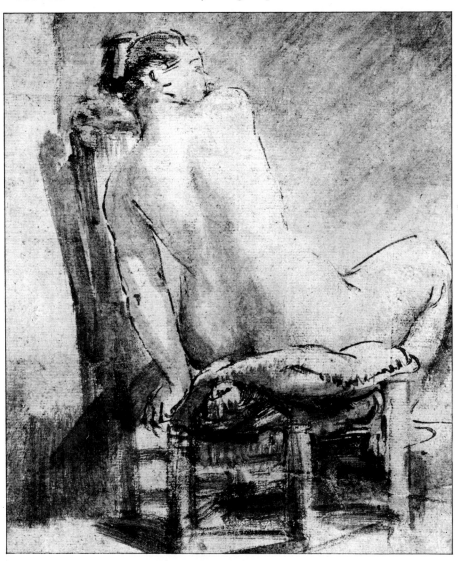

The Dutch artist Rembrandt van Rijn was a master of the medium of pen and wash, which lends itself to conveying quick impressions. Rembrandt captures the vitality of his subject well, conveying its atmosphere and intimacy. The great flexibility which the medium offers enables the artist to delineate the many subtle variations of light and shade. The figure *(LEFT)* is outlined in strong lines while the back and shadowy area around the buttocks are depicted in paler, more muted tones. The pose of the figure, its centre of gravity and balance show in practice many of the ideas on movement and volume discussed in the previous section (pp 84-89). This study demonstrates how a drawing can be used as a way of working out, for instance, the pose, areas of light and shade and general relationships between the parts of the composition. As is often the case with drawings done for the purposes of enquiry, relatively little attention has been paid to the background, while the stool which is crucial to the composition and the position of the figure has been treated in more detail.

Rembrandt's great skill and very acute perception enabled him to express the vitality of the figure with great economy of means.

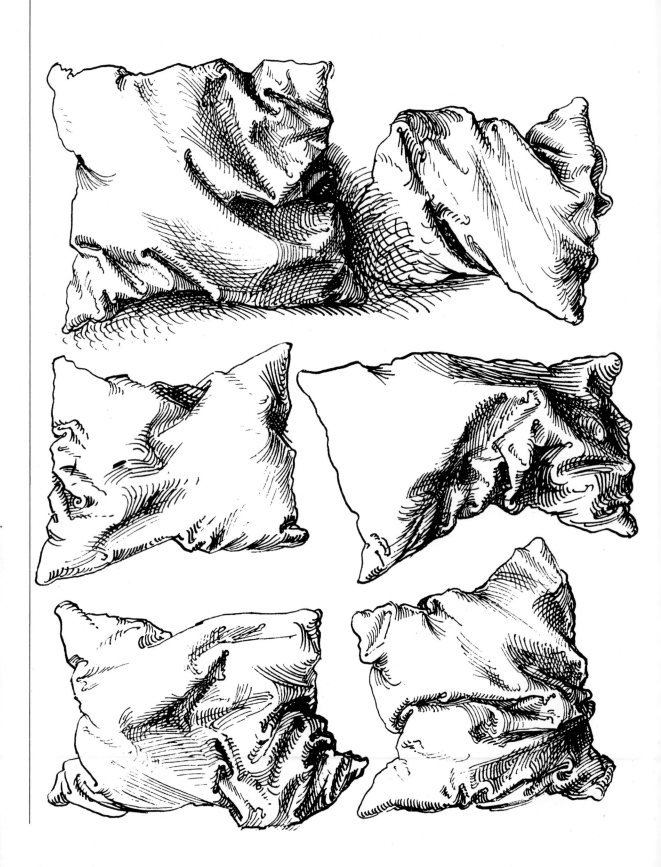

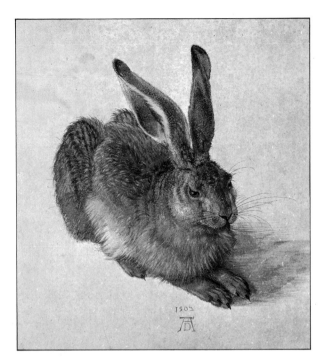

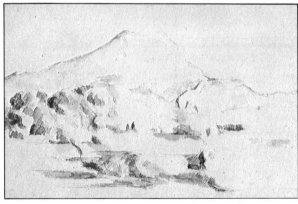

Albrecht Dürer (1471–1528) and Leonardo da Vinci should be closely studied in this context, as they provide exemplary evidence of this type of investigation.

These types of decision can be made partly intuitively as well as consciously. It is not uncommon to hear an artist say 'I put that feature in because the drawing seemed to need something there to give it tension and interest', or 'I left something out because it spoilt the overall unity of the composition.' In other words, even drawings done with analysis in mind require some intuitive or imaginative activity to give them aesthetic validity. This is the subjective aspect of enquiry.

You should consider the composition. Ask yourself how you should arrange the elements of the drawing in the most functional and satisfying way and which media best suit the drawing. Is it to be bold and vigorous, or subtle and delicate? Make your decision in response to your own predilections, feelings and sensations when confronting the subject. At this point you may need to decide whether you wish to re-arrange the components of the composition to follow aesthetic promptings rather than to give simply an accurate representation of the composition's structural elements.

Other approaches to landscape are also possible. For example, you could examine conventions used in other disciplines, such as geological and geographical diagrams, grid lines, contours and other features derived from maps and land surveying. Photographs, films or satellite pictures, could also be investigated for visual information and stimulus. In this case, the work might well appear diagrammatic, but it would in fact be based on landscape and be just as valid an exploration of aesthetic possibilities as drawing directly from the landscape. It is a common experience, in fact so common as virtually to amount to a rule, that artists regardless of experience or training need to explore a theme through a whole series of drawings in order to arrive at a vocabulary of forms and technical treatment that satisfies their intentions. Of course, there is no single definitive solution to the problems that are being dealt with. These principles can be applied to any subject of study, such as landscape, figure, still-life, or any other aspect of the world.

First you should be as clear as possible about the intention of the work, what it aims to achieve. This clarity of aim is not always easy to come by, and it may take a series of experimental drawings to discover it. Next, you should decide on your approach—is the work to be analytical, 'expressive' or experimental, for example? This should be linked to whatever knowledge of the work of individual artists and art move-

Many of Albrecht Dürer's drawings are excellent examples of visual enquiry. In this pen drawing of pillows *(LEFT)*, Dürer has focused his attention on a mundane domestic object and, in a clear and incisive way, has examined its varied characteristics. The lines follow the direction of the forms and the details of the folds, however complex, never destroy the expression of volume in the whole. Another facet of Dürer's talent were his drawings of animals. The *Young Hare (TOP)* is a masterpiece of sustained visual analysis. Each aspect of the animal has been scrutinized, but all the detail, however refined, is subordinated to the whole. The watercolours and pencil drawings of the French artist Paul Cézanne reveal a very different way of expressing his fascination with nature and form. In *Mont St Victoire (ABOVE)* the image is organized in terms of closely articulated marks and strokes. For Cézanne, the way the marks structured the surface of the paper or canvas was as important as their function in defining tone. Try to compare and contrast the approaches of Dürer and Cézanne and the ways in which they use their chosen medium.

ments can be advantageously brought to bear on the subject. You should, however, never use this as a means of imitating someone else's style or idiosyncrasies, but as a form of stimulus to your imagination and as a method of bringing an informal intelligence to bear on the problem.

Next you should decide on the most appropriate medium or media, either by a considered choice or through experiment. To do this, focus your attention sharply on the subject, make your mind receptive to the stimuli from your perceptions and open to the promptings of your imagination. The next step is to select material for transcription and, if you are doing more than simply taking visual notes, to arrange this material into an effective composition. Here you must beware of ready-made answers, such as the sort of formulae which suggest, say, certain proportions of land to sky. These can deny you the opportunity to find personal and original solutions. You should consider the questions of scale, and experiment with handling your chosen medium. For instance, you may

## ENQUIRING INTO NATURE

**The purpose of drawing as enquiry is to help you develop ways of making images, to stimulate your imagination and to encourage you to experiment with media and techniques. You should always beware of** ready-made answers, do not simply copy, or draw as others have done. You should always approach a new subject with an open mind.

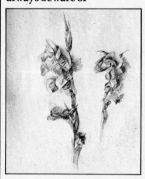

*One of the main purposes of a sketchbook is to enable you to examine different facets of the subject you are treating. In these delicate studies of gladioli, the artist has chosen to draw the object from different angles. The artist has chosen to use coloured pencils as her medium and has used them effectively to explore the subtle modulations of colour on the petals of the flower's. For the artist, one of the fascinations of flowers is that they present such a challenging variety of forms and shapes. Here the artist has attempted to convey the interplay of light and shadow in the curl of the petals using combinations of colours and tones.*

## USING ENQUIRY

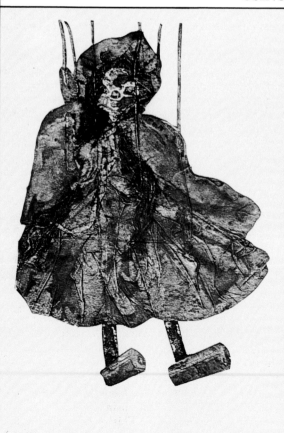

**Choose a subject and make a series of studies in your sketchbook. Experiment with as many different media and combinations of media as possible. Look at the subject from different angles and in varying ways. Look critically at your efforts, and assess which combination of approach and media suits your purposes best.**

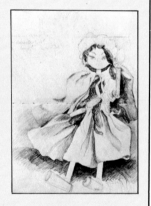

*The subject of these drawings is a puppet. However, you could select any material you like, the object of the exercise being to examine the subject in as many different ways as possible. The first sketch (RIGHT TOP) uses pencil. The tones created help to convey the volumes of the figure. Particular attention was paid to the folds of the dress. The pen and ink sketch (RIGHT BOTTOM) uses line to depict the folds of the drapery. The pattern of lines in some ways resembles the veins on a leaf. Here the dress is not well differentiated from the background. Building up the use and combination of techniques, the third study (LEFT) uses colour washes, bleach and embossing. The embossing adds a three-dimensional quality to the image. These are excellent examples of sketchbook work which explores visual ideas and experiments with media. Visual curiosity combines with inventiveness, revealing a willingness to develop new responses to perceptions and ideas.*

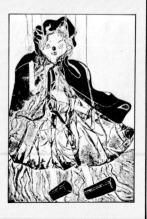

find that the breadth and intensity offered by charcoal is best used in quite large-scale drawings. As art is very much an individual matter, it is important that you evolve your own means and methods. Many of the factors involved in drawing from objects in the natural world also apply to other forms of drawing.

# Abstract work

If you are interested in abstract art, you will be as concerned with articulating an aim—whether by decision or through experiment—as an artist working in figurative areas. Questions of scale and appropriate medium are also pertinent. In abstract work, however, there may be a greater need to experiment with different ways of applying media. Drawing techniques like frottage and decalcomania were evolved as new processes by the Surrealists and have particular application to abstract work. Collage, blotting, dribbling, stencilling, spraying, scraping, cutting-up and reassembling are all technical processes which you should consider for their possible relevance to the work in hand. In addition you should give full reign to your inventiveness—anything that makes a mark or creates a shape can be used to draw with.

It is important to decide what type of abstract images you are interested in—do you prefer free and flowing, delicate and sensitive, symmetrical or asymmetrical images? Do you want to rely on line, mass, tone or texture, or, indeed, a combination of these? The possibilities are limitless.

In abstract work, it is especially important to find out about precedents and artists working in the genre to help you recognize the context of the work you are producing, the particular form of abstraction you have chosen, and its main features, technical qualities and the ideas or theories behind it. There are no rules, but if you want to combine types of abstract image, it is useful to know something about them. This, of course, applies to all styles of art, not just to abstract art. Without this type of knowledge, the work might be capably executed, but not responsive to the wealth of ideas that are such a feature of modern art.

There is a vast range of possibilities in image-making that lie between the extremes of drawing objectively from nature and working with abstract forms. This is a rich field for exploration and experiment, and the ability to evaluate results in an informed and critical manner is vital. However, one essential attribute for any artist wishing to draw and paint objectively in any context is visual curiosity. This is especially vital in early training as an artist.

## ENQUIRY AND SELF-PORTRAIT

If there is no model handy and you want to practise some figure drawing, use your self as model. You do not have to draw the whole of yourself, you can practise drawing parts of your body. For instance, look at one of your feet and draw it several times using different media and techniques. Drawing your own foot presents some interesting problems of dealing with scale and perspective.

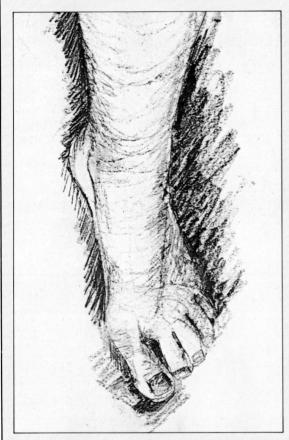

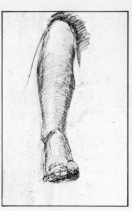

*A good sketchbook should include drawings of anything and everything. These charcoal illustrations show that much valuable visual information can be derived from drawing parts of yourself. You are always conveniently available as a model. Visual curiosity is an essential attribute of any artist and it is important that you stimulate your curiosity in as many ways as possible. This is why the sketchbook is so important because any impression or thought can be noted down, even if only briefly, for you to develop later. You should not feel constrained in any way by what you put in your sketchbook.*

# DRAWING FOR ITS OWN SAKE

The immediacy of drawing, the fact that little or no preparation is necessary, and the ready availability of paper, has commended the process to most artists as a means of making works of art with the same status as paintings or sculpture. In some instances, it is impossible to make a complete distinction between what is drawing and what is painting. For example, a Chinese brush drawing in ink on paper or silk is usually referred to as painting, yet a Rembrandt study in ink applied with a brush is called a drawing. Some marvellous examples of drawing transferred to paper by semimechanical means are called prints. Does this mean they are no longer drawings? Works done in watercolour are often referred to either as drawings or as paintings depending on the attitude or purpose of the author.

Little is known of drawings as independent works of art before the Renaissance. During the Renaissance, however, artists began to compose pictures using only drawing techniques. Sometimes they were produced as a gift for a valuable patron, or as a token of respect and affection for a friend or lover. Naturally, collectors were not slow to begin to acquire these less expensive works of art. *Archers Shooting at a Herm* by Michelanglo (1475–1564) is a fine example of his unsurpassed draughtsmanship. The rhythmic movement of the whole composition is echoed in every figure. The drawing is in red chalk, and Michelangelo has used this medium with a light and sensitive touch to reveal the subtleties of anatomical structure. He achieved this without any diminution of the feeling of physical and spiritual energy, for which his work is renowned. The work clearly demonstrates that drawing can be as valuable a process as any other for the realization of an artist's ideas.

Not all drawings of this type are as refined in their treatment. The drawing by the Spanish artist Francisco de Goya (1746–1828) called *The Stabbing* uses a bold and vigorous brush technique to express the horror of the event. Goya produced many drawings and prints that make strong social and political comments. Drawing is a perfect vehicle for transmit-

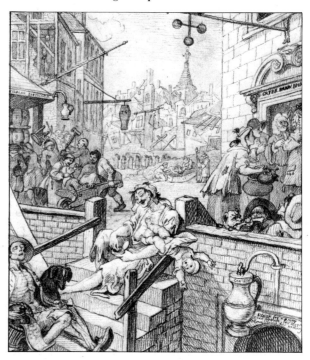

Drawing is a medium which has appealed to caricaturists. The eighteenth century English artist Thomas Rowlandson was renowned for his bitingly satirical works. His drawing *An Epicure (ABOVE)* conveys its spirited wit through the use of line and cross-hatched shading.

Drawing has often been used as a vehicle for social comment or criticism. In the eighteenth century two British artists Thomas Rowlandson and William Hogarth used drawing as a medium in itself and as a preliminary to engraving. It was in this era that the mass media really began to develop. Hogarth's *Gin Street (ABOVE)* was a sketch later turned in to an engraving. Note the strong graphic qualities and examine the spatial relationships.

In *Face of a Man* by George Grosz the artist used fine pen strokes to build up the image and give an impression of solid lines. This is an example of a somewhat understated but nevertheless bitingly satirical style of drawing.

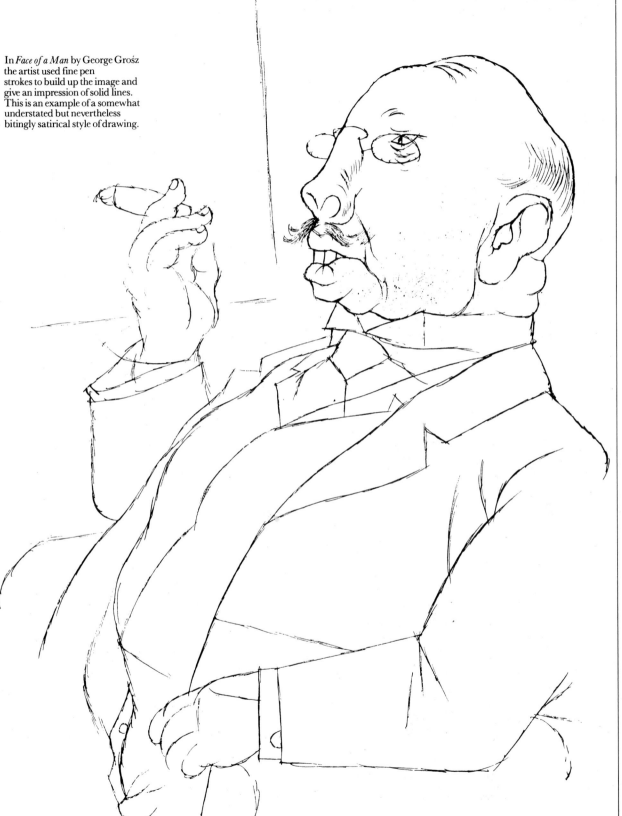

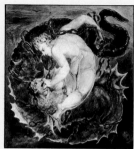

*Angel Michael Binding Satan (ABOVE)* and *God Creating Adam (RIGHT)* are fine examples of William Blake's linear style. As a youth, he was apprenticed to the engraver James Basire and Blake's mature style reflected this training. He looked back to the linear style of the Middle Ages and to this extent was very different from his contemporaries. His expressive use of line was remarkable. In both these works line is used symbolically and aesthetically. Tension and movement, respectively, are expressed clearly. In the first, the binding of Satan is stressed by the constricting, curving lines. In *God Creating Adam* the sense of creation and metamorphosis is enhanced by the feeling of movement achieved through the use of line. But besides these things, the linear qualities are used to enhance the aesthetic nature of the works. The spectator can respond to them simply as formal structures, as rhythms and patterns. The patterns do more than this because they lead the eye around the composition and through them the spectator comes to terms with the subject.

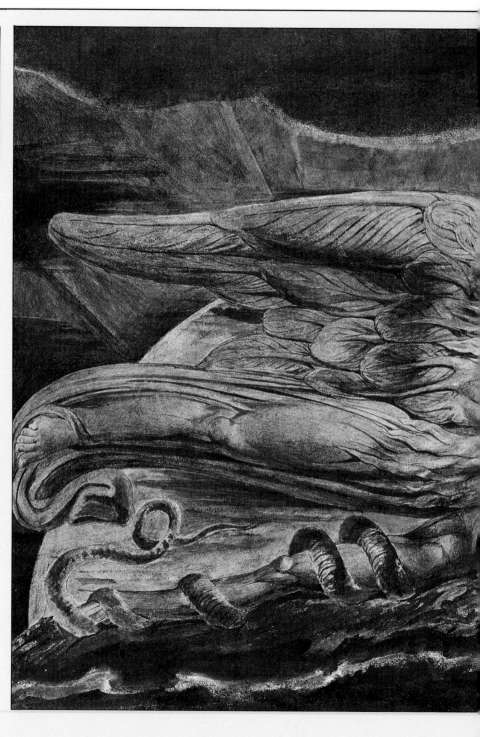

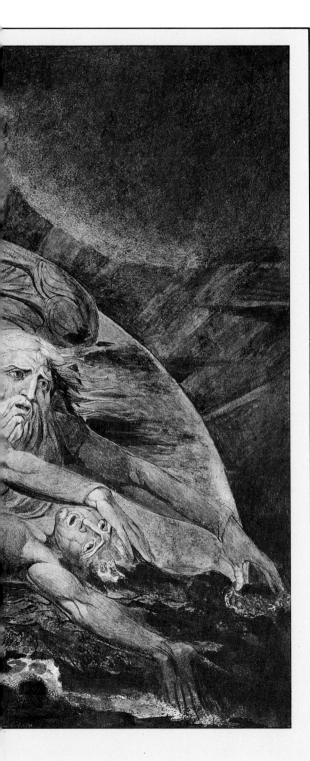

ting ideas with impassioned energy and intensity. The immediacy and assurance of Goya's technical skill transmit the idea directly without having to go through the various stages of a painting. In this way, spontaneity is preserved and the subject is expressed with the urgency Goya felt it warranted.

Drawings, particularly when turned into prints, are especially suitable for art that has a strong ideological message. The speed of turnover and wide dissemination possible in printing mean that political and social events can be subjected to satirical criticism while they are still in the public mind. This is, of course, the function of the political cartoonist, but occasionally an artist of real stature uses these means and elevates the genre to the level of fine art. Typical examples are William Hogarth (1697–1764), Honoré Daumier (1808–1879), Thomas Rowlandson (1756–1827) and George Grosz (1893–1959). The power of their imagination has created images that not only transcend the local scandals of the day in terms of social comment, but also provide a great deal of aesthetic pleasure. Their wit and invention is of the highest order. As in all true works of art, technique and idea form a perfect match. It is not for ease of mechanical reproduction alone that artists working in this mode often use pen and ink. There is something sharp, biting and unequivocal about direct strokes of the pen that is particularly apt for satire.

The English artist William Blake (1757–1827), a controversial figure in the history of art, combined drawing and painting techniques and used printing to produce his imaginative works. Blake experimented with various techniques for printing. In *God creating Adam*, for example, the image was probably produced in two stages by first painting the outlines boldly and swiftly on board (perhaps in egg tempera) and, while the paint was still wet, taking an impression of it on paper. Then colour was added to the design on the board, the paper carefully registered, and a second impression taken. This produced an interesting mottled texture which was then further coloured by hand to enhance the total effect. The design could be renewed on the board when another impression was required.

Mono-printing (a simpler version of Blake's process) is an interesting technique for you to experiment with. Using oil or acrylic on glass and working quickly so that a print can be taken before the paint begins to dry. The textured quality of the image can be quite attractive and may suggest a variety of possible further elaborations.

Another artist of vision and imagination who often used drawing or printmaking to express his ideas was the nineteenth century French artist Odilon Redon (1840–1916). For example, *Head of a Martyr* is a charcoal drawing in which Redon has used the two major qualities of charcoal with remarkable effect. The soft, rich qualities are used as a general background texturing and the intense blackness used to give added dramatic effect to the profile of the face, the eye, and the structural qualities of the bowl and supporting forms. The picture has all the completeness of a painting, and the addition of colour, rather than intensifying the image may well have diminished its powerful effect. His works are well worth studying.

Such examples show how drawing can be used to make works of art that hold their own with painting. These works also show something important about technique. Firstly it is important to understand the special qualities of various media—what they do well, how they can be applied and so on. You should try out and experiment yourself, perhaps augmenting this with other technical information from a book, a

number of which are readily available.

The personal technique which you will gradually develop is normally referred to as 'style'. It is a very individual matter, involving the artist's vision, the intentions of the work and the degree of inventiveness the artist is capable of.

In all the examples discussed here the artist has selected the medium most suitable for the expression of the ideas and feelings and has used this in a personal way. This, and the way the forms of the image are drawn, together with the use of colour, form the basis of an individual style. This is another aspect of Blake's work, where his highly personal treatment of the human figure, the way he uses watercolour and other processes and his visionary inventiveness in composition all come together in a masterly unity of idea and technique.

At this level, technique or style cannot be taught. All you can do is constantly question the appropriateness and use of the medium in your work, experi-

## USING TONE

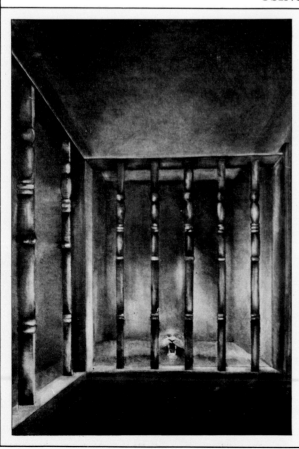

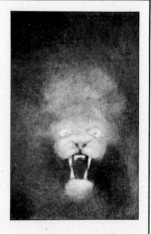

Drawing for its own sake is a useful way to explore some more unusual images and approaches. For this project, try either to create an image which is aiming to surprise or shock the viewer, or, alternatively, make a more conventional image using extremely unusual media. The purpose of this is to encourage you to explore both new images and new media. It is especially important for you at all stages in your development as an artist to be willing to consider new ways of looking at the world and new ways of producing images.

*Both of these works have distinct Surrealist overtones. The larger drawing (LEFT) combines two images which, in themselves, are quite ordinary and everyday – a bannister rail and an animal skin. However, the artist has altered the conventional context and viewpoint by putting the animal skin behind the rails instead of, for example, showing it as part of the decor of an interior. The juxtaposition which the artist has made seems alien to everyday experience, and this makes the whole image rather disturbing. The image also relies on the use of dark tones, a wide range of which*

*creates the impression that the forms are emerging from a mysterious and undefined space. The second drawing (ABOVE), also in black crayon, depicts only the head. The effect of the head emerging from a dark void is much greater than in the first image. However, this picture loses something of the dramatic effect of the first because contact with 'normal' reality seems to have been lost. Dispensing with the bannister rail and not including any other everyday objects lessens the shock effect which the first image produces. It is nonetheless a strong and well executed work.*

## URBAN VIEW

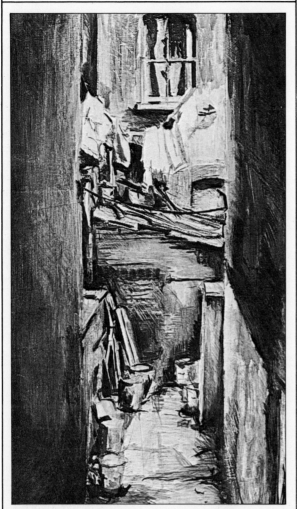

**Do a detailed drawing of a landscape. This does not have to be of a country scene, it could also be of an urban setting. Indeed, urban views have great potential for the artist because of the wide variety of line and tone – shadows of buildings, angles of overlapping buildings, spaces between them. Consider the medium or media carefully. Most drawing media offer excellent possibilities for varying tone and texture. Try one work in monochrome, perhaps using white or black paint for highlighting.**

*This strong and evocative drawing was done in charcoal and acrylic wash. The composition is well conceived. The two flanking walls are left blank, giving greater emphasis to the complex build-up of forms in the centre. The dark tone of these walls leads the eye in towards the feeling of light in the central section. The tunnelling effect of the side walls also helps emphasize the limited space in the back yard and alley, and helps create the rather claustrophobic atmosphere of the image. The scene is viewed from an interesting angle and this helps the effectiveness of the image. The image shows good handling of the media and an ability on the part of the artist to depict light and shade in many tonal variations.*

ment with alternative media to try to achieve a better coincidence of idea and image. This type of questioning has also to be done by any artist desirous of improvement or of breaking new ground. Only by so doing can you develop the all-important ability to be self-critical.

Finally, for any painter, drawing is simply an on-going process. The division of drawing activities into enquiry, drawing for painting, and drawing for its own sake is inevitably arbitrary. All these functions overlap and support each other. Many thousands of drawings are done without a specific function being attached to them other than to keep exercised an artist's manipulative skills, powers of perception and invention, visual curiosity and commitment to art. There need be no other justification for drawing. It is a fundamental occupation for all visual artists, an intellectual and expressive discipline that provides the unique pleasure of making meaningful marks and creating images.

## EXPLORING DISTORTION

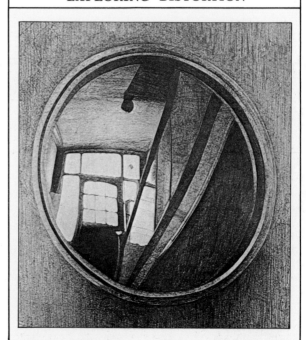

**Draw an everyday object in a way which makes it look unusual. You could try drawing a close-up of an object or something seen from an unusual angle.**

*The image is taken from a circular mirror which frames the drawing and focuses the viewer's attention. The unusual shapes stem from the distortions produced by the convex mirror and the source of light. The dramatic effect is enhanced by strong tonal contrasts. The image owes much to photography.*

# DRAWING FOR PAINTING

The principles of drawing as enquiry also apply to drawing which accompanies or is a preparation for painting. There is, however, a difference in emphasis depending on the type of painting you are aiming for. For example, the use of a wide range of media in exploratory drawings for abstract work might trigger new interests in tone, colour, texture or mark-making, and suggest new ways of applying paint to produce 'equivalents' for those qualities. The same range of media might not be necessary for working out a figure composition or experimenting with still-life groupings, where the emphasis is on the arrangement of the elements in the composition.

## Preparatory drawings

Drawing for painting is an ancient but still vital tradition. The great national art galleries and museums of the world hold many thousands of drawings by artists which were made in preparation for paintings or sculpture. Relatively little remains of preparatory drawings done before the beginning of the Renaissance, simply because they were not valued in themselves and were discarded once they had served the purpose of defining an image and transferring it to panel or frescoed wall.

However, the Renaissance brought a renewed interest in the natural world, prompted curiosity and stimulated new ways of visual thinking. As a consequence, artists not only made drawings which explored the human figure, animals, anatomical specimens and virtually all aspects of nature, but they also experimented with variations on compositional themes before deciding on the final version. They also made many drawings to refine their knowledge and pictorial understanding of problematical parts of their compositions. These included explorations of foreshortening, folds on drapery and perspective. In order to achieve authenticity of detail, artists made careful drawings of forms of architecture, costume and nature. All these

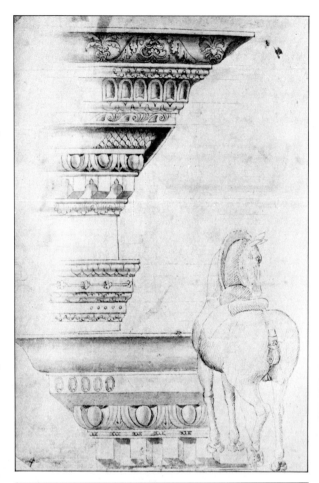

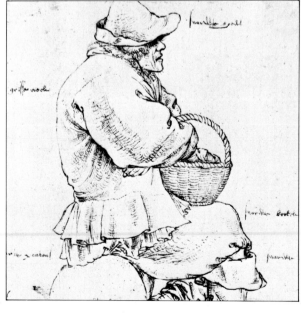

Artists have widely differing approaches to their sketchbooks. For instance, the Florentine artist Benozzo Gozzoli used his sketches to explore details of architectural forms and the figure of a horse (*TOP RIGHT*). Gozzoli used ink and wash to explore various aspects of the pillar tops. Much of Gozzoli's work was in fresco.

A more fluid approach is evident in the drawing in pen and brown ink by Pieter Brueghel the Elder (*BOTTOM RIGHT*). Sketched initially in black chalk, the *Seated Peasant* is of particular interest because it includes the artist's own colour notes, jotted down beside the figure. Try using the same approach in your sketchbook. Notes on the colours in your sketch will act as a useful reminder when you transfer it to a more fully worked out drawing or painting.

The studies for *Raft of the Medusa* by Theodore Géricault which, together with the finished painting, are illustrated on this and the following pages, give some indication of the many ways in which drawing can be used as a preparation for painting. The subject was a shipwreck off the West African coast in July 1816, which at the time caused widespread controversy. The captain and crew took to the lifeboats after the frigate *Medusa* sank, leaving the many passengers to fend for themselves on an open raft. Some 13 days passed before the survivors were rescued. By then they had resorted to cannibalism. This horrendous tale gripped the imagination of the French public. Géricault read widely about his subject, had a scale model of the raft made, compiled a dossier of material and even went to the French coast at Le Havre to study the sea and sky. Initially Géricault was uncertain where to concentrate his interest. His first studies dealt with the rescue of the survivors by the brig *Argus*.

He tested alternative approaches to the scene. In the first, the survivors are seen from the viewpoint of the rowing boat *(1)*, in the second from the viewpoint of the survivors *(2)*. The artist then moved on to the mutiny on the raft. An early study *(4)* shows the scene parallel to the picture plane, while a later elaborated version *(6)* shows a full rendering of the subject in an ambitious composition which shows the influence of Michelangelo and Rubens. The survivors hailing the boat shortly before their rescue interested Géricault next. In this sketch *(5)* the viewer is, as in *(2)*, almost on the raft, but the figures are turned away, straining towards the middle distance. For his studies of other elements of the composition, particularly the various figures, Géricault not only made many studies *(3,7)*, he also even studied cadavers in order to render the severed head satisfactorily *(8)*. Groups of figures also came in for extensive scrutiny *(9,10,11,12)*, as the artist developed his ideas on position, relationships and angle. Finally Géricault did a detailed study of the composition *(13)*. He added two figures to the final

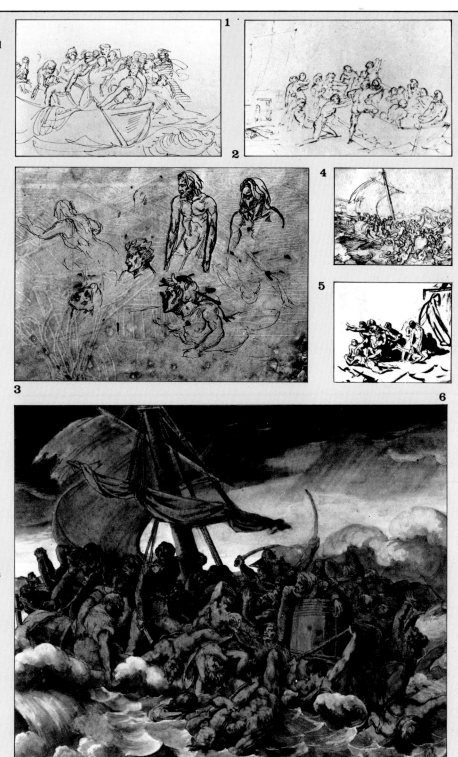

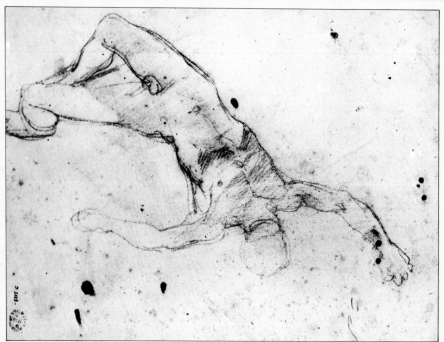

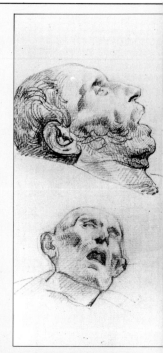

7

13

version *(14)* after the picture left his studio. These provided a more stable base for the general pyramid shape of the composition. Three main lessons can be learned from Géricault's studies, which you can apply in your own work.
First, drawing is used to clarify and determine the intention of the work.
An initial hazy idea can be elaborated and developed in this way. Secondly, drawing is used to explore the variations of composition once the idea has become reasonably clear.
Finally, drawing helps the artist gain valuable knowledge about individual components of the picture by recording relevant details of surface and structure. These insights are invaluable where you want to work on an idea in your studio, relying on previously gathered information to develop the theme.

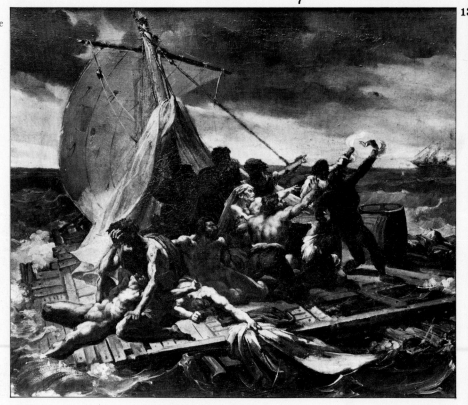

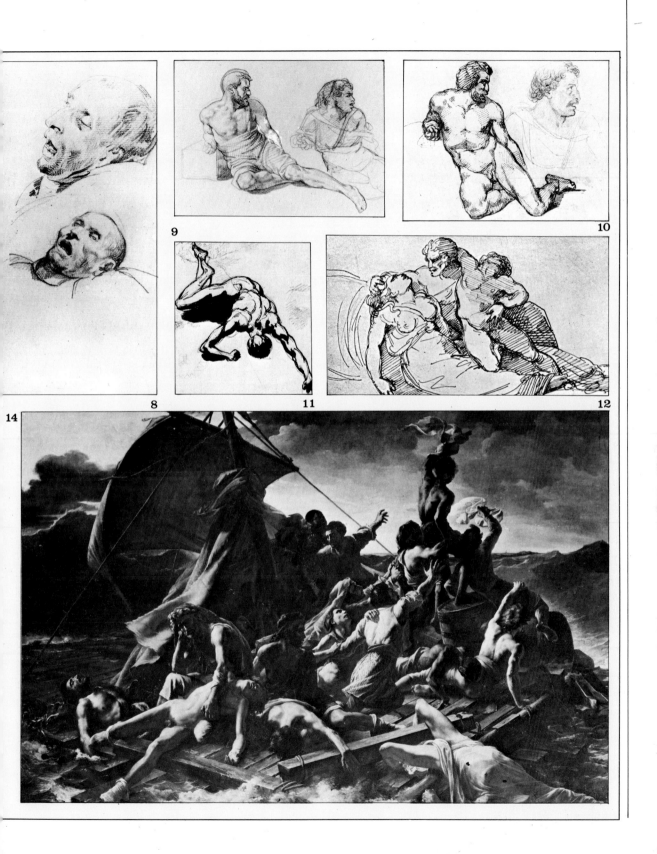

8

9

10

11

12

14

aspects were systematically worked out and the quality of the drawing brought to a very high standard before the artist carried out the idea in the final medium. Eventually patrons began to value these preparatory studies and added them to their collections.

When all the drawing problems had been solved the artist would make a full-size drawing, known as a cartoon, and this would be transferred to the prepared surface of the wall or panel by means of pouncing. Pouncing is a way of forcing dry pigment through tiny holes pricked round the contours of the design. In later periods, the technique of pouncing was largely superceded by tracing, and eventually most painters began to draw directly onto panel or canvas, working from

## STILL-LIFE STUDIES

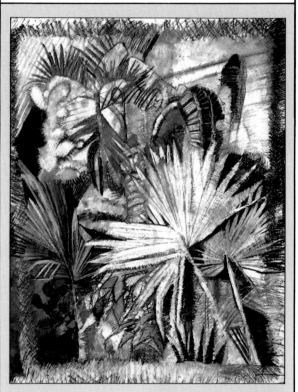

## CUBIST STUDY

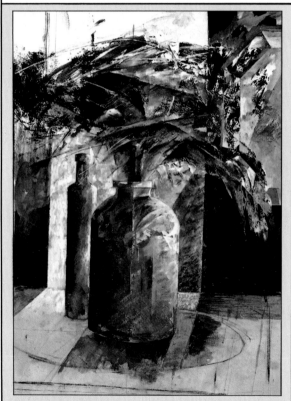

**Do a still-life drawing in the style of one major artistic movement.**
*This picture shows the artist's interest in Cubism. The image is based on still-life objects. However, the leaves springing from the jar in the foreground are reduced to a series of bold sweeping gestures. The organization of lines, tones and planes have a virtually abstract quality. The pattern created by the*
*strokes of the leaves adds a quality of movement to the image. The media — charcoal with black and white acrylic paint — are well used, although perhaps lacking subtlety in their application.*

Make a series of studies of natural forms. Your subject could, for example, be plants in their natural environment or in a vase or container. In doing a drawing for painting, think before you start of the kind of painting you want to produce, and the medium or media you want to use. Use the studies to work out the general approach and quality you wish the painting to have. Think about whether you want to use bold, adventurous strokes or fine detailed line and tones. What impression do you want the final picture to convey? What particular problems can you foresee? Use your studies to work out some of the difficulties before beginning on the painting.
*These two studies of plants show an initial study in pencil (RIGHT) using some tone and a more fully developed drawing (ABOVE) using chalks and charcoal. The general shape of the leaves was, in both cases, more*

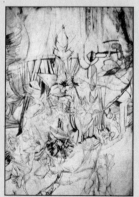

*important to the artist than the detailed rendition of form.*

## INTERIOR VIEWS

Make a number of studies – at least four – to explore different approaches to a subject which you are interested in turning into a painting. It might be a good idea to choose an interior scene, something which you are familiar with and of which you have interesting memories. Try using media with which you are less familiar. If you have been working with ink, experiment with wash as well. Do not worry if your drawings lack detail. The purpose of drawings as a preparation for painting is to enable you to work out your initial ideas, find out what problems they present and evolve the approach you want to take.

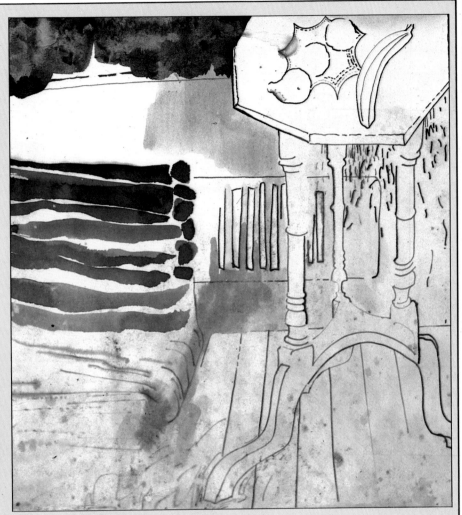

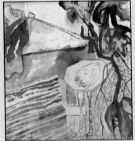

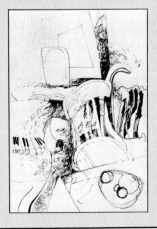

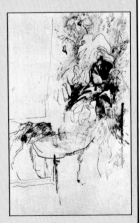

*These four ink drawings show how one artist explored a theme before embarking on the painting. The idea in the artist's mind was nostalgia — memories of past places, times, people and objects. The artist has used the basic forms of a room and the objects in it. The drawings are abbreviated. In them the artist is working out a number of visual ideas, testing out compositions and the degree of stylization, distortion and abstraction which suits the theme of the work. Drawings like these help the artist to build up a vocabulary of forms which can be used in future paintings. Compare the composition in the four images — the positioning of the tables on the painting surface and in relation to the other forms in* the pictures, such as the plants. *Examine how the variety of tones which can be arrived at with ink, staining and wash gives an expressive impression of the different textures in the subject. Look, for example, at the relationship between the horizontal and vertical lines in the first drawings (ABOVE, ABOVE LEFT) and the curving lines of the chairs (RIGHT) and tables and plants (FAR RIGHT).*

smaller preparatory drawings which were enlarged and transferred to the prepared surface by means of 'squaring up'. If the artist felt the need to make alterations during the painting process, this was done by painting out the unwanted area and substituting the new idea.

For the aspiring artist, the process of developing a theme and working out a satisfactory composition is best demonstrated by examining in some detail the work of established masters. The wide variety of preparatory drawings for paintings and sculpture show the artist's quest for excellence. They reveal the creative mind at work perhaps better than any other type of drawing, because the processes of recording information, exploring various compositional alternatives, accepting and rejecting solutions, restating and refining imagery, which lead to the production of a major work of art, can be followed in detail.

Much of the preparatory work for the *Raft of the Medusa* by the French artist, Theodore Géricault, (1791–1824), has been preserved. This comprehensive collection of working drawings provides fascinating, even awe-inspiring evidence of the dedication, patience, creative intelligence and skill of a great artist. Géricault's impressive preparatory work can be divided into two categories—experiments with composition, which cover testing alternatives and evolving new combinations of forms in the search for dramatic and aesthetic unity, and, secondly, gathering visual information to give power and authority to the various components of the picture.

Géricault's picture was based on a shipwreck of 1816 which attracted much contemporary comment and caused a huge controversy. Géricault's main concern was not to comment on the rights or wrongs of the incident but to make a powerful work of art, which attempted to treat a contemporary incident in the monumental style associated with the great artists of the past. The huge painting, which measures 16 feet by 24 feet (3 metres by 7 metres), is purged of topical sensationalism and stands as an epic account of human suffering.

Géricault was steeped in his subject. In addition to reading the full account, he had talked to survivors and had a scale model of the raft on which the shipwreck survivors were marooned. He had compiled a dossier of material relating to the disaster and drew on this both as a means of giving authenticity to his work and as a stimulus to his imagination. In addition, he travelled to Le Havre to study the sea and sky. The story of the raft of the Medusa contained a series of dramatic situations. To begin with, Géricault made drawings of a number of these in an attempt to discover which suited his purpose best. At

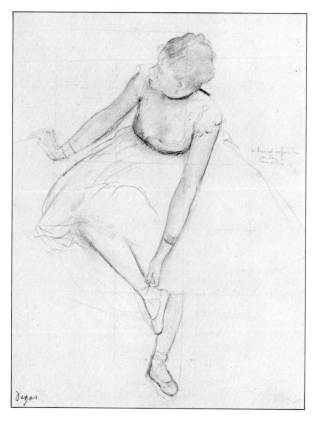

Drawings as a preparation for painting can either be very detailed studies or brief sketches. Both can be good ways of developing your ideas. In his study *Dancer adjusting her slipper (ABOVE)* the French artist Edgar Degas used pencil and charcoal on pink toned paper. Some white highlights were added. The sketch concentrates on capturing the dancer's pose, conveying the positions of the main parts of the body and their relationship to one another. The relationship between the supporting hand and the angle of the head, and between the dancer's left arm and right ankle are especially important.

this stage he was not at all clear as to where he wanted to concentrate his interest. In exploring a theme artists are often only vaguely aware of what they are searching for. The important thing is to recognize developments in your ideas when they take place.

The twentieth-century masterpiece, *Guernica*, by Pablo Picasso (1881–1973) provides some interesting parallels with Géricault's *Raft of the Medusa*. Both paintings are huge. Both were produced in response to terrible events causing ghastly suffering—in Picasso's case the 1937 bombing of the ancient Basque town of Guernica by German warplanes during the Spanish Civil War. Both works are examples of the 'modernism' of their times. Both transcend the topicality of

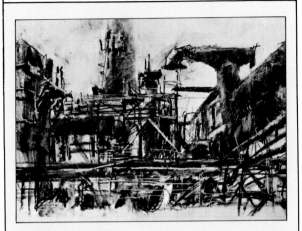

**Make a study of an industrial landscape as a preparation for a painting. Choose a scene which you feel is typical of that kind of landscape. Before embarking on your study, think which medium and surface will be most suitable for your painting.**

*This is a strongly expressive drawing. The charcoal is handled with great vitality. The heavy,* *vigorous lines give the work a fine dramatic quality. The thickness of the lines conveys the starkness of the lines in the subject well. When approaching a subject like this, think how best to convey in paint the tonal differentiations which you can attain with charcoal. In the painting taken from this preparatory sketch, the artist used long and short strokes of heavy paint in the same way as the charcoal strokes in the drawing.*

painting than was the case with the *Raft of the Medusa.* Nevertheless, the whole process is a major example of the use of drawing in the evolution of a major work of art.

An examination of Géricault's method indicates three general principles that can be applied to the production of preparatory drawings for painting. First, drawing is used to clarify and determine the intention of the work. Often an idea is vague and ambiguous to begin with, so the drawing process helps to formulate the idea and often suggests useful elaborations from the first hazy impulse. Secondly, drawing is used to explore variations of composition once the idea has become fairly clear. Finally, drawing is used to gain valuable knowledge about individual components of the composition by recording relevant details of surface and structure.

These principles apply to all forms of figurative work that are not painted directly from the object, and are invaluable where it is necessary to pursue the idea in the studio and rely on gathered information to develop the theme further. Figure compositions and landscape (including the urban environment) are typical examples of where these principles can be used effectively.

# On-the-spot drawing and photographs

Another traditional method of recording information is the drawing done 'on the spot'. The drawing could be a landscape, townscape, an interior or elsewhere, but it is done in circumstances which do not permit a thorough study of all the visual information available. In such cases, it is useful if the drawing is accompanied by written notes indicating special qualities of tone and colour or other features that will serve as a reminder once the painting has been started in the studio. Small patches of tones and colours can be noted in a corner of the paper as a scale of values to be used later as a 'key'.

In addition to drawing, many contemporary artists rely on photographs to provide the visual information they require for their work. This has now become an accepted practice. It is also possible to project a colour slide of a subject or parts of the composition directly onto the canvas and to trace round the outlines.

It remains a matter of personal choice as to which method is to be used. You should use the method or combination of methods which seems best suited to the work. Nevertheless, it is worth remembering that a practised eye can usually spot where photographs have been used as source material.

their subjects and are timeless in their evocation of human suffering. Both draw on the inspiration of past masters, and, of particular relevance in this context, both use the method of an intensive period of preparatory work.

However, there is one significant difference. Whereas Géricault returned again and again to making searching studies of the human figure, drawing directly from living and dead models, Picasso had already invented a quite new vocabulary of forms to express his pictorial ideas through his innovatory Cubist works and subsequent experiments. He had studied the artistic conventions of most of the world's art and had taken from them whatever he needed to construct his revolutionary visual concepts. He drew on this store of imagery for the elements of *Guernica.* In every other respect Picasso's preparatory work followed the long established tradition of using drawing as a means of clarifying and developing ideas and testing out alternatives of image and composition. A number of variations on the various groups and individual figures were explored. The image of the horse in particular underwent a series of transformations and far more changes were made in the actual

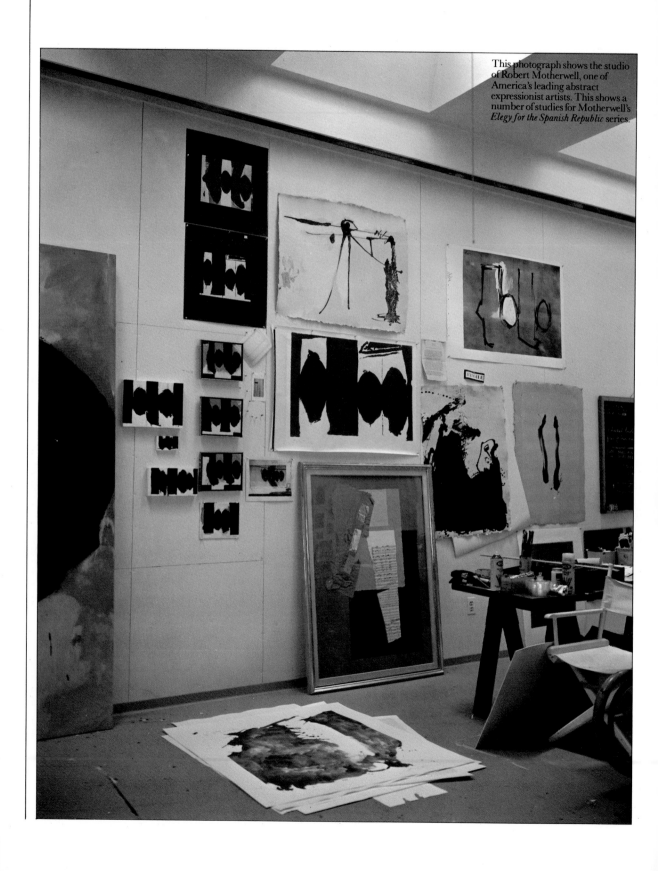

This photograph shows the studio of Robert Motherwell, one of America's leading abstract expressionist artists. This shows a number of studies for Motherwell's *Elegy for the Spanish Republic* series.

# Abstract and other work

Sorting out compositional problems and gathering visual information before transferring the idea to canvas, helps solve most of the drafting problems before painting begins. However, many artists are not inclined to follow this system because they feel that the painting merely adds colour and scale to an idea that has already been resolved at the drawing stage, and thus painting can only too easily become a merely mechanical process that denies the painting any life of its own. In other words, they feel that extensive preparatory work may prevent them from acting spontaneously on an impulse while the painting is in progress. For such artists, it is imperative that changes occur in the painting itself, each stage challenging the previous one and the final solution being the product of many reworkings. In this case, forms are repeatedly redrawn in the canvas and colours changed and shifted about in the quest for a greater dynamic unity. It is not uncommon to find traces of earlier stages showing through and becoming integrated in the total image.

This is a common practice among some abstract artists. Where drawing and painting become synthesized into one activity, and freshness of colour and texture are maintained, the result can be 'muscular' and vital. In these instances, preparatory drawings—if

## ABSTRACT STUDY

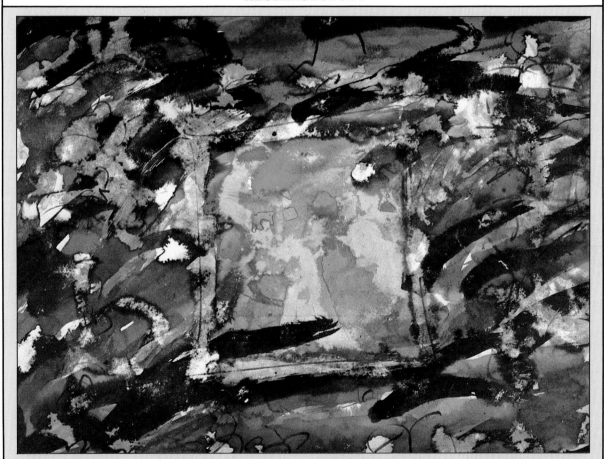

**Explore some ways of making abstract images. Try out several media and approaches.**

*This abstract drawing in gouache and coloured inks was made with the paper lying horizontally. Gouache was applied to selected areas, and layers of ink were washed on using Japanese calligraphic brushes. The whole drawing was then washed under a running tap. The gouache acted as a resist. The artist repeated the process a number of times until the final image was produced. The interesting combination of colours and tones which the wash technique created makes this a good example of one approach to abstract image making. Do not be afraid to try out different ways of making such images.*

any—may take the form of a few summary notations exploring one or two basic arrangements of shapes, perhaps repeating, with minor variations, an obsessive form personal to the artist. Robert Motherwell's *Elegy* series is an excellent example of this. The American artist Motherwell (born 1915) has already produced over 100 paintings using variations of the same theme. Many artists working with abstract forms paint directly onto the canvas without using any preliminary drawings. In this case, drawing and painting are synonymous.

This approach does not just appeal to abstract artists. Many other kinds of artist, painters of portraits, landscapes and still-lifes for example, also work directly onto the canvas. The image is reproduced from observation by means of pencil, charcoal or diluted paint, and, when the composition and delineation of the objects is considered satisfactory, tone and colour are added. Redrawing, by which is meant either the more accurate representation of what is there or a modification of the forms to express the artist's personal vision, can take place at any time during the work.

There are, of course, many variations in approach between the use of drawing as a means of evolving a definitive image and the whole process of image-making taking place on the canvas itself. Many artists are exploring areas that fall between strict representation and total abstraction. Even artists working at such extremes use drawing to work out personal ways of using media and develop a style of image-making that suits their temperament. Their explorations are carried over into painting which, in turn, suggests modifications to their drawing activity. A good example of this would be someone who is painting figuratively but is attempting to get away from a naturalistic form of representation. Through a series of drawings, attempts could be made to develop a different style. If at any stage in working towards a new style you feel that you are not achieving satisfactory results, do not be afraid to go back to an earlier stage. For example, if you are doing a figure drawing, try returning to carefully observed studies of the figure in order to understand its structure more fully, as a basis for attaining less superficial formal variations.

For almost all types of painting, drawing is an essential accompanying and preparatory activity. However, there is one important point still to be made. A recurring problem for both amateur and professional artists, especially those working in non-figurative areas, is how to carry over from drawing to painting the particular freshness, vitality and spontaneity often found in a preliminary study. It is a common complaint that the painting lacks the liveliness of the drawing. To avoid this difficulty, bear in mind that drawing media are quite different from oil and acrylic paints and make adjustments accordingly.

One difference is that most preparatory drawings leave areas of paper untouched and often make strong use of line, whereas, in most paintings, the entire surface of the canvas is covered with paint, often in successive layers. A line in ink, charcoal, or pencil drawn on light coloured paper makes its visual impact not only through the verve with which it is drawn, but also by virtue of the strong tonal contrast it makes with its background. This quality cannot be achieved so easily in many forms of painting. The fact that colours, tones and textures work together over the whole surface of the canvas diminishes the possibility of achieving the same effect as the bold simple contrast of a drawn line.

To ensure that the painting retains its vitality, the artist has to find equivalents for this quality. Colour contrasts, rhythmic movements of form, bold handling of brush or palette knife or inventive techniques, such as splattering, staining, dribbling, wiping and scraping, can all be used as an effective substitute for the energy of drawn lines or the uninhibited use of other drawing media. Also it should be borne in mind that developments in twentieth century painting have opened the way for virtually any approach that can be made into a vehicle for the ideas being explored. The maxim 'anything goes' holds as long as the result is effective. In this light, drawing and painting conventions should be examined and tested in terms of their relevance to the intentions of the work. If necessary, you should give up established habits in favour of new directions. In this context, experiment is vital and provides the only way to break new ground.

The appropriateness of technique is important. For example, hard-edge or geometric drawings usually require a choice of media and method of execution which are conducive to precision. There would be no point in using, say, pastel to produce this type of work, unless a stencil technique was being used. For freer, more expressive abstract images, it would be logical to use media that could be applied freely, perhaps using brush, rag, or fingers. Gouache, acrylics, watercolours, inks, or even unconventional media—such as creosote and varnish—could be used. Oil paint on paper can also be used effectively as a drawing medium. On absorbent paper, the 'creep' of the oil provides an interesting neutral tone round the brushmarks. Collage techniques can also be used to work out ideas. Torn or cut paper shapes have the advantage that they can be shifted about and rearranged until a satisfactory composition is arrived at.

## COMPLEX ABSTRACT STUDY

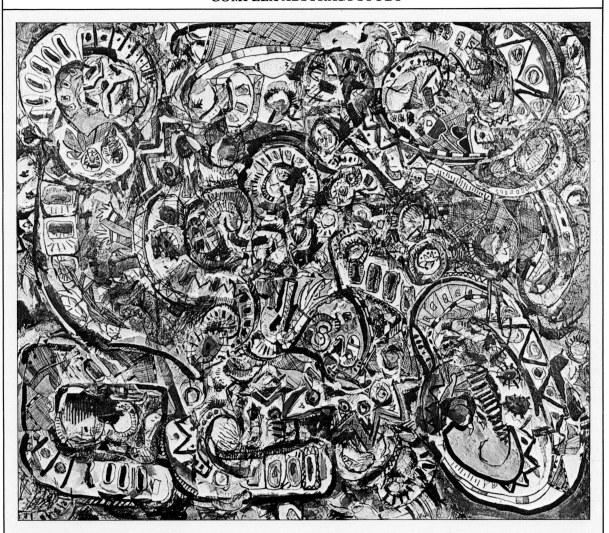

**Make a series of drawings which explore abstract images in a freely drawn way. Use different media and a variety of surfaces. Try to free your mind from making images of objects and concentrate instead on the possibilities of pattern and texture. However, you should also attempt to make your image more than just a pattern.**

*These abstract compositions were executed in pen, coloured inks and charcoal . The artist was interested in art outside accepted conventions and traditions as well as in primitive and aboriginal art. Based on these ideas, he made a large series of drawings investigating different relationships between form and rhythmic elements. He was trying to find a type of imagery which avoided being just pattern making. In order to stimulate his imagination, the artist ripped up some drawings and stuck them together again in different configurations. He rubbed out some parts and worked over others. If you are interested in this type of image making, you might find it useful to look at works by artists such as the American Jackson Pollock or the British artist Alan Davie.*

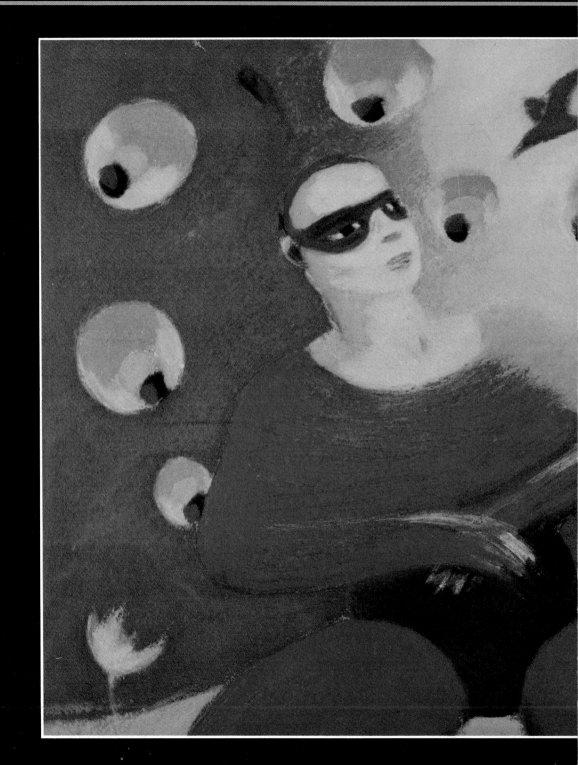

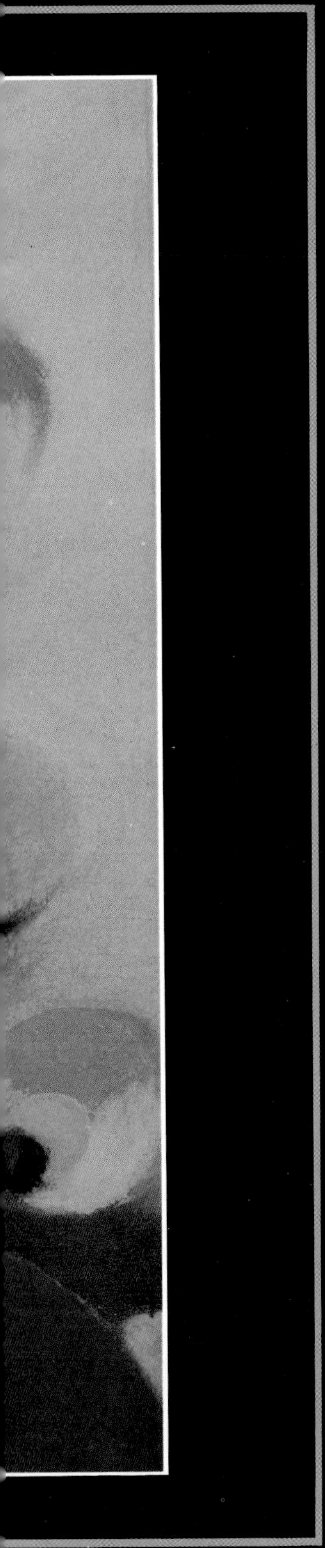

# 4

# COLOUR

- INTRODUCTION
- EQUIPMENT
- EXERCISES

Gary McCarver
*The Acrobat*

# THEORY AND PRACTICE

When you begin to paint you will be confronted by two main problems—how to relate the intense colours of your manufactured paints to the colours of the world which you wish to portray, and how to relate the colours to each other on the painting surface. The natural environment consists largely of broken colours and a myriad of subtle greys. This is unlike a child's simple conception of the world, where, for example, sky is thought of as blue and grass as green. Nevertheless, it is surprising how people view the world through these sorts of preconceived ideas without actually perceiving how it is. You need to be able to create those colours which you detect, greys which combine subtle qualities of green or red for example, and this is an absorbing and complex task. In addition, you will have to learn how colours behave and how they relate to one another. This requires familiarity and practice in mixing and in laying colours down beside each other. This section of the book sets out to familiarize you with colour and how it can be controlled.

*The principles of harmony and contrast of colours and their application to the arts* by the French colourist Michel-Eugène Chevreul (1786–1889) was first published in France in 1839, and later in Britain in 1854. Chevreul's colour theories dominated the strategies employed by the Impressionists, the Neo-Impressionists and other painting schools, and, in essence, his colour theories have provided the foundation for all colour teaching in art schools since. The structure of this colour course has also been influenced by the theories and practice of the Swiss artist and Bauhaus teacher Paul Klee (1879–1940), by Joseph Albers (1888–1976) who also taught at the Bauhaus as well as at Black Mountain College and Yale University in the United States, and, finally, by the influential British art teacher of the 1960s, Tom Hudson. These individuals jointly and with others developed Chevreul's theories into an educational course.

The aim of this section is to develop an understanding of the behaviour of colour through experience, through practical observation and experiment. Only by practical investigation can the relativity and instability of colour be clearly demonstrated. While undertaking the practical study outlined in the section, it is suggested that you have a look at the work of Chevreul. His hemispheric colour solid is one to which repeated reference will be made.

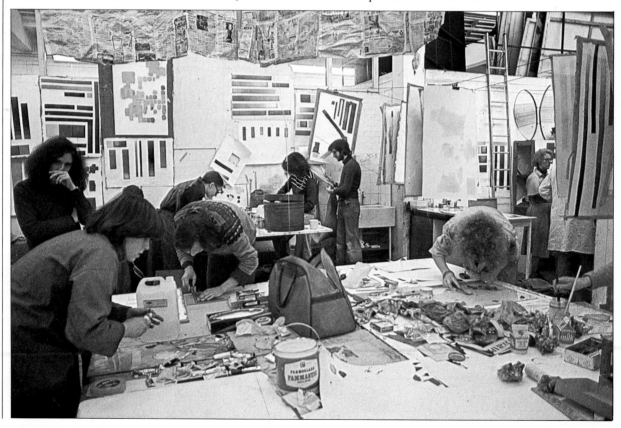

# Materials

You will also require two plywood boards to fix your paper to and a square of clear perspex glass with polished edges to use as a palette, two glass jars and turpentine. In addition you will need rolls of kitchen paper and rags, a trowel palette knife and a flat blade palette knife, paper adhesive tape, clear adhesive tape (2 in/10 mm wide) and masking tape (2 in/10 mm wide), a 1 inch (2.5 cm) house painter's brush and several art brushes, including a No 1 sable brush. You will need cartridge paper and various coloured papers, crayons and pastels. A collection of water-colour pigments, gouache and acrylic pigments would also be useful. Note that a tube of black acrylic pigment and a half-gallon (2.5 litres) of white emulsion are essential. The following range of pigments, all manufactured in this instance by Winsor and Newton, are recommended: Winsor red, Winsor violet, Winsor orange, Winsor green, Winsor blue, Winsor yellow, cadmium orange, cobalt blue, cerulean blue, scarlet lake, French ultramarine, chrome yellow, emerald green, chrome orange, cadmium yellow, magenta, cadmium red, lemon yellow, rose madder, geranium lake, viridian, vermilion red, Alizarin crimson, cobalt violet, titanium white and lamp black.

Having acquired all the necessary equipment, the next step is to stretch some paper onto your boards in preparation for the exercises which are outlined in this section. Take a sheet of cartridge paper (about 0.5 yard/metre square) and dampen it with a sponge. Then secure it to the board using the paper tape. Allow the paper to dry and stretch gradually and naturally. When the first sheet of paper is completely dry, you can carry out the same procedure on the other side of the board.

All the projects in this section should be done using oil pigment as the basic material. There are many arguments in its favour. It is manufactured in an extremely wide range of colours; it can be manipulated and mixed easily; it can be applied with a palette knife in flat, even areas of colour, painted with a fine sable brush and even washed or stained. Oil pigment is slow drying and can therefore be mixed slowly and precisely. Lastly, its tone does not change upon drying. While oil pigment is recommended as the most appropriate material, some of the projects might also be carried out using water-

These students *(LEFT)* are at work on colour projects. The importance of a good working atmosphere in the studio is apparent in this photograph. Charts and examples of previous work hanging on the walls provide the context for current exercises and, as the project progresses, the full range of effects becomes visible. The students are surrounded by visual reference and evidence for the investigation in hand. Notice that work takes place on broad, flat tables so that colours can be mixed and transferred directly to the paper in even light.

### Equipment for colour projects

Paper is stretched while wet and fixed to a board with adhesive paper tape *(3)*. Adhesive tapes *(1, 2)* will also be useful. You need clean jars *(4)* for water or turpentine *(9)*, and kitchen paper *(6)* or rags. Flat and rounded brushes in hog's hair and sable *(7)* give precision but use decorators' brushes or palette knives *(8)* to spread broad areas of colour. Water based emulsion *(5)* and acrylic *(10)* paints need a plastic palette *(11)*, but oils are mixed on glass. Coloured pencils *(12)*, papers *(14)* and pastels *(13)* enable you to observe optical effects quickly and cleanly.

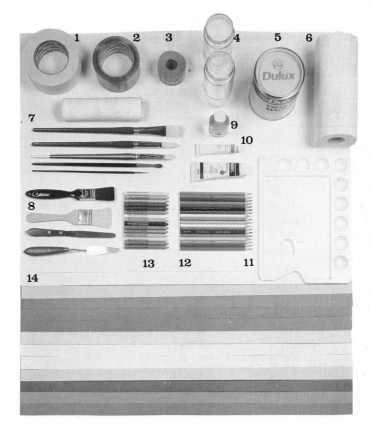

colours, acrylic colours and, in some exercises, even coloured papers.

# The colour sphere

Before beginning the first exercise, it is important to consider the various systems of notation employed by colourists when formulating and explaining their colour theories. A colour solid represents a means of charting colour within a three-dimensional framework or structure. There have been colour cones, double cones and several spheres. The sphere which is illustrated here is based in that patented by Albert Munsell in 1900 and later used by Paul Klee when he taught at the Bauhaus in the 1920s. Its purpose is to describe and measure hue, chroma and tone or value. Hue is the pigmentation—such as red, yellow, blue and green—and is

When mixing pigments and making colour scales, it is important to make a careful note of what you do as you go along. You are, after all, learning about how various colours are made and when you later start producing paintings you do not want to rely solely on chance encounters between all the various pigments.

measured around the circumference of the sphere. Chroma is the intensity or brightness and is measured horizontally through the sphere. Chroma decreases towards the centre of the sphere where a neutral grey is located. Tone or value is lightness or darkness, measured vertically so that the top pole cap is white and the bottom one black. It is important to remember that these are the three fundamental colour attributes. By using this method of notation colour can be arranged into systematic scales of equal visual steps.

# An achromatic scale

To begin with, you can consider the movement of white through grey to black. This scale is referred to as an achromatic scale because it is devoid of all traces of colour and cannot therefore be traced in the colour sphere. It should not be confused with the grey pole or axis of the colour solid for that is made up entirely of colour greys, greys produced by mixing different pigments.

If you mix white pigment with black pigment in

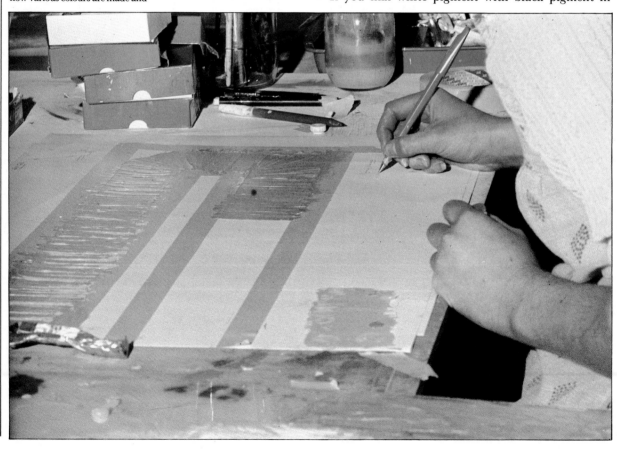

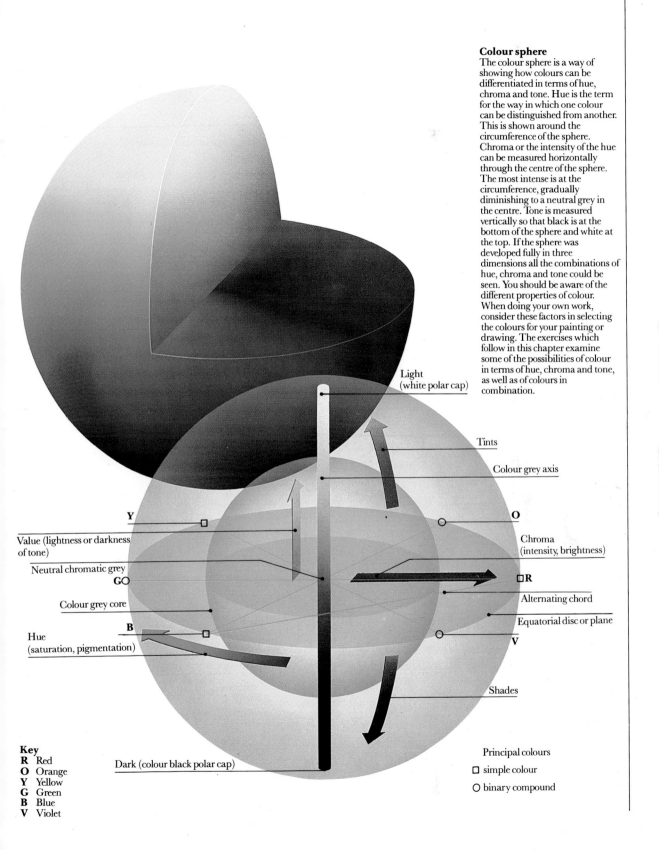

**Colour sphere**
The colour sphere is a way of showing how colours can be differentiated in terms of hue, chroma and tone. Hue is the term for the way in which one colour can be distinguished from another. This is shown around the circumference of the sphere. Chroma or the intensity of the hue can be measured horizontally through the centre of the sphere. The most intense is at the circumference, gradually diminishing to a neutral grey in the centre. Tone is measured vertically so that black is at the bottom of the sphere and white at the top. If the sphere was developed fully in three dimensions all the combinations of hue, chroma and tone could be seen. You should be aware of the different properties of colour. When doing your own work, consider these factors in selecting the colours for your painting or drawing. The exercises which follow in this chapter examine some of the possibilities of colour in terms of hue, chroma and tone, as well as of colours in combination.

Light
(white polar cap)

Tints

Colour grey axis

Y

O

Value (lightness or darkness of tone)

Chroma
(intensity, brightness)

Neutral chromatic grey

GO

R

Alternating chord

Colour grey core

Equatorial disc or plane

B

Hue
(saturation, pigmentation)

V

Shades

Dark (colour black polar cap)

Principal colours

□ simple colour

○ binary compound

**Key**
**R** Red
**O** Orange
**Y** Yellow
**G** Green
**B** Blue
**V** Violet

varying proportions, the result will consist of a series of tonally different greys. Such a collection of greys can be arranged in a sequence from white through light greys, through progressively darker greys to the very darkest grey, and so to black. If you mix the pigments in a random fashion, you will see that the progression from white to black is uneven, that is, the tonal steps are not consistent. Your next task is to select a neutral grey tone, one that is equidistant from the polarities on the scale. To do this, you will have to produce a more precise and comprehensive achromatic scale. To achieve this gradation, a very small quantity of black pigment should be introduced into an amount of white pigment. It should be mixed thoroughly and the resulting pigment placed alongside the original white pigment. Repeat this procedure, adding progressively more black to the preceding mixture, taking care to maintain an even gradation. Continue to add more and more black until such time as the original mixture ceases to be grey. Needless to say there will always remain the slightest fragment of white in the black-grey so the final stage in the gradation should be a black taken straight from the tube.

Now is the time to choose your neutral grey, that is a grey which is equidistant between black and white. This is a subjective choice, but, if greys are juxtaposed within white and black fields, it will be observed that white will tend to make a neutral grey appear darker in tone while the black will make the neutral grey look lighter in tone. The reasons for this will be discussed later. To help you examine the nature and behaviour of colour you should carry out the rest of the exercises on grey surfaces. You can do this by mixing white emulsion and black acrylic pigment into the neutral grey which you will have discovered on the achromatic scale and applying to your surface before painting.

## Primary pigments

If you spread the range of pigments that are available from the paint manufacturers on your palette, you will observe that some are obviously very intense, pure and bright. Others are, by comparison, darker and less intense. They all differ, in fact, in hue chroma and tone. It is those pigments that have the highest level of intensity that you should look at now. These pigments are referred to as the primary colours and are identified as red, yellow and blue. Begin your examination of these primary colours by firstly inspecting the colour potential of the family of yellows, laying them down beside each other on the grey surface or field so that

each touches the next. You can then assess the relative changes of hue, from lemon yellow through to cadmium yellow. Varying the juxtaposition of all the yellows will modify and exaggerate the hue differences. To conclude this experiment, select and name what you believe to be the most intense yellow of all.

A similar exercise can be repeated with both the red and blue families. It should be noted that a very small addition of white pigment into some of the darker blue and red pigments will help you to distinguish the hue or pigmentation more easily. It is again the most intense

red and blue for which you should search. Coloured papers might also be used to help in the quest. Once you are satisfied that you have found the three primary hues, you should lay them out in a large square each touching the adjacent one, at the top of a newly stretched and primed grey worksheet.

You should remember how important it is to acquire the habit of cataloguing the pigments and mixtures on your study sheet. The continued maintenance of a log book for observations and discoveries about colour is also essential.

# Secondary colours

The next project involves carrying out a series of experiments that explore the range of hues that exist between the primary colours. These are known as the secondary colours and include green, violet and orange. First make a gradation scale (like that in the achromatic series) of even steps from pure yellow to pure red, a red and a yellow which have absolutely no trace of any other colour in them. Theoretically, at a point mid-

## MIXING PRIMARIES

**Explore the range of hues which exists between the primary colours. Now, taking yellow first, lay down a narrow strip and then proceed to add increasing quantities of red. At the end of the scale there should be no yellow involved, the last strip being pure primary red. You should repeat this exercise making scales from yellow to blue and from red to blue.**

*These exercises show clearly what happens when the three primary colours are mixed in the three scales outlined. As is often the case practice has failed to match up to theory. In the yellow to red scale and in the yellow to blue scale, the secondary colours orange and green appeared. This is what would have been expected, In mixing red and blue, however, the artist did not produce violet, which would have been expected. In mixing red and grey. You will have found this when mixing the colours yourself. In the bottom three scales the artist has managed to achieve a violet by mixing in additional colours at various points along the scale. You should experiment with this yourself. You will find that the most useful colours for this exercise are French ultramarine, Winsor violet, cobalt violet and geranium lake. You can make further experiments by using slightly different hues, for example if, in the first instance, you used chrome yellow, repeat the same exercise using lemon yellow.*

distance along the scale, the secondary colour orange should be located.

A similar exercise should be repeated making a scale from pure yellow to pure blue. During this exercise, gradually add white to the mixtures, and, in doing so, control the tonal level throughout the scale. By doing this you will be articulating hue and tone simultaneously and it is recommended that all the mixtures included in the yellow to blue scale should be pitched in tone approximately equal to yellow. In practice this means that the blue will be very pale indeed. Again, in

this series, at a point halfway along the scale, the secondary colour green should occur. If a similar procedure were adopted with a movement from pure red to pure blue, the result would be found only to approximate to the secondary colour violet, for the pure red/pure blue scale shows the greatest inconsistency or irregularity between the theory and practice of colour.

If white is added to the centre mixture of the pure red/pure blue scale, the result is an approximate grey/brown. To accentuate the discrepancy between theory and practice, you should try to make a gradation scale from a blue that tends towards green, and a red that tends towards orange, adding white throughout in order to maintain a tonal level equal to the orange-red. If more white is added to the centre mixture, the result will almost certainly be a convincing grey.

These tests show the paths described by mixing simple colours. In the colour solid they are seen to move in towards the broken and grey core. Some of the mixtures can be described as broken colours for they are

You will have discovered that when mixing primary red and primary blue you create an approximate grey colour rather than the violet you would tend to expect. In order to make that violet you will need to inject a number of secondary colours. On the colour sphere *(BELOW)* the four secondary colours are located. They are geranium lake, cobalt violet, Winsor violet and ultramarine blue. When these are injected in the right proportions, they help to create an intense violet.

You will have by now discovered how the primaries behave when they are mixed and how secondary colours are made. You should now go a step further and, using the same primaries, see how many different identifiable hues you can create. By doing this you will discover the enormous range of secondary colours which can be produced using the three primaries. Remember that you will have to add a number of other colours in order to create your range of violet hues.

*Here the artist has explored oranges, greens and violets by plucking them out of their scales and juxtaposing them in different configurations. In this way the tones of the different hues have been compared. Furthermore, the range of hues has been increased employing different pure pigments. For instance, in the blue scale in the middle, cobalt blue has been mixed with cerulean blue. Repeat the exercises using different combinations, this will help you see how colours work together.*

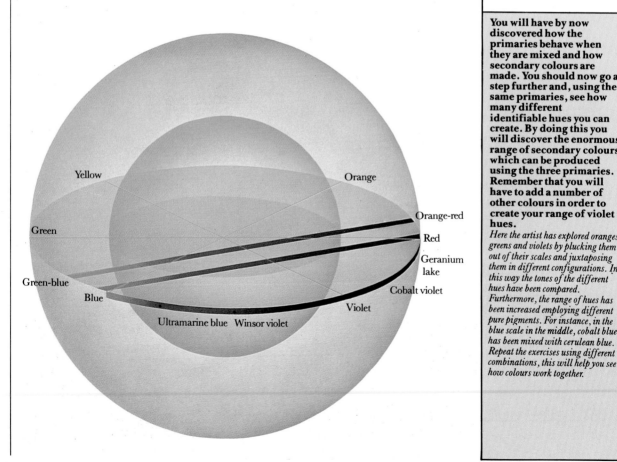

Yellow

Orange

Orange-red

Green

Red

Geranium lake

Green-blue

Cobalt violet

Blue

Violet

Ultramarine blue    Winsor violet

low in chroma and located far away from the region of high chroma which is on the surface of the colour solid. In order to correct this loss of chroma, you should make a further gradation study from pure red to pure blue maintaining equal tone throughout, but in this third scale you should attempt to revitalize the series with additional pigmentation. This can be achieved by introducing, for example, French ultramarine, Winsor violet, cobalt violet and geranium lake at appropriate points on the scale. The relative differences in chroma between the centre mixtures of the three blue to red scales can be examined by juxtaposing samples from the different series. The addition of manufactured secondary pigments into the other scales will also help increase their chroma and intensity. A continuous colour band of three primaries and three secondary colours together with an unlimited number of subdivisions could now be assembled.

Other historially important colour circles include A. H. Munsell's version. This consists of 10 major hues, five principal (red, yellow, green, blue and purple) and five intermediate set out as follows—yellow-red, green-yellow, blue-green, purple-blue, and red-purple, with other subdivisions.

Paul Klee employed a spectral colour disc of six hues, violet, red, orange, yellow, green and blue, while in Michel Chevreul's colour circle there were three primaries, red, yellow and blue, three secondary colours, orange, green and violet, and six intermediate colours, red-orange, orange-yellow, yellow-green, green-blue, blue-violet and violet-red, with further subdivisions.

The Englishman Moses Harris created the very first colour circle in 1766, in which the primaries were red, yellow and blue. The German writer Johann Wolfgang von Goethe (1749–1832) made a similar circle in 1810, after which the red, yellow and blue circle became the common working instrument of most colour theorists. It is the Paul Klee model to which this study most closely corresponds.

## EXPLORATORY SECONDARY COLOURS

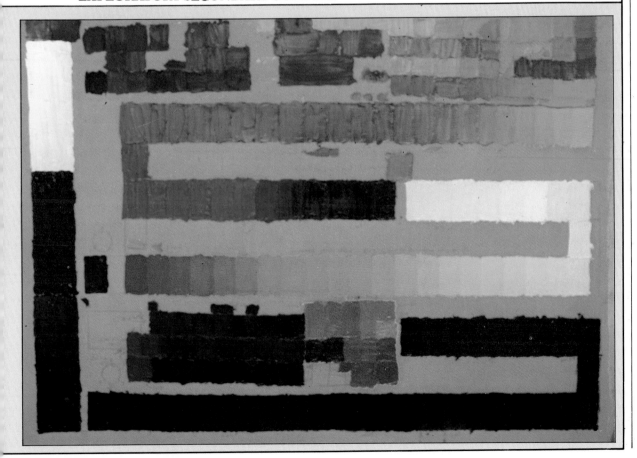

**Secondary scales**
The diagrams show the orange to
violet secondary scale as well as
the blue-violet to yellow-orange
scales. A equals the centre mixture
of the violet to orange scale and B
the centre of the blue-violet to
yellow-orange scale.

# Secondary colour harmonics

This fourth exercise examines the harmonic series which exist between pairs of secondary colours, when the movements created by mixing these colours by-pass the intermediate primary colours. These series include the scales of orange to violet, green to orange and violet to green. White should be added to the individual components of the gradated colour scales where appropriate in order to maintain an even tonal level throughout. This tonal level should be equal to that of the secondary colour, orange. The white will help you to see the hues more clearly and will also encourage the hues in the middle of the scales to incline towards grey.

The middle mixtures in these scales are referred to as broken or tertiary colours. In order to accentuate this tendency for the central mixtures to veer towards grey, you might examine the effects achieved by introducing a blue-green to a red-orange, a red-orange to a blue-violet, and a yellow-orange to a blue-violet. White should be introduced as before. The selection of hues forming the basis for this exercise will test your understanding of the principal colour boundaries. If the principal colour limits were not recognized accurately then this series may have inadvertently involved diametric colour relationships or colour opposites, for example red and green, yellow and violet, or blue and orange. When colours are arranged in these relationships, they are referred to as complementary colours.

## MIXING COMPLEMENTARY PAIRS

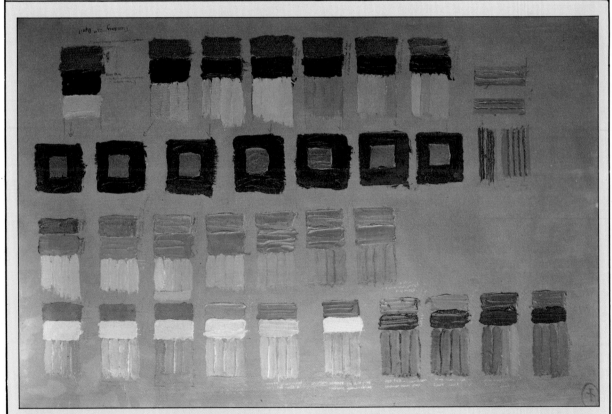

**By mixing secondary colours you create broken or tertiary colours. These broken colours tend towards grey and they are the ones which approximate most closely to the colours in the natural** environment. In this exercise, you can explore how pairs of complementary colours mix. Through the mixing of the primaries you will have created a whole series of secondary colours. From these you should now select your complementary colours – orange and blue, violet and yellow, and green and red – and then mix them in their pairs. Vary the proportions of each in order to explore a wider range of broken colours.

*In these exercises the artist has taken four sets of secondary colours, mixed them in different proportions and laid the results underneath the complementary pairs.*

# Complementary colours

Complementary colours are pairs of colours which are widely separated on the colour sphere. Examples include yellow and violet or red and green. In effect, the study of complementaries is the study of colour opposites. In the following exercise, you should begin by placing any simple colour next to its opposite. The opposite colour must contain no traces of the primary colour found in the first of the complementaries which you have laid down. White should be added to the darker hue of the combination in order that both hues can be recognized simultaneously. Be careful to avoid an inversion of the natural values of the hues. Yellow is the lightest colour, followed by orange, green, red, blue and violet. Comparing and judging the brightness of one hue against another is not an easy task, though you will become more adept at it with practice.

You should now make mixtures of each complementary pair of colours. In principle, when two opposite pigments are mixed, an achromatic grey should be the result. In point of fact, some deviation nearly always occurs. Where there is deviation away from the achromatic grey, you will find that the selected hues are not in fact directly opposite and that there are traces of one primary colour in both pigments. A range of the principal opposites, namely blue-orange, yellow-violet and red-green should be examined using the procedure outlined here.

# Simultaneous and successive contrast of colour

You may have noticed that, when the complementary colours were placed next to each other, the intensity and brightness of the two colours were enhanced. Their hues, however, have not changed. When two colours which are not diametrically opposed to each other are compared, they have a modifying or even a cancelling effect on each other. These enhancing or modifying effects can be explained by the principle of simultaneous contrast, that is, the instantaneous increase or decrease in intensity and hue of colours when they are perceived in adjacent positions. The enhancing effect that is evident in a pair of complementary colours can also be attributed to the phenomenon of successive contrast, by which, in principle, after-images are induced in the eye when you study an area of intense colour for a period of time. A complementary colour relationship is one in which a principal colour is accompanied by its after-image.

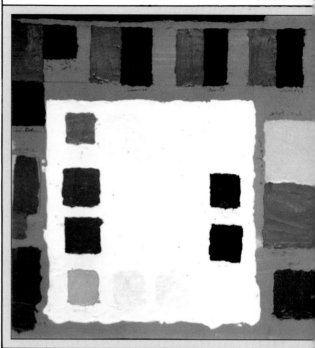

## COLOUR INTERACTION

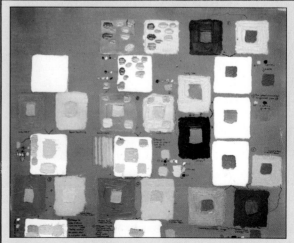

Paint two colour fields of complementary colours. Paint a small square of a third colour below. Now, mix two colours similar to the colour of the small square, but sufficiently different so that when they are placed on the two larger colour fields their colour appears to be the same as that of the small square outside. When you have achieved this, place those two colours next to that of the small square and you will see how different they in fact are.

*You will find that the pigments which seem the same on the yellow and violet backgrounds look very different on a white ground.*

TER-IMAGES

**This is no easy task and will require great concentration. Paint a white square onto your usual grey background and onto that paint a small coloured square. Stare at this for up to 40 seconds and then concentrate on the white area on the paper and wait for the after-image to appear. This will be an approximation of the coloured square's complementary colour. Now try to make this colour using your pigments.**

*In this exercise the artist has painted a number of colours on the white squares and then painted their after-images beside them. In the top lefthand corner of the lefthand square, for instance, a violet square was painted. Laid down beside the violet square is its yellow after-image. The colour is pale, but that is an accurate interpretation of an after-image. If you do not manage to do this exercise satisfactorily at first, keep trying. With practice, you will develop more facility.*

# Mixing pigments, coloured light and optical mixing

Mixing pigments is known as subtractive mixing. As more colour is added, the darker the resultant pigment becomes. If all the three primaries are mixed, the resultant effect will be black. You have seen how pigments behave when they are mixed during the preceding exercises and projects.

The effects of mixing light are very different. When coloured lights are mixed the process is additive, so that the movement is towards light rather than dark. With the light primaries, red and violet-blue will produce magenta, red and green when mixed will give yellow; this result is perhaps the most astounding of all. Green and violet-blue will give cyan (blue-green). When red, green and blue-violet are mixed, they will produce white light. Black occurs when there is an absence of all three light primaries.

Finally, you should understand optical mixing. The effects of optical mixing—or the mixing of colours in the eye—which are due to the successive or after-image phenomenon do not precisely follow the laws of pigment mixture, nor do they precisely follow the laws of light mixture. After-images are visual opposites, and the

results of optical mixture resemble most closely the mixing of coloured lights. To explain modification of colour on the retina of the eye and thus the phenomenon of after-image, the mechanisms of the rod and cone cells found in the human eye and their function in colour appreciation are important. The rods serve primarily to register sensations of brightness, and they operate at low levels of light intensity. The three types of cones respond to the blue-violet, green and red regions of the spectrum respectively. In combination, these cells provide full colour discrimination. The rods and cones of the human retina are tuned in such a way as to receive any of the three primary light sensations—red, green and blue-violet—which make up all colours.

If you stare at red, you will fatigue the red-sensitive receptors so that with a sudden shift to white (which consists of red, green and blue-violet) only the mixture of green and blue-violet occurs. This blue-green colour—or cyan—represents the after-image. Cyan is the light complementary of red.

You can test out this concept of the after-image yourself. You should locate pairs of complementary colours and then take aside the most saturated and intense hue of the combination. Now stare at this isolated hue for more than 30 seconds, then direct your focus to a small pencil spot in a sheet of white paper and wait for the after-image to appear. If you blink, the after-image will be regenerated. You should repeat this exercise over and over until the optical sensation of the after-image can be measured accurately for hue, intensity and value, and then mixed using pigment. You will find this a particularly strenuous and demanding task, but in the end you should have produced a thin, approximate version of the complementary colour. If you refer to the previous section on colour mixing, you should experience no difficulty in explaining the after-image effects in terms of light and pigment primary mixtures.

# Colour intensity

Coloured papers with high chroma and pigment saturation could be used to help demonstrate the effects of contrast. Arrange small samples of coloured paper into complementary fields of colour and observe the increased intensity. While doing this try to provide plausible explanations for the increasing or decreasing intensity.

It has already been demonstrated how, through the effects of simultaneous contrast, a hue can be made to seem lighter or darker depending on juxtaposition and the comparative tonal level of its neighbour. This effect is deceptive and illusionary, for an actual tonal change in the hue itself does not take place.

Simultaneous and successive contrasts have been outlined, now by studying the accompanying illustration you will gain a greater idea of how colour relationships work. The two green figures, or centre squares, are identical, but they in fact appear quite different. In the righthand portion of the diagram, the red field maximizes or enhances the greenness of the figure. The colour of the square has a similar effect on the red colour field. They are complementary and both are intensified as a result of their diametric positioning on the colour sphere. In the lefthand portion, the two greens are harmonic and adjacent on the colour sphere, and their tonal values are close. The larger blue-green field does influence perception of the green figure, but the two colours in fact have a cancelling-out effect upon each other.

Matching perception with theory is not easy, but there is sufficient visual evidence to support the following explanation. Both the green figures cause optical fatigue to occur in the eye's green receptors. As a result, the better functioning red and blue-violet receptors switch over and provide a magenta after-image, which, when added to the righthand red field regenerates or enhances it. In the lefthand section, the magenta after-image added to the blue-green has a cancelling-out effect. Modification of hue occurs therefore in the

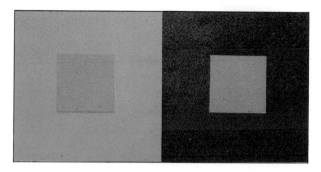

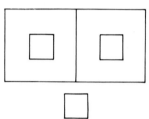

out effect on one another, whereas the colours of the magenta square, which are complementary, intensify one another. Hence the two central colours appear so different.

Follow the line drawing *(LEFT)* firstly using the colours shown *(ABOVE)* and then experiment with other colours and combinations. Grey is a particularly good example to try. You can also try the exercise in reverse, by making the central colours *look* the same. Then look at the colours you have created against both a white and grey background. Try the same exercises with other main colours, starting with the other complementary colours.

**Colour relationships**
The two green squares in the centre of the large squares *(TOP)* are the same colour, but they appear very different. The two greens *(LEFT)* are close together on the colour sphere and the tonal values too are close. The two colours seem to have a cancelling

**SUCCESSI**

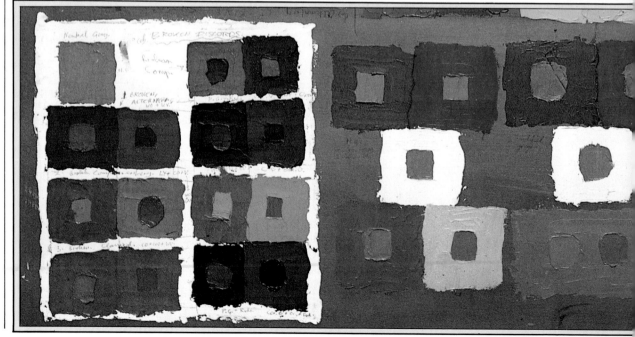

lefthand section, while intensity or brightness increases in the righthand section.

In the righthand section, the red field causes a blue-green light complementary after-image which enhances the green figure within it. In the lefthand section, the blue-green field causes a magenta after-image which cancels or modifies the green figure within it. The contrast here is mixed.

Another exercise will give you some help in analyzing colour interaction and deception. You should attempt to make three colours appear to read as five colours, and also make five colours appear to read as three.

## Mixed contrast

Mixed contrast is the creation of another colour through the superimposition of an after-image on a hue. Because of the tendency of the eye to see complementaries in the form of after-images, the appearance of hues undergoes constant change. If the after-image of the field of blue is deliberately imposed or allowed to drift onto the green centre figure of the previous illustration, the section where the overlap occurs will appear as a new colour. Mixed contrast is therefore an extension of successive contrast. At this point remember that the superimposition of an after-image upon a subtractive pigment surface does not match the subtractive mixing of those

two colours; neither does it match the instantaneous change of hue that occurs as a result of simultaneous contrast.

You should look at a field of intense primary red. After about 30 seconds, shift your focus to one side and allow the after-image to develop. Then slowly allow the after-image to drift back over the principal colour red. Then calculate the hue, intensity and consistency of the overlap or new colour, and measure and mix carefully the illusionary image with pigments.

## Optical fusion and additive colour mixing—Pointillism

Mixed contrast, you will have observed, has the effect of desaturating and reducing the chroma of colours when they are correlated over large areas. This cancelling effect can be pronounced if two opposite colours are juxtaposed in small areas, either in thin parallel stripes or in dots. Optical fusion or additive colour mixing is the mixture of light stimuli in such a way that they enter the eye simultaneously or in rapid succession, and affect the same area of the retina, so that the eye cannot easily resolve them into individual colours.

When looking at juxtaposed dots, the eye is confused by the simultaneity of colour stimuli, and is induced to register a new or third colour sensation. The retina

NTRAST

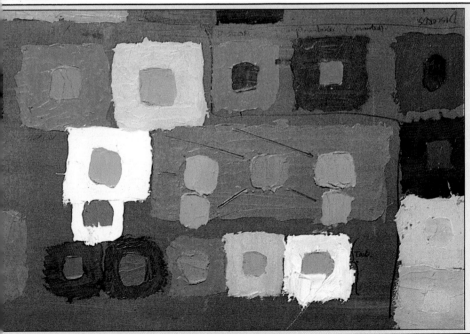

Choose two complementary colours, such as yellow and violet. Paint one square of each colour close together. Underneath paint a square of white. Into the first square paint a smaller square of a different colour, such as a neutral grey or beige. Then create a colour which will look the same on the second square. Finally, on the white square paint a small sample of each of the colours in the centre of the complementary squares.

*These exercises are being done outside the context of any painting or finished work so that you can concentrate solely on the colours, their qualities and the effects they have on one another. You will find that to practise these projects will be of great help to you when you come to decide on the colours and the effects they have in your own work.*

cannot easily differentiate in these circumstances. It is important to realize that, although the materials used are pigments, these reflect coloured light, and thus their combination will be guided by the principles of additive, not subtractive colour mixing. If two diametric colours are employed in this format therefore, the third colour illusion will theoretically appear as white because this is, after all, what happens when light primaries are mixed. In fact, the result of colour fusion normally has a slight hue bias towards one or other of the principal hues involved.

In passing, you might look at the work of the Impressionist analyst and Chevreul enthusiast, Camille Pissarro (1830–1903), who employed complementary hue contrasts to intensify and cancel. Pissarro's technique of assembling colours in small areas interested the French artists Georges Seurat (1859–1891) and Paul Signac (1863–1935), prompted them to examine the principles involved and subsequently to develop a more exact and scientific application. Chevreul's observation that colours were capable of being mixed in the eye led ultimately to the nineteenth century movement called as Pointillism.

The following projects demonstrate the effects of the optical fusion of colour and colour vibration. Firstly you should paint a pair of complementary colours in narrow alternating stripes. Care should be taken to ensure that the tones of the pair are close. The stripes should be little more than 0.1 in (2 mm) wide and aproximately 4 in (100 mm) in length. It is important to consider the effects of fusion, and also to assess the hue and tone of the new or third optical colour mix. The experiment should be repeated with blue-orange, yellow-violet and red-green pairs.

The same diametric opposites may be used in a pointillist configuration of dots. Again in these tests, the tones should be pitched close, and equal proportions of each pair of complementary colours should be used. You should measure the level of fusion yielded by different complementary pairs seen from different distances.

**FUSI**

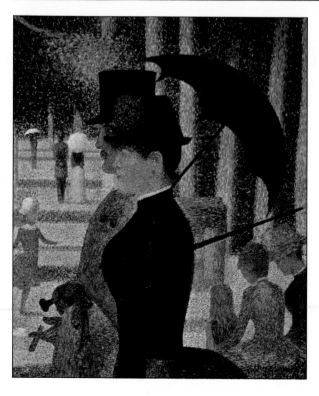

In this detail from *La Grande Jatte* by Georges Seurat *(RIGHT)* you can see clearly that Seurat has built up his images using a multitude of small coloured dots. Seen close up, these dots can be clearly identified. At a distance however, they blend with each other so that the spectator sees broken or tertiary colours. Seen close up again it is possible to pick out dots which are made up of pure colour, often yellow or pure red. The blending effect is caused by optical fusion. After-images of one colour combine with other colours around and thus modify them. When studied for a long period the spectator will become aware of the painting becoming increasingly lighter in tone.

**...LOURS**

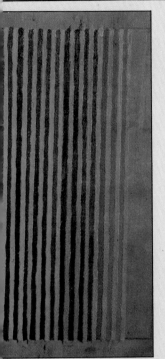

In this exercise you should attempt to create optical fusion through the juxtaposition of complementary colours. Make sure that the tones of the colours are close. First make a series of red and green stripes, then orange and blue followed by yellow and violet. The stripes should be approximately four inches (10cm) long and about half an inch (1.25cm) wide. The same colours which you use for this experiment can be used in a configuration of small dots. When seen from a distance you will find that the visual effects of both are very similar.

*In this exercise the artist has not made all the pairs of colours complementary, nor are all the juxtaposed colours of the same tone. In those areas where this has happened, it is noticeable that the stripes do not fuse well. For example, in one section of the blue orange area, the blue is too light in comparison with the orange, so that the colours appear to clash rather than fuse.*

# Neutral colour grey, the light and dark polar caps, colour blacks and colour whites, tints and shades

Now that you are familiar with colour opposites and have gained some confidence in selecting true diametric opposites, you can begin a systematic search for an absolutely neutral chromatic grey, that is, a grey that originates from the principal colours but shows no bias towards any hue. Such a colour grey should contain no trace of black pigment. To produce a range of colour greys from which to select a neutral grey, make a series of gradated scales employing diametric opposites. The tones throughout should be kept as near as possible to the tone of the achromatic grey identified at the beginning of the section. In other words, the diametric scales should be discernible from the grey background by hue and not by tone. This accumulation of colour greys will require cataloguing or sorting into appropriate colour groups. Those greys which appear to have no bias should be set to one side for later assessment, for your final choice will be made from this group of apparently neutral greys.

In the colour sphere, the tonal pole joins the light and

## COLOUR GREYS

In this exercise you should try to create a neutral grey, similar to the one you have been working on so far, but this time by mixing coloured pigments not just black and white. This should be done by mixing complementary colours. Mix all the different pairs of complementary colours and experiment with adding white and altering the proportions of the colour mixes. You should put to one side those greys which seem to be neutral, that is, close to the achromatic grey which you mixed in the first place. You should also make up blacks by mixing together colour pigments.

*In this exercise the artist has laid some of the greys on to a white base while the others have been placed on a grey ground. At the top a black has been mixed using colour pigments and the tone has then been heightened by adding white in order to ascertain the hue of the mixture.*

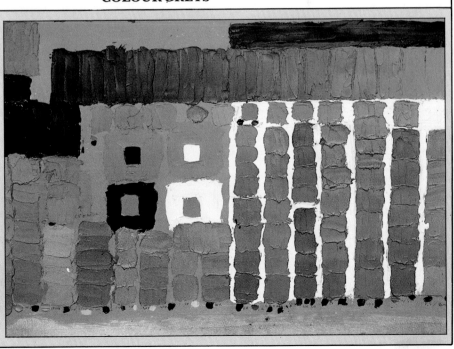

dark caps. Tonal notation measures the lightness of colours, independently of their hues, and extends from absolute black to absolute white. Theoretically, the three subtractive simple colours when mixed will yield black. In fact, a combination of red-blues, green-yellows and orange-reds is more likely to produce an opaque, dense, unbiased neutral black. You should make many colour blacks from various permutations of principal colours, and, in order to assess the relative hue or pigmentation levels, you can raise the tones by adding white pigment. This exercise will yield even more colour greys. You can now see that the tonal pole is not made up of achromatic greys, but instead constitutes a range of light and dark colour greys that results from mixtures of complementary colours.

The light, or white, polar cap of the colour sphere should be considered briefly and a range of colour whites compared. It will be sufficient to juxtapose various pieces of white paper. This will reveal that the colour range varies from blue-whites and yellow-whites to red-whites. You can sort the papers into groups of colours as was done with colour greys. It is important to remember that, by adding white to a principal colour, its hue undergoes no change, only its tone is heightened or lightened. Similarly, if white is added to a broken or tertiary hue, only its tone is changed. Likewise, colour

## DISCORDANT COLOURS

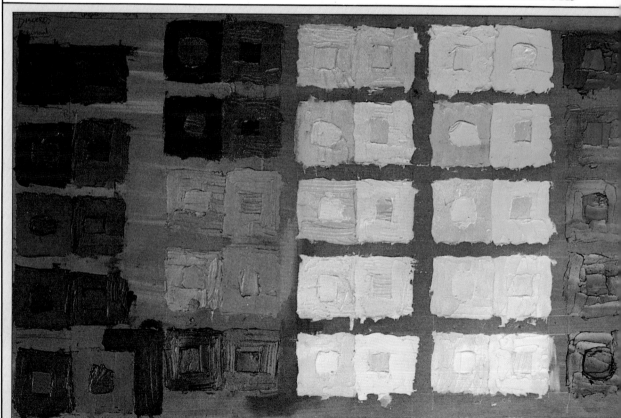

**This exercise involves arranging a discordant design. In order to do this, you will have to make the tones of all the colours equal to or higher than the lightest colour. If you incorporate a yellow, for instance, all the other colours will have to match it or be higher than it. Now** **lay down strips of colour, about half an inch (1.25cm) wide and about four inches (10cm) long. Where colours are adjacent their natural values will be inverted.**

*In this exercise the artist has chosen a yellow as the lightest colour. As you will have learnt, there is a strict natural value order for colours. The darkest is violet so that in order to* *raise to the value of yellow it has to be made very light indeed. This accounts for the paleness of the violets and blues in this particular exercise. The interaction of discordant colours is important in painting and drawing, so study the effects achieved in this exercise closely.*

greys only undergo tonal modification if white is added. Conversely, if a colour black is added to another colour, all its characteristics of hue, chroma and value are modified or changed. The darkening of a hue is referred to as shading.

When you are satisfied that a chromatic neutral grey has been identified through the process of elimination and juxtaposition, you should compare that grey with the original achromatic neutral tonal grey which you mixed during the first of these exercises. The original grey will probably have a blue bias while the neutral colour will probably look orange when placed in the grey field.

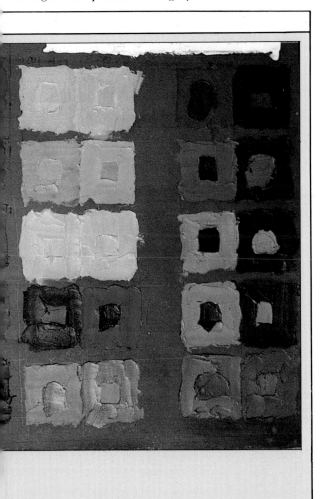

## Colour greys and broken colours in natural objects

The grey core of the colour sphere expands out towards the broken colours which are all biased towards the hues around the periphery. Consider the colour greys and the broken colours which can be found in the environment around you and collect a number of small natural objects including, for example, rock samples, leaves, lichen-covered wood, and perhaps even a fish or stuffed bird. Study these colour greys and find approximate equivalents by mixing pigments. During this exercise, take care to measure the arrangement of colour and configuration accurately. Only a detail of an object need be attempted.

## Discord, vibrating colours, value control, lightness, brightness and luminosity

The previous exercise will have shown you that the natural environment consists largely of broken hues and colour greys. In addition, the earlier study of harmonics will have also helped to highlight the incidence of colour harmony and gradation which exists in nature. Some colour relationships, however, are not harmonic, they are discordant. Before searching for examples of the discord phenomenon in the natural world, you should first examine colour discord in the abstract.

Colours arranged in a discordant relationship will compete or clash. In order to achieve the exciting effect of colour vibration, the natural indigenous tonal order of colours must be reversed. This order was mentioned earlier. This introduces an element of opposition into a colour relationship that would normally be harmonious, albeit sometimes contrasting. For example, a visual screaming effect can be achieved by juxtaposing two complementary colours in which the normal tonal order has been marginally reversed or inverted. For example, in a blue-orange discord, blue should be made fractionally lighter than orange. Blues are normally darker than orange. Red is generally considered to be brighter than blue, and yellow is brighter than red. The most saturated red is lighter than the most saturated blue; and the most saturated yellow is lighter than all the principal hues. Any two colours, whether they are adjacent or diametric, can be made to clash, either by making tonal values equal or by creating an inversion of the natural tonal order of hues. You will find that some pairs of colours will be more difficult than others. Of the complementary pairs, violet and yellow will probably cause the greatest difficulty. Remember that violet must be made as light as or even lighter than the yellow. It will therefore appear almost white, and will seem to have lost its hue or saturation of pigment. However, this is not so, because, as was said before, the addition of white does not alter the hue in a colour.

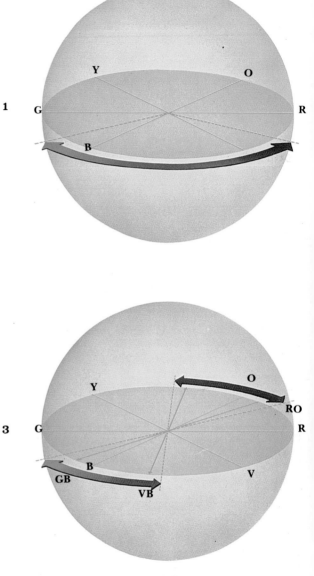

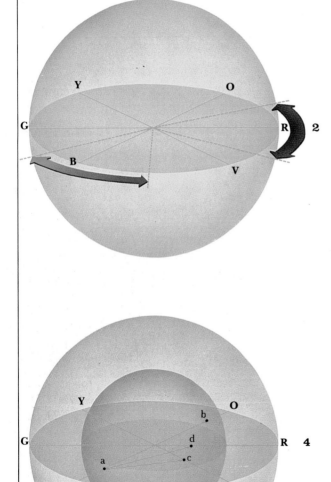

### Colour discords
These diagrammatic representations show the different main colour boundaries and categories of colour discord. The diagrams show: classical or adjacent discord (*1*) (blue and violet boundaries), alternating discord (*2*) (blue and red boundaries), complementary discord (*3*) (blue and orange boundaries) and broken, tertiary or colour grey discords (*4*). Here the line a-b is the complementary discord, a-c the broken or grey classical discord and a-d the broken or grey alternating discord.

| | |
|---|---|
| **Y** | Yellow |
| **R** | Red |
| **O** | Orange |
| **G** | Green |
| **B** | Blue |
| **GB** | Green-blue |
| **VB** | Violet blue |
| **V** | Violet |
| **RO** | Red orange |

# Discord, orchestration studies, discordant colours in nature

The next exercise uses the principles of discord. It will also test your understanding of lightness and brightness, and your success will depend on sensitive tonal control. Taking an example of commercial packaging, try to transcribe the design into a compound series of discords. That is, every colour in the original design should be altered to appear discordant along its edges with all the other colours. The design should be made to appear entirely discordant. If yellow is found in the design, then all the other hues should be raised to or above the tonal level of the yellow.

Finally, arrange a series of parallel vertical stripes 4 in (100 mm) deep in widths varying from, for example, ½ in (12 mm) to 4 in (100 mm), in such a way that every adjacent colour relationship appears discordant along the edges. Remember, to achieve discord throughout the series, all the tones must remain consistent, and none darker than the lightest hue.

This section has introduced you to the principles of harmony and contrast, the main colour relationships, colour adjacents and diametrically opposed colours, to colour blacks, colour whites, colour greys and broken colours, to colour deception and induction, to simultaneous, successive and mixed contrast, to optical

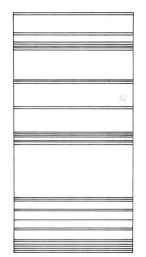

This linear diagram *(LEFT)* illustrates one method of orchestrating colour discords. The suggested colour sequence should be closely adhered to, including the width of the bands. From *(TOP)* to *(BOTTOM)* the colours are: blue, grey/broken colour, orange, grey, blue, violet, red-violet, red, red-orange, blue, neutral chromatic grey, orange, blue, orange, yellow, violet, yellow, yellow-orange, orange, orange-red, red, green, blue, violet (including white), white yellow-orange, grey (orange-blue subtractive mixture), neutral colour grey, grey (orange-blue subtractive mixture), blue, orange, blue, orange, blue, orange.

fusion, after-image and, finally, to colour discord. You should now try to apply these ideas in as many different ways as possible. Your new knowledge and awareness of colour can be applied to whatever area of art you are interested in. Drawing in charcoal or pencil can use your knowledge of greys, blacks and whites, while, in painting, you can apply the whole range of theories and practice. When using colour, remember to consider the colours in relation to the ideas in this section, and that colour can only be assessed in context. Never be afraid try out new colour moods and themes.

## COLOUR DISCORDS

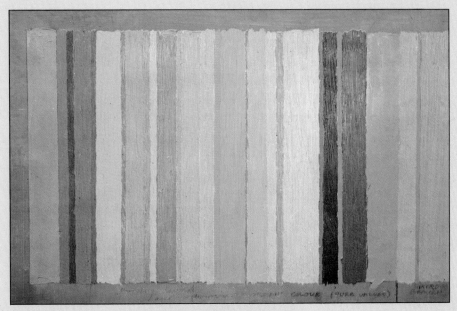

**The object of this exercise is to arrange a series of stripes of varying widths but all 4in (100mm) long so that each colour appears discordant with the one next to it.**

*All the tones in this exercise must remain consistent and so none must be darker than the lightest hue. Otherwise you will not be able to achieve discord throughout the series. If you use yellow you should make sure that all the other hues are raised to or above the tonal level of the yellow.*

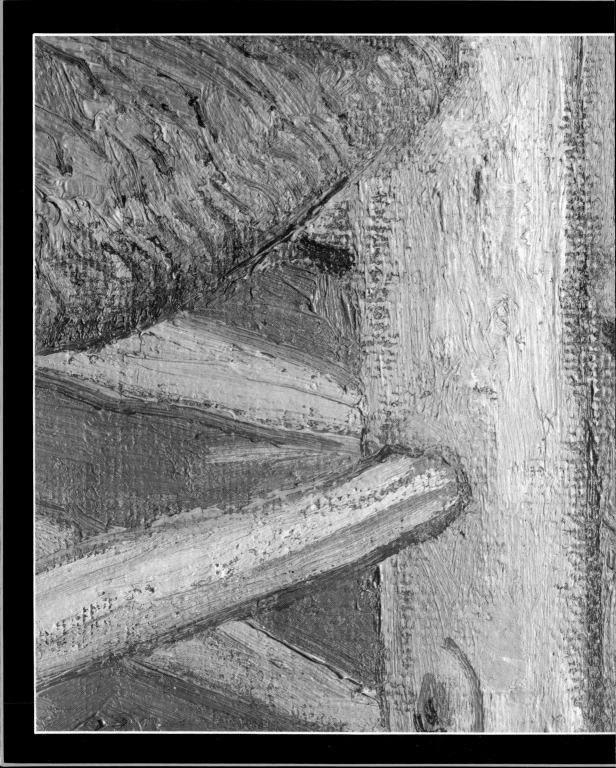

# 5

# PAINTING

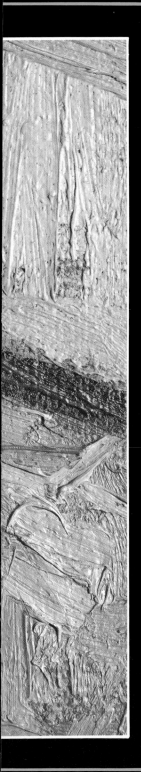

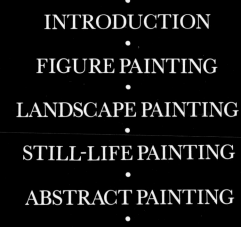

- •
- INTRODUCTION
- •
- FIGURE PAINTING
- •
- LANDSCAPE PAINTING
- •
- STILL-LIFE PAINTING
- •
- ABSTRACT PAINTING
- •

Vincent van Gogh
*Chair and Pipe (detail)*

# INTRODUCTION

The role of the artist today is in many ways an enviable one. Artists have at their disposal, either in the original or in excellent reproduction, the entire history of painting. However, the artist's position in society is an ambiguous one. Whilst restrictions of style, technique and content are all but non-existent now, the painter has a much less well defined role than in the past. Until recently, the terms artist and artisan were more or less synonymous. The job of the painter was not dissimilar to that of the carpenter or the stonemason. Painting was considered to be the occupation of a craftsman, and apprentice painters spent many years learning to create a visual image as much in the style of their teachers as possible. Painting as a means of self-expression is a relatively new idea.

The best way to learn a skill has always been to observe someone who has already mastered it. The history of art is populated by pupils and masters, while of course, the pupil has often gone on to become the more important artist. Some of the greatest innovators began their careers as assistants to comparatively unknown masters—first learning the rules of painting before going on to break them in the search for new ways of creating an image. An investigation of most of the great masters will usually show a transition from the traditional methods to their own characteristic way of working. It is continuing a long tradition, therefore, to look at what has gone before as a means of instruction. By examining the techniques and methods of great painters, the student can learn the language of painting more easily.

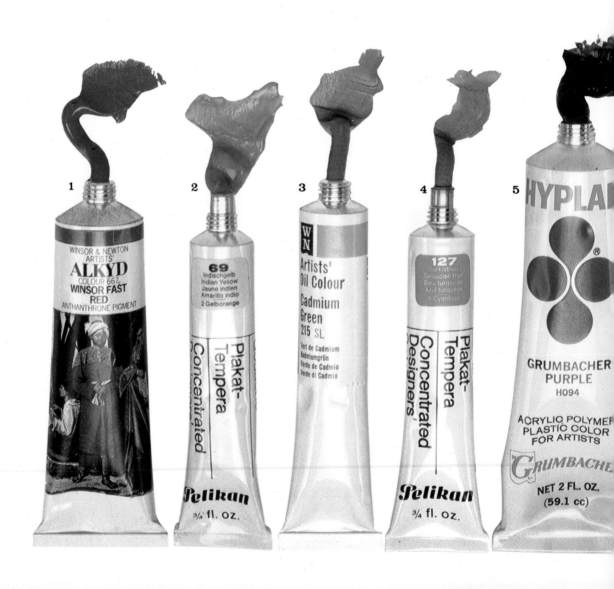

The term 'painting', broadly speaking, refers to any system of applying pigment to a support. There are, however, certain common categories into which most methods of painting fall, and it is these which will be dealt with here. Whilst it is by no means essential for an aspiring painter to be familiar with the history of the development of paint, it is not only interesting but also helpful to understand how and why certain techniques of painting were evolved. Freedom from the necessity of arduously manufacturing their own materials is one of the major advantages artists today have over their predecessors; but the choice of commercially available paints can be overwhelming. With experience, it becomes easier to select from materials and equipment those which most closely meet with requirements. Because these needs vary from individual to individual, the ideal way to discover which method of working suits you best is by constant experiment.

# Painting media

For most people, their first experience of painting is probably with a child's watercolour box, and this may have left the impression that this is the easiest type of paint to use. This is a great mistake. To use pure watercolours to full advantage is an exacting technique requiring a high degree of skill. Watercolours are very finely ground pigment bound in gum, usually gum arabic, which is water soluble. Traditionally, pure watercolour is laid in transparent washes, working from the lightest tones and progressing to the darkest, allowing the support, the surface to which the paint is applied, to sparkle through. With watercolour the support is usually paper.

Gouache, similar in many ways to pure watercolour, differs in that it is an opaque paint. This means that it is possible to lay lighter tones over the top of dark areas. Many gouaches now contain plastic which means that, once the paint has been applied and allowed to dry, it is possible to work over it without the underlying layers leaking through.

A paint which is little used today, but which has a fine pedigree, is tempera. Its lack of popularity may be because, although it is possible to buy ready-made tempera paint in tubes, these are not really as satisfactory as the home-made variety. Tempera paint is made by combining equal quantities of powdered pigment with a solution of egg yolk and distilled water. With tempera it is usual to work onto a support prepared with a gesso ground which can be sanded to provide a perfectly smooth surface, particularly sympathetic to this method of painting. The paint must be laid on fairly thinly as, if put on too thickly, there is a danger that it will all simply peel off again. However, there is no limit to the number of transparent layers that can be built up, one upon the other. Although quick drying, and therefore requiring a degree of facility, tempera paints can be extremely versatile and lend themselves to a variety of approaches, including stippling, splattering and, scratching back through the surface.

Fresco is another method of painting which, for practical reasons, is hardly used nowadays. This is a pity as the quality of a frescoed surface is an especially appealing one. The technique of fresco painting is lengthy and arduous, based upon the chemical changes which take place when pigment, held in pure

**Painting media**
The range of paint available to the artist today is extremely wide and the quality very high. The main types of paint are oils *(3)*, acrylic *(5, 7)* and tempera *(2, 4)*. Watercolour *(6)* also comes in pans and bottles. Gouache, also called 'designer's colour' comes in tubes and is like an opaque watercolour. Alkyd paints *(1)* are quick drying resin-based paints used with an oil medium. When choosing brushes and other equipment, it is better to have a small selection of high quality equipment than a large selection of poorer quality materials. The same applies, of course, to paint and surfaces.

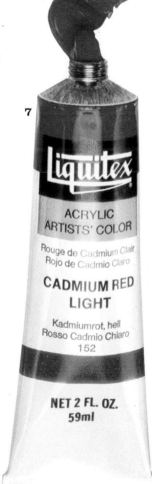

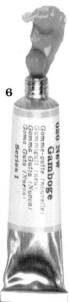

water, is painted onto freshly laid plaster. Since the paint can only be applied to wet plaster, the design has to be thoroughly worked out beforehand and the picture must be made in daily stages. As the plaster dries, the pigment becomes crystallized into the surface; if too great an area of plaster is prepared at one time, it may dry before the pigment can be applied and has then to be chipped away again before work can progress. Although laborious, fresco is a method which has the advantage of extreme durability, as well testified by fine Roman examples.

For about the last 400 years the most popular painting medium has been oils. Oil paint consists of dry pigment suspended in a vegetable oil, usually poppy or linseed oil, which has a very slow drying time. Oil paint is versatile and can be used to give a wide variety of qualities and textures by the choice of additives and means of application.

A recent rival to the popularity of oils has been acrylic paints, the use of which has been properly developed only in the last 30 years or so, although they have been available in industry since the 1920s and 1930s. Acrylic paints are pigments held in a synthetic resin and, although it has been suggested that their use has superseded that of oils, they should not be used as a substitute. In fact, the techniques involved in acrylic painting have much more in common with watercolour and gouache, using transparent layers over a light ground which can be allowed to shine through.

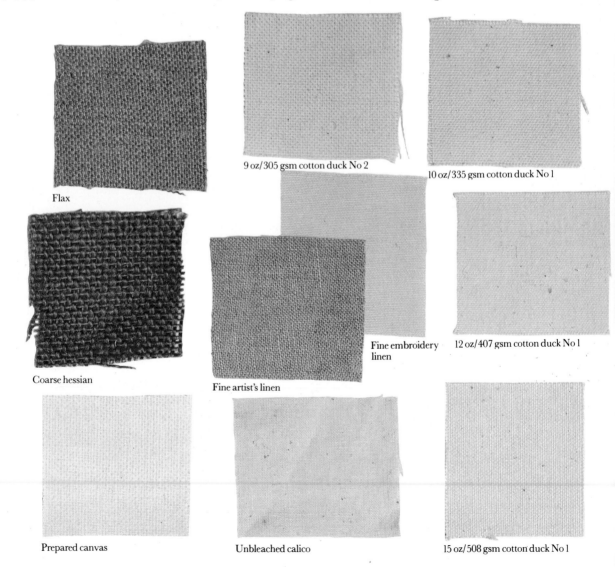

Flax

9 oz/305 gsm cotton duck No 2

10 oz/335 gsm cotton duck No 1

Coarse hessian

Fine artist's linen

Fine embroidery linen

12 oz/407 gsm cotton duck No 1

Prepared canvas

Unbleached calico

15 oz/508 gsm cotton duck No 1

# Supports

Whatever sort of paint is used, the choice and preparation of support requires careful consideration. A great variety of supports has been used during the long history of painting, but the most popular have proved to be paper, canvas and wood. There are good and practical reasons for this popularity. Wooden panels, prepared with a suitable ground, which were worked on before the use of oil on canvas became widespread, have never been entirely superseded. Wood is relatively light, portable and much more durable than a fabric support, although offering a less flexible surface on which to paint. Although the use of canvas is associated with the development of oil painting from the fifteenth century on, its history in fact goes back at least 4,000 years and possibly longer. Certainly, for the painter today, it is the most obvious choice because ease of storage and transportation are usually extremely important considerations. Thin board and paper, more suitable for use with water-based paints, and available in a vast number of colours, weights and textures, offer a relatively cheap and easy surface on which to work.

The preparation of the chosen support is important, because, without a suitable ground, the paint may become absorbed into the surface, causing the colour to sink and the texture to become dull. The ground consists of a filler mixed with a binder, usually either size or oil, or an emulsion of the two. When preparing a ground for panel painting, the traditional method was to mix gesso, or calcium sulphate, with a binder. This ground is ideal for tempera painting as the surface can be rubbed down until it is as smooth as glass, but it is less suitable for canvas painting as it is rather inflexible. Canvases may be prepared with an emulsion made from oil and size. The colour of the ground can help to set the tone for the painting, particularly as pigment can be added to the filler.

Paper, which is available in a variety of surfaces, is already sized and ready for use. However, many people prefer to stretch their paper by first damping and then fixing it to a drawing board or other suitable support with gummed tape. This prevents buckling when using very wet paint.

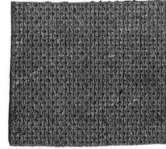
Card

Rough hardboard

Chipboard/Masonite

Brass

**Painting supports**
The various painting media require different kinds of support. This selection of supports shows some of those suitable for oil and acrylics. For watercolour, good quality paper is best. Sized wood or board with a gesso ground is suitable for tempera. Any well-prepared, oil-free surface is suitable for gouache.

Mahogany

Smooth hardboard

# FIGURE PAINTING

It is not surprising that over the centuries the human figure in all its many aspects has been the most commonly chosen subject for painting. It is natural that people should be interested in themselves. The cause for surprise should rather be in the originality continually demonstrated by artists who are, after all, only painting what countless numbers of others have painted before them.

## Self-portrait

Paint a self-portrait of the head and shoulders only, using a mirror and one source of natural light. This means that the head itself and the features within will have one positively lit side and a shadowed darker side. The importance of reflected light in this exercise is considerable. The area in shadow is given depth and

This self-portrait by Edgar Degas *(RIGHT)* is a sensitive tonal study of the artist when he was about 18 years old. The slight imprecision in depicting the mouth shows the artist's relative youth and inexperience. However, the muted brown and flesh colours are well balanced, and the face is shown in an interesting semi-profile position, lit from one direction.

solidity because of the way it reflects light and colour from surroundings. Before starting work, experiment with coloured drapes, placing yourself between them and your source of light. Brightly coloured drapery will obviously throw back more light than darker coloured drapery, and the atmosphere and mood of your painting will be altered accordingly. Decide which of these most closely reflects your own feelings and prepare yourself for work.

**Preparation** First make yourself comfortable, so that you are able to work for sustained periods of time, and so that you are able to return to precisely the same

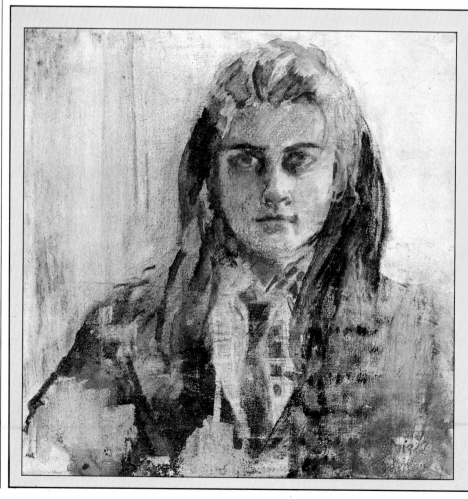

This self-portrait was painted in oils. The artist applied the paint very thinly. She also allowed the texture of the canvas to show through by scraping back the paint after she had applied it. The canvas texture adds to the effectiveness of the image. The figure has been well positioned on the canvas and there is an interesting modulation of the pink/grey tones from the left to the righthand side of the canvas. The shape and generous cast of the features have been portrayed with a good feeling of solidity. The whiteness of the support, however, perhaps shines through too much, giving a rather stark effect. This could be avoided by toning the surface before beginning the piece.

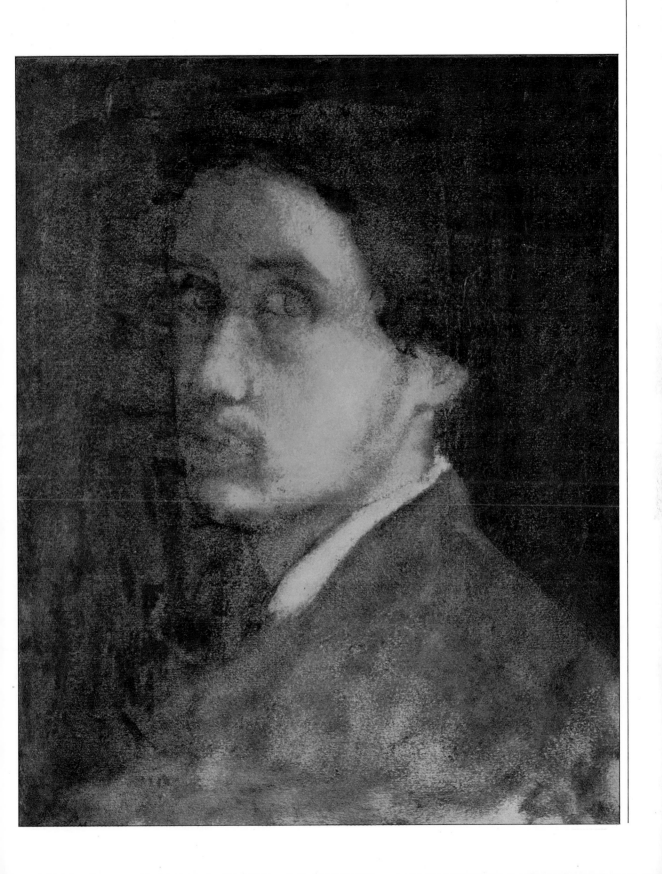

position should you need to rest. Then begin to consider the problems. Before you now is the most infinitely subtle of human forms—the complex series of hills and valleys that constitute the human face. Further, there are psychological overtones. Short of plastic surgery, there is little anyone can do to alter the features they are born with. However, the way in which you use your face will alter the way in which it appears to other people. It is easy to recognize the mood of the moment—a person who is happy usually appears so, and it is the expression on the face which makes this apparent. Similarly, the face of someone who is unhappy will be likely to reflect their misery. Of course, these are extremes between which there are an infinite number of varying human emotions which can, to a greater or lesser extent, be interpreted in the way the mouth is held, by the creases around the eyes and nose, and so on. Examine your own face as objectively as possible and see how your inner feelings manifest themselves.

From the viewpoint of the work in hand, however, what you should initially be concerned with is a solid form, lit as directed, and sitting with space all around it. What you are about to paint can be seen as an object in space, with a distance between the viewer and the object, and between it and the background. Mastering this concept is of prime importance. Observe how the air seems able to move around the head and how the strong contrasts of light and dark render it solid and substantial.

**Shape** After thinking about the structure inside the painting, you should then consider the surface of the picture itself. You must decide what sort of interpretation should be made and how best to use the arrangements of shapes, colour and tone. Now look into the mirror and place yourself in as simple and symmetrical a position as possible, head in the centre with equal space either side. You must ask yourself if this is too obvious—does it lend a 'classical' and perhaps inappropriate mood, does the line through the face, which also becomes the precise centre of the picture, divide the whole too simply into two halves? If this is the case, try then moving the head sideways so that the two background areas flanking it are asymmetrical. Try positioning the head so that there are virtually no background shapes, and decide whether this tends to cramp and confine the face. Try the opposite, by travelling back and allowing the head to become surrounded by a good deal of space. Does this now make the head 'float' as if disembodied? These thoughts, questions and experiments must continue in this way until you are satisfied that you have a fair idea of what will give a good balance in the picture.

**Colour and tone** Now consider the colour. Think not

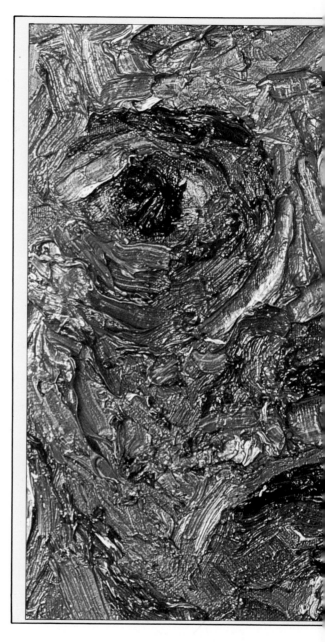

only about the flesh, although this is very important, as there will be such a great variety of tones and colours, but give thought also to the other and equally important elements in the piece. These are the shapes which make up the space beside and behind the head and must be as much a part of your work as the features of the face. Cooler colours tend to appear recessive, warmer ones to advance. This can be used to advantage in portrait painting. The subject of your picture, yourself, may well be best rendered in

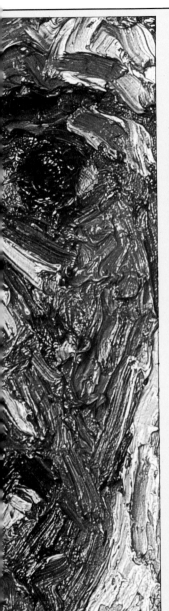

These two self-portraits are
extremely striking interpretations.
The thickly applied oil paint gives
a surface texture which is an
important element in the final
image. In both pictures the head
virtually fills the canvas so that the
face seems almost trapped within
its frame. This impression is
increased by the emphasis given to
the staring eyes. In the first self-
portrait (LEFT) the main
highlights on the nose, cheeks,
mouth and temple are painted with
only one or two firm strokes, while
equally strongly applied touches of
darker color add to the solidity of
the face. In the second self-portrait
(BELOW) the ear is somewhat
clumsily rendered, but even this
seems in keeping with the artist's
overall approach.

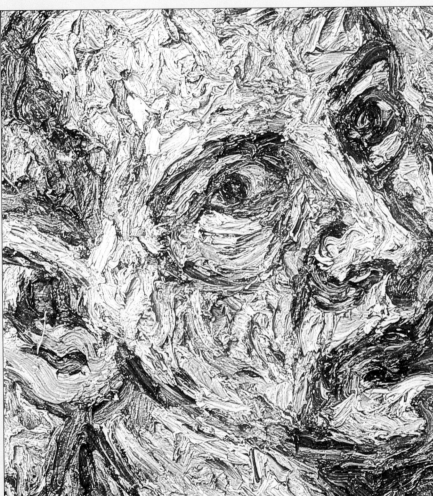

warmish tints, saving the cooler ones for the background, thus greatly assisting the illusion of space.

A further important aspect to consider before you
start to paint is that of tone and what can be called the
tonal organization of the picture. Those areas which
have the greatest contrast in tone, that is to say those
parts which contain the lightest lights juxtaposed with
the darkest darks, will appear nearer to the viewer
than areas where the range of tone is narrower.
Besides making use of tone in this way, make sure that
this aspect of your painting is as well balanced as are
its linear and colour aspects. You may choose to work
with a rather high key of bright tones, or alternatively
to keep your tonal values rather sombre and low. This
can be extremely effective, always provided that you
are consistent.

**Technique and medium** You should now be ready
to begin painting. It is up to you whether your
approach is going to be as objective as possible or
whether you are going to attempt to produce a piece of

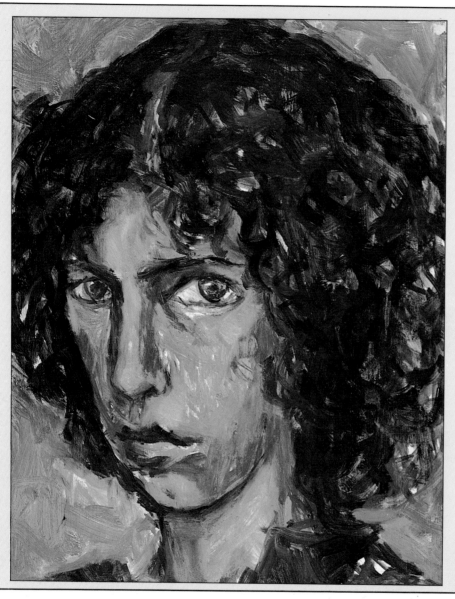

*This self-portrait was painted in oils on board. It shows a direct view of the sitter in a mirror. The composition is interesting in that the sides of the canvas cut the shape of the artist's hair. This allows the oval of the face to dominate the picture. The colours of the face are complemented by those of the background, which, however, are left rather general. This too lends emphasis to the face. When you are embarking on a self-portrait and using a mirror, experiment with viewing yourself from different angles and distances. A close-up image can be strong and effective, but interesting effects can also be achieved with a less direct approach.*

work which is more subjective. It would be a good idea to execute more than one painting, trying out a number of different approaches. In painting self-portraits, as with any form of painting, it is a very good idea if you experiment with as many different media as possible. So, if you have produced your first painting using oil colours, then perhaps your second should be done with acrylics or watercolour. It must be emphasized that all these different types of paint are a matter of individual preference, and that the only way to discover which are in sympathy with your own methods of working is by trial and error.

Sandro Botticelli's *Head of a Boy* (RIGHT) is painted in tempera. The artist began by doing a careful and detailed underdrawing, over which cool terre verte and ochre washes were laid. Next the tones were added in with careful brushwork and cross-hatching. The clear eyes and gaze of the sitter add to the impact of this image. The hair has been painted with numerous fine strokes.

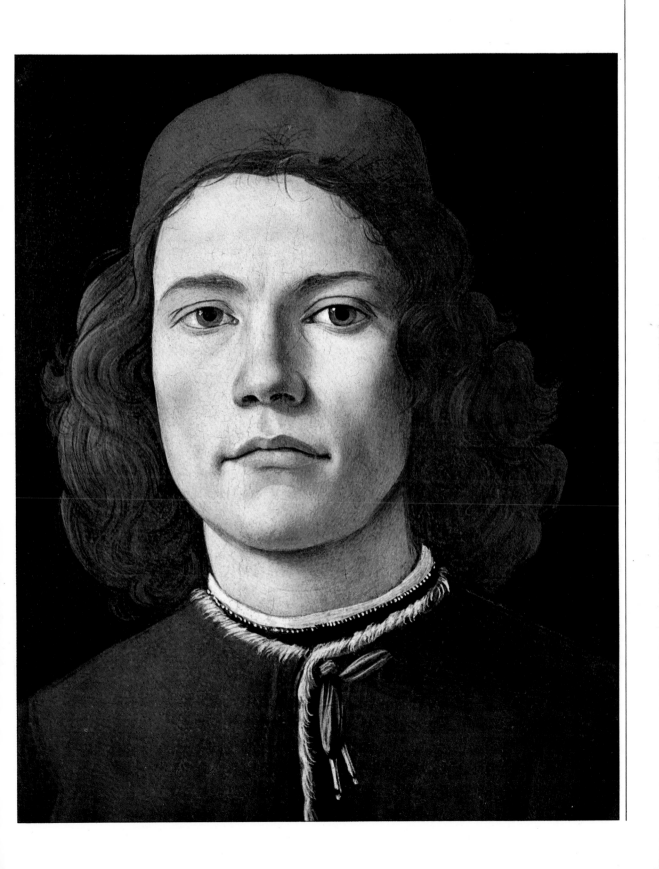

# Portrait

Painting a portrait of someone other than yourself may be a much more daunting prospect, as you can become too concerned with depicting a 'likeness'. This should not, however, be your primary concern. Approach painting a portrait in the same way as you did the previous self-portrait, giving thought to arrangements of colour, tone, line and form. If you are methodical and accurate, then it is probable that the finished painting will be not only a likeness of your model but that it should be a well balanced and professional piece of work.

**Preparation** Seat your model against an uncluttered background and in a position where you will be able to set up your canvas or board at a sufficient distance to enable you to view both the painting and the subject at the same time. Whilst you are working, you should compare the two continually.

Because the previous exercise specified the use of natural light, you may prefer to try some form of artificial light this time. It is possible to achieve a huge variety of effects simply by changing the direction of the light, and, if you intend to work using artificial light,

then you should begin by trying out as many variations in lighting as you can. The nearest approximation to natural lighting will be achieved by placing your sources of light above and to one side of your subject, and at some distance apart. You will find that light from directly above and, more particularly, directly beneath your subject will lend a strange and rather unreal atmosphere to your picture. Used deliberately this can be an interesting way of adding drama and mystery to the finished piece. As a rule, however, it is as well to concentrate on simplicity as the effects of extreme and unusual lighting can be difficult to control.

Throughout the history of painting, there have been widely varying preferences for the way in which the model should be lit for a portrait. The strong contrasts of light and shade favoured by many eminent painters, of whom Rembrandt (1606–1669) is perhaps the most notable, were particularly avoided by others. For example, Hilliard (1547–1619), court painter, miniaturist and jeweller, refers in his treatise on painting technique, *The Art of Limning*, written around 1600, to a request made by the English Queen Elizabeth I that her portrait should be done 'in the Italian Manner'. This meant it was to be painted without extremes of tone because the image was 'best in plaine lines without shadowing, for the lyne without shadowe showeth all to a good judgement, but the shadowe without lyne showeth nothing.' This serves as an excellent reminder that people are always at the mercy of fashion, in painting as in other aspects of their lives. It is as well to be aware of this and, rather than becoming victims of the fashion of the moment, try to use fashion to your own ends.

Your general composition should be fairly similar to that of your self-portrait, although you may if you wish include more of the figure. It would be wise not to start painting a full length figure. Make sure that you allow your model plenty of rest during which you can consider other parts of the painting.

You may, if you wish, work from a nude model, but if you intend to paint your subject clothed, then try to avoid a costume which is over-elaborate. Remember too that large areas of bright colour can be overwhelming unless treated with caution. This does not, of course, mean that you should avoid the use of positive colours, only that they should be used with discretion and an awareness of the effects that can be induced.

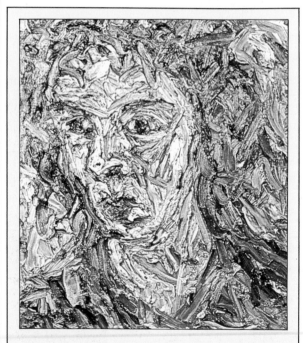

*The use of colour in this portrait is extremely interesting. There are no local flesh paint tints at all, but a series of strongly marked touches in very thick and juicy paint, which combine to produce an effect of shimmering and an interesting and unconventional rendering of flesh. The face is strongly placed and dominates the image.*

This striking portrait of Federico da Montefeltro by Piero della Francesca *(RIGHT)* shows a stark profile against a detailed landscape. The precise handling of the paint and the detail of, for example, the lines around the eyes are especially noteworthy. Many early landscapes in fact formed the background to portraits or figure groups.

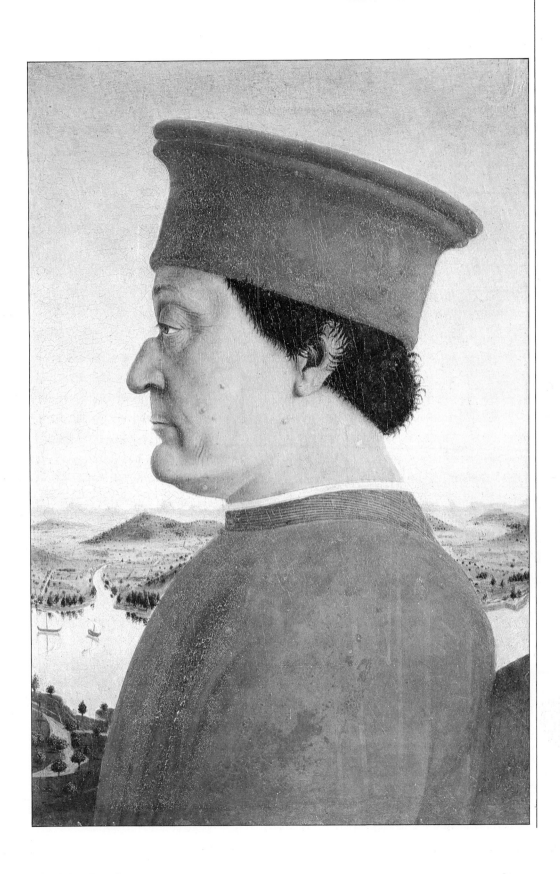

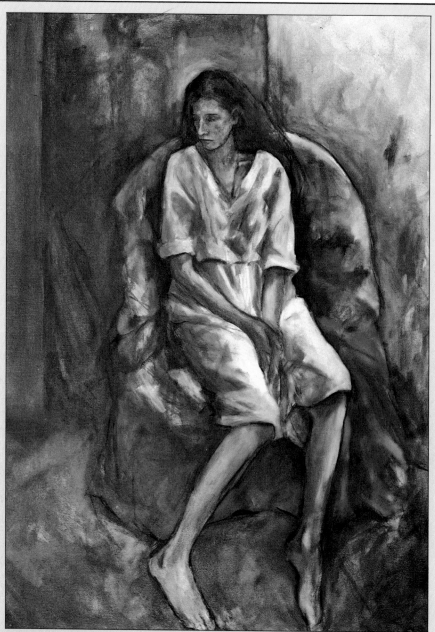

Henri Matisse's portrait of his friend the artist André Derain *(RIGHT)* is an excellent example of Fauve technique. The Fauve artists were interested in the expressive potential of colour in conjunction with the surface of the canvas, the quantity of paint and quality of the brushmark and line. The picture shows a series of clearly definable colour relationships. The background colours are cool greens and blues and these are counterpointed against the warmer oranges, yellows and reds of the figure. The combination of colours and complementaries (orange against blue and red against green) help focus the viewer's attention on the head. The smock is painted fairly lightly using long strokes of yellow with varied tints of brown and green. The head receives the main weight of pigment. In several places the ground shows through and this plays an important role in unifying the image. The angle of the head and the position it occupies on the canvas are also vital in the impact of the image on the viewer.

*This portrait has a good deal of character. It is full length in order to show the languid slimness of the sitter. The pose too emphasizes this. Dividing the background into three vertical stripes adds life to the image, as does the juxtaposition of the red and green colours. The tints used in the background are picked up in the chair on which the subject is sitting. When posing a model for a portrait, think not only about the*
*actual pose and how to achieve the impression you want for the sitter, but also consider the background in some detail, because this will have an important effect on how the image appears. Do you want the background to be detailed and exact? In such a setting the figure of the sitter might tend to disappear. Do you want the viewer's attention to focus on the sitter? In this case, a muted or*
*understated background might be more apt. Consider too the shapes in the background, think about the shape which the sitter occupies in that space and how to achieve the best composition. Before starting to paint, experiment with some sketches of the subject from different angles showing various arrangements of the figure and background. Try out several media too.*

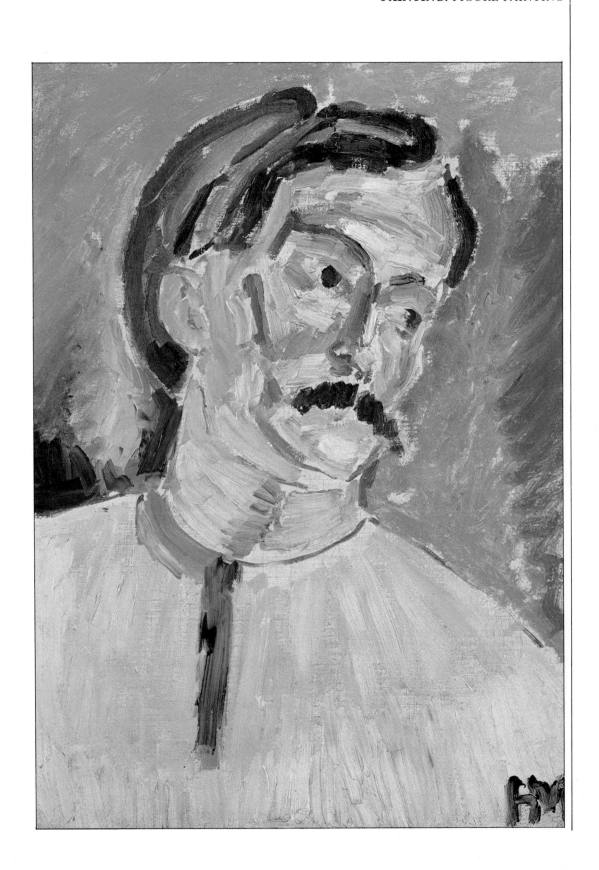

# Figure in an interior

The projects so far have dealt with relatively simple picture concepts. By keeping to a straightforward composition, it has been possible to give full attention to harmony of colour and tone, line and form. These are aspects of picture making which remain constant regardless of subject matter. However, dealing with these problems becomes increasingly difficult as soon as the entire human figure is introduced as an element within the picture.

The human figure is a complex yet infinitely subtle series of continuously changing forms which has always preoccupied artists. Without a knowledge of anatomy, however, it can be exceedingly difficult to understand the structure and movement of the figure, particularly if your model is clothed. Artists in the past have often made nude studies towards paintings where the figures would actually be depicted clothed, because by so doing they were better able to represent the underlying structure. Certainly you should take advantage of every possible opportunity for practising drawing from a model, either nude or clothed.

It is easy to see the point of the old fashioned system of art school training. Students were obliged to serve a long apprenticeship before being allowed to draw and paint from a live model. They spent their time copying from examples by the old masters and drawing laboriously from plaster casts. Having completed this part of their training, they spent a further period of time drawing from the life model. Only when a satisfactory standard had been reached here would they be allowed to embark upon colour representation. This is obviously a rather time-consuming approach to what is nevertheless a perennial problem. A sound grasp of anatomical

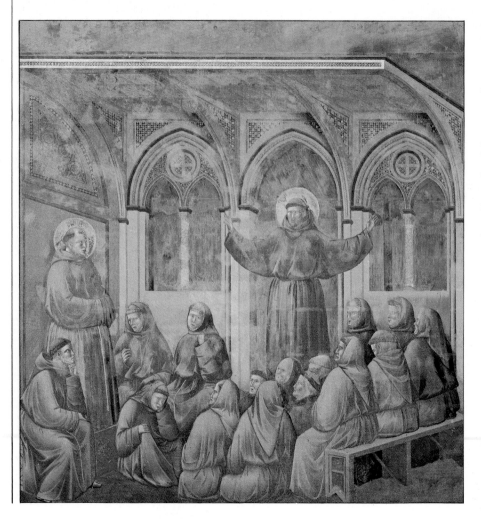

Giotto was a master of the demanding medium of fresco, a technique of painting onto walls. Because fresco involves applying paint to wet plaster, a large surface has to be divided up into a number of sections and each one painted separately. This means that changes in the design are difficult to make, and therefore preparatory drawings have to lay down the major components of the design. The fresco of *Saint Francis (LEFT)* shows how Giotto has organized the figures to emphasize the figure of the saint. The treatment of the drapery is also noteworthy.

Jan Vermeer was perhaps the major Dutch seventeenth century genre painter. Genre paintings show scenes of everyday life. The intimate domestic atmosphere of *The Music Lesson (RIGHT)* is created in part by the arrangement of two figures – the teacher and the student. The figures are placed towards the back of the scene, lit by the light streaming through the latticed window on the left. The black and white tiled floor and richly coloured carpet lead the viewer's eye to the figures. Vermeer used a variety of techniques for painting lights ranging from thin layers of translucent glazes to thick opaque paint applied directly to the surface without preliminary underpainting.

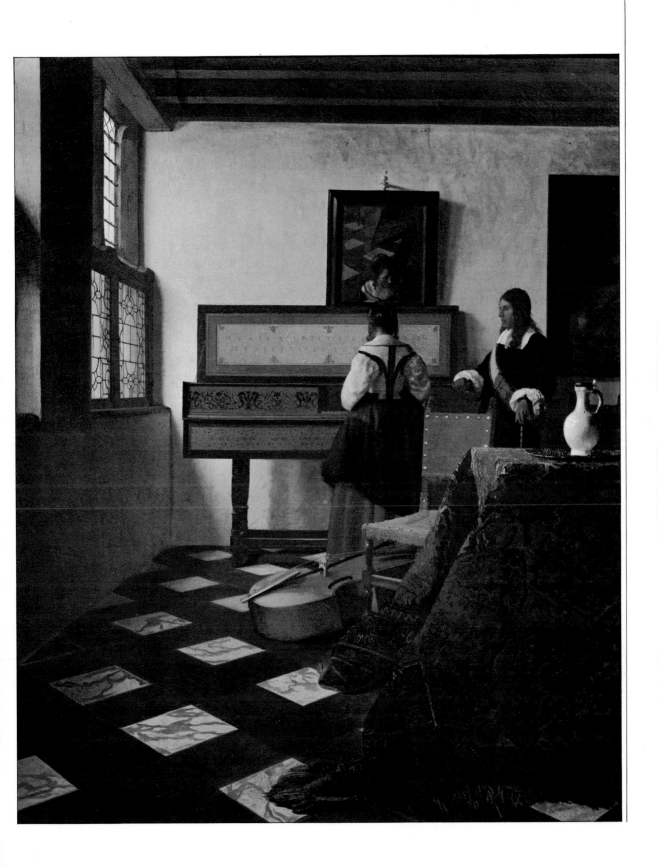

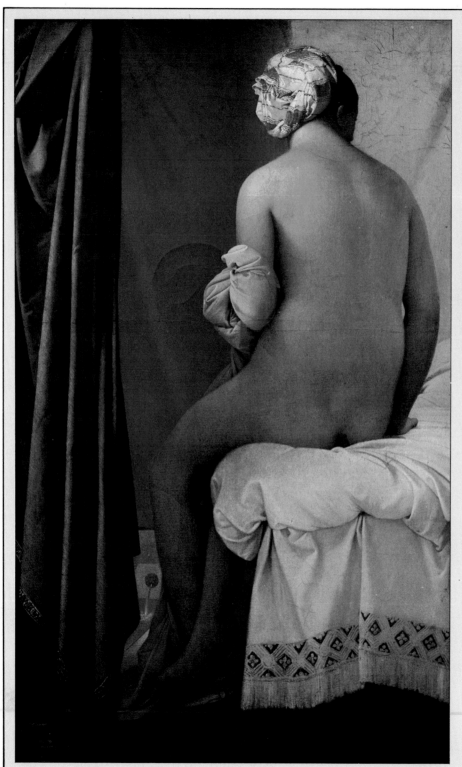

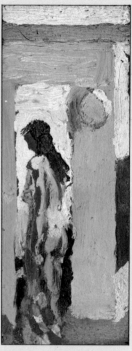

These two examples of figures in interiors show slightly different approaches. Woman Bathing by the French artist Ingres (LEFT) shows a three-quarter back view of the softly lit figure with the face in shadow.

The flesh tones are softly modelled, contrasting with the darkness of the drape in the background. The carefully executed drapery folds add to the impression of solidity. Examine how the textures and colours are combined and contrasted. The artist paid attention to all parts of the composition. Note how the bath in the background is filling with water. In the small-scale student work (ABOVE), the figure is in a similar position but seen much more as part of the interior rather than dominating it, although the figure is still the most important element in the picture. In both pictures it seems as if the artist is peeping in on a very private scene and as if the figures are quite unaware of the artist's presence. This is a useful device when planning your own compositions.

drawing is of vital importance to anyone who wishes to be an artist. Even those who intend to move onto abstract work will not find that their time has been wasted if they persevere in mastering this facet of the language of drawing and painting. A glance at the early work of any artist of note, whatever their style, will amply demonstrate this point.

**Preparation** For this exercise you are required to paint a human figure in an interior. You should choose a room which is of interest to you and possibly one with which you are already familiar. It is always easier to make a statement about something which you know well and for which you have positive feelings, and it is good to put yourself in a position where you are forced to examine a known environment anew.

It is up to you whether you paint your figure nude or dressed. If you intend to work with a clothed model, then make sure that the choice of dress is not arbitrary. This should be considered as carefully as all other aspects of the painting; you should pay particular attention to the colours and textures which you intend to introduce. When positioning the figure take care that it does not become dull and predictable. Remembering the pitfalls of dividing your canvas equally, set your figure slightly to one side and ensure that it relates naturally to the environment within which you are placing it. There are a number of ways

*For this figure in an interior the artist used oil paints. The composition is very enterprising. The still-life objects in the foreground set the scene for the picture. Instead of concentrating on the figure, the spectator only sees what is virtually a sneak view of the figure in the mirror. The mirror gives the image great depth. The surface of the canvas has been well divided. Greens, yellows and oranges predominate, and these colours have been contrasted with a strong, dark emphasis creating vertical and horizontal stresses. This more complex type of composition is well worth experimenting with as you become more confident in handling simpler shapes and configurations of figure and object. The same considerations of arranging space, trying out different approaches in preliminary studies and trying to evolve an image gradually apply also to this more complex kind of composition.*

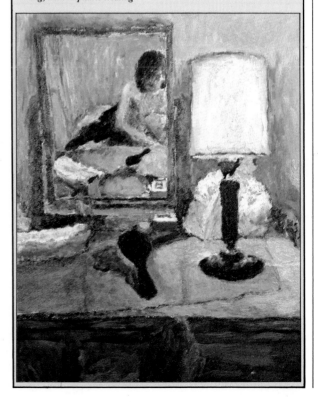

The French artist Pierre Bonnard used colour in an exciting and individual way. The main colours in *Nude in an Interior (ABOVE)* are the complementaries orange and blue. Examine the composition and how the colours are combined. For example, the colours of the floor in the bottom righthand corner relate closely to those of the wall. The arrangement of the composition is also interesting. The orange figure is bending forward in a position which hides her face. The vertical lines and strong contrasts are typical of Bonnard.

that this can be achieved—perhaps the colour relationships can be arranged to create a total harmony, or you can use lighting to create tonal unity.

How you light your subject for this exercise, as for any other, will largely dictate the mood of your painting, and, of course, the best way to discover what suits you is by experiment. Natural light will vary enormously depending upon the weather, but can also be controlled by the use of drapes or blinds, often with interesting effects. On the other hand, rather strident artificial light may be used deliberately to create a particular atmosphere, or spotlights may be set up to produce a fairly subdued illumination.

Objects only become visible because of the light which shines upon them. Some colours and textures almost totally absorb light and others almost totally reflect it, with an enormous variation between the two extremes. Human flesh happens to have a highly light-reflective quality which makes it at once a subject of absorbing interest and great complexity. When assessing a hue it is not enough simply to take note of the local colour. You must also look for the effect which one colour has upon another. As light is reflected from object to object, there will be a complicated interaction of colour which will be increased depending upon the variety of local colour within the setting you have chosen.

As with drawing, painting is largely a matter of learning how to look properly; in this it is important to be constantly aware of what you are looking for. If you think of painting as a language, then making a picture is like translating a series of shapes and colours from three into two dimensions. The Swiss artist Paul Klee (1879–1940) once said that 'art does not reproduce what can be seen: it makes things visible.' This is what you must set out to do.

When planning your composition, think about how you are going to suggest depth within the picture plane. Try to think of the atmosphere as having a tangible colour and texture and make use of changes of scale to create an illusion of depth. You may, perhaps, place a large unit of furniture in the foreground, allowing the figure to be glimpsed through and beyond. Alternatively you may prefer to place your figure in a more prominent position, dominating the room and its contents. However you arrange the composition, make sure that the finished painting achieves a balance between figure and environment.

At all times be aware that it is up to you how your picture is structured and how you make use of colour and tone. These are decisions which must always be made positively; this is the raw material from which you will produce your finished painting.

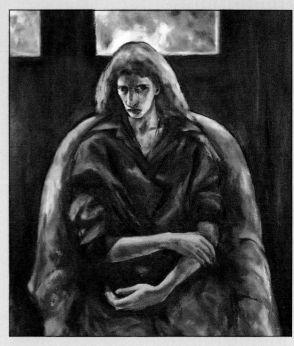

*These two pictures both make good use of symmetry and atmosphere. In the study of the figure in an interior (RIGHT) , the composition is regularly balanced to such an extent that the figure becomes almost incidental to the overall sense of space and mood. Nonetheless, the figure has such a strong presence that, despite its relatively small size, it still tends to dominate the other elements in the picture. In the portrait (ABOVE) the dominant form in the image is the shape of the chair on which the figure is sitting. The arms are well arranged and this both contributes to the overall composition as well as expressing something of the mood of contemplation which the image conveys. Both pictures are painted in oil on canvas. The paint is generally well handled and the colours combined effectively. However, in the portrait, the reflected lights are a little too light. Oil is perhaps the most popular medium and has dominated painting since van Eyck in the fifteenth century. However, it is a medium which requires patience and practice before you can master it. Oil paint consists of pigment mixed with a binder, usually linseed or poppy oil. The oil oxidizes and forms a solid skin in which the pigment is evenly distributed. The main disadvantage of oil paint is that it takes a long time to dry. It is worth making sure that your canvas is well prepared with size and ground before you start painting. It is possible to buy ready prepared canvas, but it is more expensive than preparing your own. Other surfaces such as wood or metal which can be used for oil painting should also be prepared before you start applying the paint.*

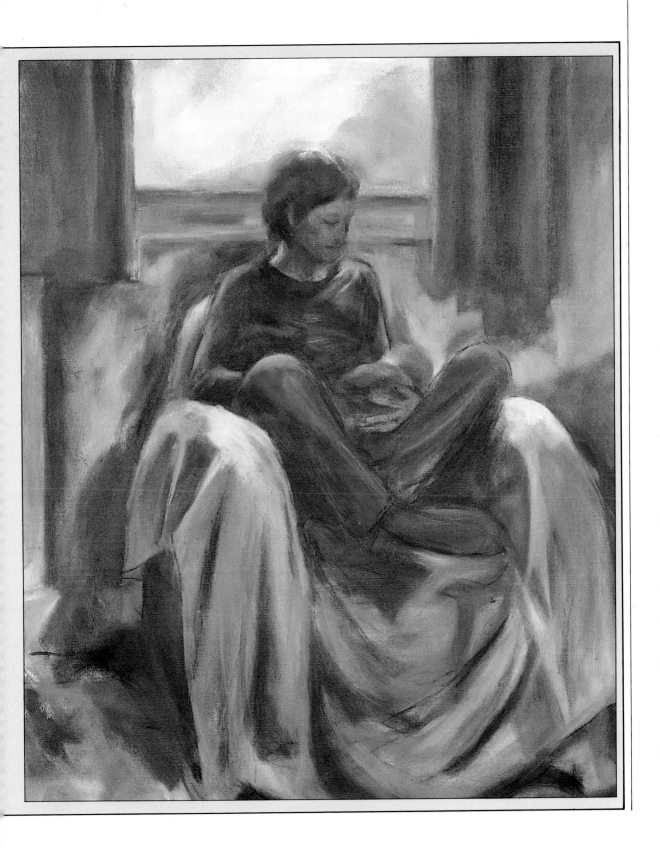

# Simple figure composition

A further progression from painting a figure in an environment is to make a painting which includes as a major element the interaction between three or more human figures. Choose the subject with care, making sure that it carries conviction. It may be a good idea to use an incident from your own life, sporting events with which you are involved, or related to one of your hobbies. You should be aware of the difference between a painting which is simply figurative and one which is narrative. The former is a painting which sets out to record a visual image and to make a statement about relationships of line and colour, to show how light affects form, and so on; this painting is termed representational. A narrative painting, whilst being concerned with all these things, also sets out to tell a story. You will probably be familiar with many narrative paintings. When it was unusual for ordinary people to be able to read and write, they relied mainly upon paintings inside churches for their knowledge of the Bible and history of Christianity, and paintings of this type were often commissioned from artists. These paintings were an important and everyday part of people's lives.

A revival of interest in this sort of painting during the last century produced large numbers of narrative paintings, usually with a religious or moral theme. With the swing away from figurative to abstract painting during this century, there have been relatively few artists working in this way, although there is evidence that the tide may be turning again.

**Preparation** Whatever your subject, you will almost certainly find it an advantage if you make a large number of preparatory sketches. Try out various ideas working on a small scale at first, organizing the separate elements of your composition into a cohesive whole. You should, in any case, carry with you at all times a small sketchbook in which you can make notes of things and people in everyday situations. You may find that your sketchbook had a record of exactly the right figure group for the idea you have in mind and, should you need further information, you can always ask a friend (or friends) to pose in the appropriate position. It is also quite legitimate to work from photographs, whether you take them yourself especially for the exercise or simply collect interesting pictures from magazines and news-

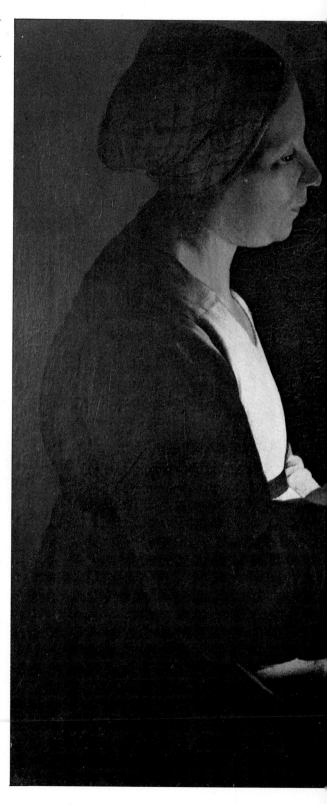

This simple figure composition *Le Nouveau Né (The Newborn Child)* by the French artist Georges de la Tour is a striking example of the combination of warm colours and strong light which concentrate the viewer's attention on the figure of the child. The light radiating out from the centre and the smooth flesh tones are characteristic of de la Tour's work.

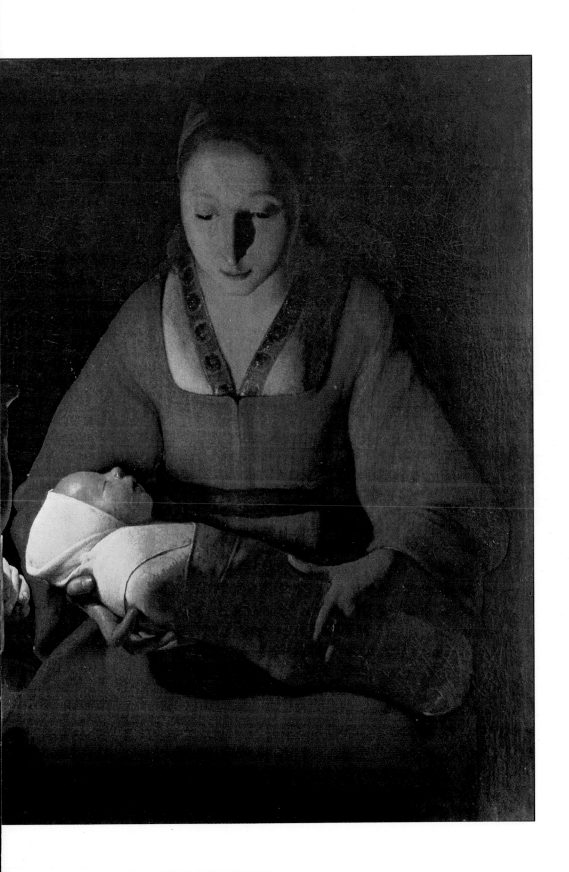

papers. There are, however, certain dangers in this, for instance it is not always easy to understand the internal structuring of a group of figures fully with only two-dimensional reference available; nevertheless, many artists work this way exclusively. Obviously, it is possible to combine the use of photographs and drawings, and, of course, working directly from life.

When deciding on the arrangement for your figure group, choose the eye-level with care. Note the way the entire mood of the picture can be altered by raising or lowering the eye-level. Try viewing a group of people from a high vantage point, by standing on a chair or table, then look at the same scene lying on the floor, and observe how the emphasis changes. Make sure that, in the event of your figures being placed at different depths within the picture, they stand on the same ground plane.

Keep your figures large scale. They should occupy the greater part of the picture plane whilst still allowing enough room to set them into a convincing environment. You may relate a large figure in the foreground to a much smaller one, thus establishing a space between and therefore giving depth to your picture.

Spend some time considering the way your figures will relate to one another within the picture plane. You may wish there to be actual physical contact between them, in which case they will form one large and perhaps complex overall shape. It is also possible that, whilst not actually touching one another, the figures overlap visually when translated into two-dimensional shapes on the canvas. It is important to establish the space between by use of linear and atmospheric perspective.

There is a further way in which the figures will interrelate—by choosing to trap these people within the frame of your picture you imply that there is some

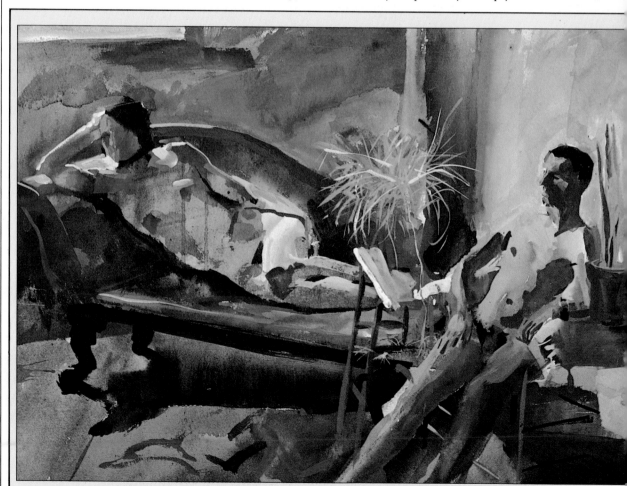

connection, however tenuous, between them. Numerous novels and plays have been written exploring the way in which human beings become involved with one another for perhaps only a fleeting moment of time—trapped in a lift, taken prisoner, and many similar themes spring to mind. In a way, you are imprisoning your figures for all time inside your picture, and the viewer will look to see how they relate to one another. You may allow this interaction to remain implicit, or you may choose to emphasize it by a gesture or expression. Much will depend upon your subject matter.

The exercises so far have dealt with forms held within a confined space. For this painting you may, if you wish, dispense with this limitation and attempt a much larger setting. Be sure to make use of good reference as, without it, your painting may lack conviction. Even quite a small space viewed over

someone's shoulder might, because of perspective, contain vast vistas of towns and cities, hills and valleys, stretching into infinity.

In drawing a simple figure composition, it is of great importance to have a sound grasp of the mechanics and structure of the human anatomy. Your preparatory drawings for this painting should, of course, have regard to accuracy, although not at the expense of making your group appear static. Having made your working drawings, there is no reason why you should not then use distortion, elongating or compressing shapes, in order to make the picture work better. Use whatever reference you wish in whatever way you feel will make the best arrangement of shapes and forms within the picture plane. If you do distort the shapes in your painting, then be sure that the decision to do so has been a positive one and that the reasons for it are good.

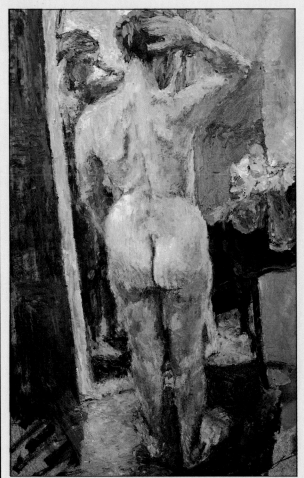

*This simple figure composition was painted in gouache. Gouache is an opaque type of watercolour paint. It has several advantages over transparent watercolour paint, particularly for the beginner. Dark tones can be laid first and lights added afterwards. Although gouache lacks the luminosity of pure watercolour, it is a good medium for subjects which need extensive elaboration. Both paper and board are good surfaces for gouache work. In the initial stages, this composition was going to include three figures, but the artist decided to delete one so that interest could focus on the relationships between the remaining two figures. It is important to note that the strong horizontal line of the chaise-longue has been placed at an angle, thus avoiding some of the problems which would have arisen had it been positioned horizontally. The plants, positioned on the right and between the two figures contribute well to the overall atmosphere of the picture. When deciding on the composition for your own pictures, bear in mind the relationship you wish to establish between the figures. In this picture the figures are looking in the same general direction, but there appears to be little contact between them. This image is interesting because of the cool atmosphere it establishes which is continued in the cool range of colours the artist has used.*

*Positioning the figure is one of the most important considerations when painting a figure in an interior. In a simple portrait, the viewer's interest can focus on the figure alone, but when an interior is being shown too, the artist has to consider the relationship between figure and setting, and the balance which should be established between these elements. For instance, do you want the figure to be the most striking part of the composition? Should the figure blend in with the setting or be overwhelmed by it? You should also consider the colour relationships between the figure (clothed or nude) and the surroundings. A figure dressed in dark colours will tend to blend in with a dark background, while clearly differentiated colours will create a stronger contrast between the figure and background. What range of colours do you want to use? In this picture, the figure is placed in the centre of the picture. Her back is towards the viewer. In this way, the figure dominates the picture. However, the pose is slightly awkward and looks a little contrived. The shadows on the flesh pick up some of the yellows and greens in the background. The large areas of warm colour contrasting with the cooler colours in the background, such as the green of the vase and wall. A mirror is a useful device to extend the range of options open to you. Here the model's silhouette can be seen as a reflection. The colours are well played off against one another to create the overall effect of light in the picture.*

# Complex figure composition

This project is the most ambitious so far attempted, and you should expect to spend a good deal of time in preparing for it, before you even begin to paint. It will probably be as well if you work on a larger size of support than you have used previously, as the complexity of this painting will demand a fair amount of room for manoeuvre. Your complex figure composition should use more than 15 human figures. Choose a subject that will allow you to show your figures in a natural setting, such as you would expect to find in a street market, for instance, or at a racecourse. You may find it more interesting to concentrate on a particular aspect of the scene, such as the way emotions are portrayed on the face, in which case you might produce a painting of a crowd at a football match or other similar gathering where this is likely to feature. You could make a complex figure composition showing current fashions in dress, hair-styles, make-up and so on, thus treating the painting as a piece of social documentation.

**Preparation** First of all you should gather as much reference as you can by making drawings and notes and putting yourself as often as possible into the situation which you intend to make your subject matter. A painting will always carry more conviction if it is about something with which you are familiar. Absorb as much of the atmosphere as you are able, and this will inform your painting as much in one way as drawings and photographs will in another.

Obviously, with a composition as complex as this, you will have to spend a long time juggling around with the various elements which you intend to include. You must be completely satisfied with the way that you have planned the composition before you begin to paint. Whilst you do not set out to copy any previous artist's work, you will almost certainly find it helpful to examine the structure of other paintings which include a large number of interrelated elements. There are certain conventions of composition which have been loosely adhered to over the years, and it is worth finding out more about them.

You should be familiar with the notion of the 'Golden Mean' or 'Golden Section'. This is an historically important convention for dividing a line or area in mathematical proportions which were generally considered 'ideal'. In a rectangle drawn according to the Golden Section, the sides would be in proportion 5:8. Even without setting out deliberately to make use of this means of arranging shapes within the picture plane, many artists have divided space in this way.

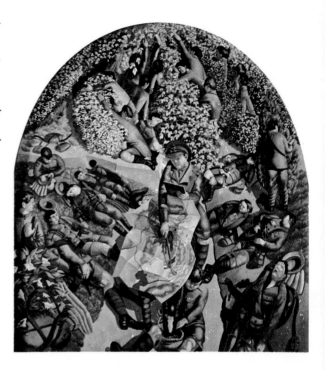

At different times in the history of painting, there have been traditions of composition which were popular. Renaissance artists tended to favour a symmetrical arrangement within the canvas, often building up the figures and other components to form a triangle with the base set firmly parallel to, though not level with, the lower edge of the picture. This gave a very stable composition within which it was then possible to introduce movement and rhythm without causing an imbalance. It is interesting to experiment with a composition based upon an inverted triangle and to observe how this affects the balance of the picture. Later painters seemed to prefer to make their compositions asymmetrical, and, in sixteenth and seventeenth century Mannerist paintings, there are often sweeping diagonals and flamboyant circular movements. Other favourite conventions of composition are the U-shape, which tends to lend a heavy and rather ponderous mood to a picture, and the sort of composition which leads the eye, by means of converging lines, in towards the focal point of the painting. Spend some time experimenting with small drawings, arranging and rearranging your figure groups until you think that you have arrived at the best composition for your subject. If you want to make a statement of a violent or explosive nature, then obviously you will not use a compositional device which is by nature static, and vice-versa.

When planning any large painting, one of the

The arrangement of complex figure compositions requires much forethought and preparation. Delacroix's monumental study *Liberty (RIGHT)* shows the figure of Liberty leading the people on the ruins of the barricades. The surrounding figures emphasize the central figure of Liberty. This emphasis is enhanced by the muted tones of the main areas of the painting which contrast with the paleness of Liberty's dress and the strong red of the flag. Allegorical, political or social comment has often been a concern of artists painting complex figure compositions. The twentieth century British artist Stanley Spencer painted several series of complex compositions which show the individuality of his talent. Compare the arrangement and execution of the figures in *Mapreading (LEFT)* which comes from the Sandham Memorial Chapel, with Delacroix's much earlier composition. Compare also the two artists' very different figure painting techniques. While Delacroix depicts his subject in a serious way, Spencer's view is rather more satirical. Brueghel's *Massacre of the Innocents (BELOW)* shows a winter scene from a more distant viewpoint than either Delacroix or Spencer. The viewer's eye is led to the central group of figures along the lines of the path.

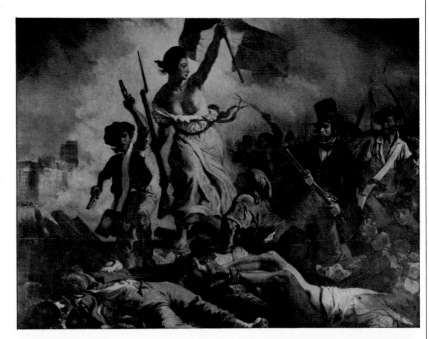

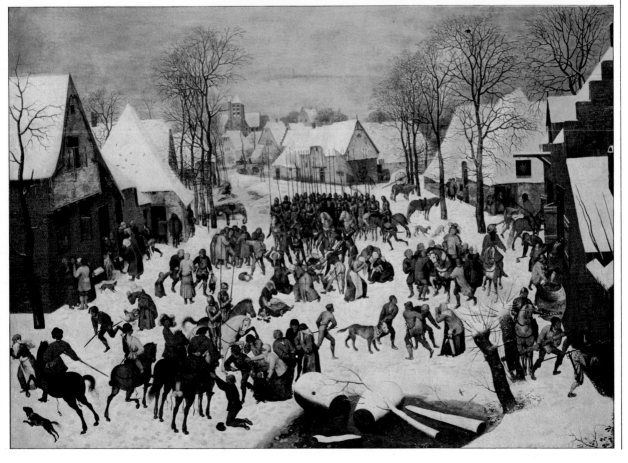

problems which you must solve is that of the visual distortions which occur at the outer edges if you have been following the rules of perspective. Mathematically calculating the linear perspective of any given scene only works if there is a fixed viewpoint. As soon as the area seen becomes too great to take in at one glance, it is natural to swing the eye in order to see what is to the right and left. When planning this out on the picture plane, however, it becomes more

difficult and the best thing to do is to avoid including any element which will draw attention to this at the outer edges of your picture. Painters such as the Dutch artist Jan Vermeer (1632–1675), who were well aware of this problem, tended to use large areas of tone and to avoid linear extremes in order to obscure any obvious distortion.

Because this picture will take much longer to complete than any of the previous ones, you must be

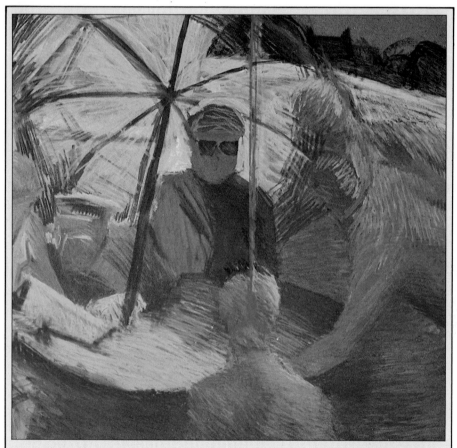

*Because the figures which form the focal point of this composition are drawn right to the edge of the canvas, the general horizontal emphasis of the design tends to lead the eye out of the picture plane. This tendency has been counteracted in this case by the strong diagonal from*

*The initial shapes in this figure composition were laid down in paint and the forms developed with pastel drawing. The decision to limit the range of colour narrows the problems in one sphere, thus allowing the artist to concentrate on the texture and form of the drawing. The pastels are handled vigorously in broad strokes of strong colour, defining the linear structure and following the rhythm of the planes and masses. The depth of the composition has been emphasized by contrasting dark shadows with vivid*

*highlights and warm colours with cool.*
*Although the varied directions of the pastel strokes add considerably to the vitality of the picture surface, in some areas they are not fully cohesive and have a slightly jarring quality. This is particularly noticeable in the righthand side of the painting, where the forms seem less well observed and not so confidently described. The spatial definition is lost, not in itself necessarily a bad thing, but in this case the result is out of keeping with the style applied*

*to the other figures. The colour is interesting, since it does not follow a conventional distribution of light and dark contrast. The broad wedge of warm colour on the left enlivens the larger areas of light yellow and mid-toned blue. The composition as a whole is not fully resolved, but the artist has attempted to structure the painting within specific guidelines while maintaining the freedom to interpret the forms with inventiveness and energy.*

sure to paint with consistency. Decide what range of colours you intend to use for your palette and stick to them throughout. It is surprising how the addition of only one new colour can alter the entire mood of a painting. In any case, using a fairly limited palette will help you to create a unity and harmony, where the sheer number of elements contained in the picture will tend to cause a visual dissonance.

Some consideration of practical matters is also necessary before you undertake a painting of this scale. You must make sure that you have set your easel up in a position where you are able to step back and examine the picture from a distance as often as you need to. It should also be possible to leave it in position for however long it will take you to complete the painting. If this is impracticable, then you should be able to store your painting and equipment in an easily accessible place.

*right to left formed by the line of swimmers, and by investing the whole surface with textural detail and lively movement which draws attention back into the rectangle. The artist has obviously considered the problems of translating the surface and movement of water into*

*painted equivalents and has studied the work of other artists dealing with this subject. Several solutions have been combined to produce the overall effect — clear, bright colour with touches of white, a loose painterly style allowing the brushmarks to develop the surface*

*texture and graphic linear marks to define shapes formed by reflected light on the water. The broken colour over the figures describes both the activity of the swimmers and the optical distortions caused by water over solid forms. The blue costume of the*

*central swimmer provides tonal contrast without departing from the overall harmony. Colour balance is given by the strong red shape placed right at the edge of the canvas, echoed in the fragment of a figure at bottom left.*

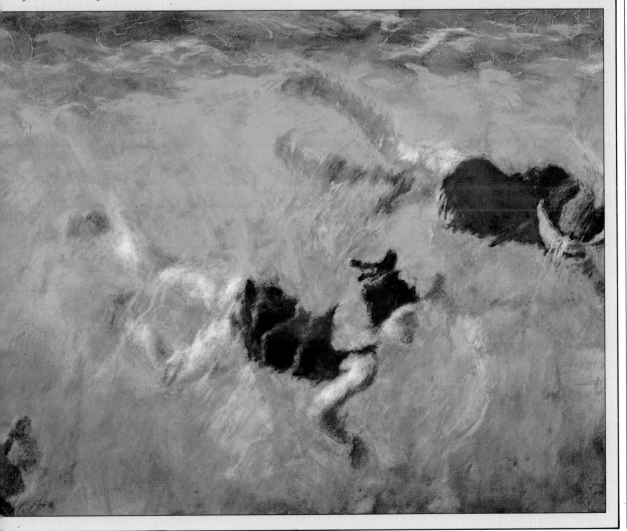

# LANDSCAPE PAINTING

The distinction between figures in a landscape and a landscape with figures is difficult to define. Only when the human content ceases to be the most important element in the picture can it really be referred to as landscape painting. The painting of landscape for its own sake is a comparatively recent development in the history of art and was more or less unknown before the late eighteenth century. This is not to suggest, however, that there were no landscape painters before this time, since this is obviously not the case; rather, a change in emphasis and approach took place. Artists have always made use of their environment as a setting for, but incidental to, their pictures, and many have been excellent landscape painters. Before the Renaissance, the rendering of landscape tended to be rather flat, especially as the rules of linear and atmospheric perspective had not yet been fully evolved. By the late fifteenth and early sixteenth centuries, artists were painting the countryside in a much more convincing manner, although still very much as a background to the real subject of painting. *The Virgin of the Rocks* by Leonardo da Vinci (1452–1519) is an excellent example of this treatment. The Venetian Renaissance artist Giorgione (1475–1510) was one of the first to give landscape a more important role, showing his figures surrounded by lush greenery, trees, hills and valleys. In his time, the British artist John Constable (1776–1837) was revolutionary because he chose not only to treat landscape as a subject apart, but because he worked directly from life and concerned himself with the effects of the continuously changing light and weather conditions. That people found his colours too bright and his free brushstrokes unacceptable seems unbelievable today, but he was a genuine innovator who anticipated what the Impressionist painters would be doing half a century later.

The practical considerations of landscape painting make it imperative that you plan carefully beforehand. Unless you have a convenient window from which to paint in comfort, it will be necessary to carry with you all the equipment that you expect you will need. A balance needs to be struck between trying to take more than you can conveniently carry and leaving behind vital materials. Even if you decide to work from sketches, you will still need to take enough with you to make full colour notes. At any rate, a few field trips will soon make it obvious what pieces of equipment are dispensable and which absolutely necessary for your particular method of working.

The next problem, assuming that you have no splendid views from your window, will be selecting a suitable location. Unless you have a car, finding the

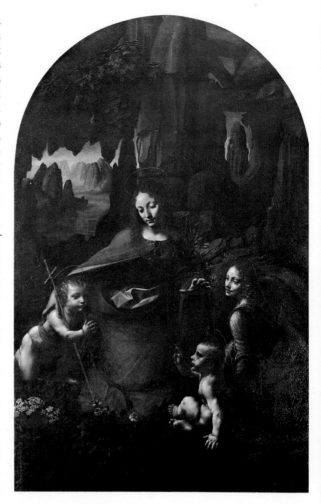

*The Virgin of the Rocks* by Leonardo da Vinci *(ABOVE)* shows a group of figures in an almost surrealistic rocky landscape. Leonardo was extremely interested in nature and did many fine botanical, anatomical and geological drawings. The muted tones and subtle flesh tones of the Leonardo contrasts sharply with the bright colours of *Vision, After the Sermon* by Paul Gauguin *(ABOVE RIGHT)*. It combines strong colours – red, white and yellow – with distinctive curves, producing a striking composition. The visionary quality of the works of Samuel Palmer show a third, very different approach to landscape painting with religious overtones. *Shepherds under a Full Moon (RIGHT)* is one of Palmer's many explorations of the effect of moonlight on the landscape. Landscape painting – or even painting figures in a landscape –

requires careful preparation. You will probably find it a good idea to do several preliminary sketches to help you work out how to arrange the composition on your surface. What balance do you wish to have between sky and land? Where do you wish the eye-level to go? Try looking at the landscape through a hole cut to the shape of your surface in a piece of card. This will help you to see how the area of the painting will appear on a canvas. Do not feel that you have to paint a large expanse of landscape. A close view of a small area can be of great potential to the artist. Above all, select a subject which interests you and treat it in the way you feel is most appropriate.

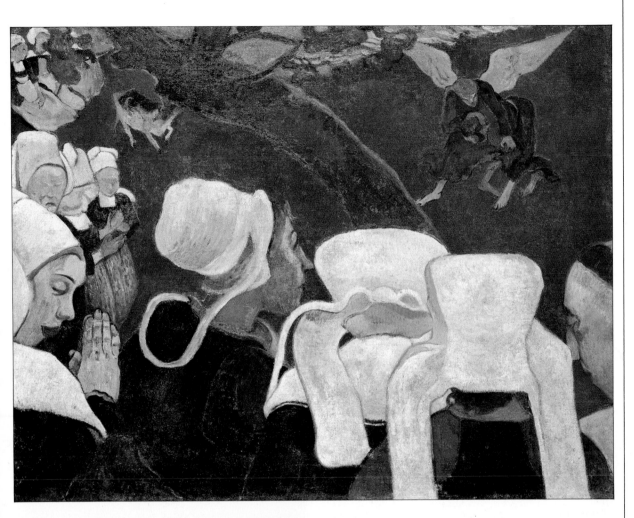

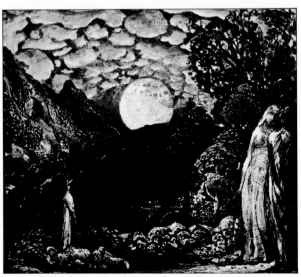

area you wish to paint may require some expenditure of energy on your part, but getting to know your environment can be very worthwhile. Depending on where you live, it may be that you have to walk some distance or make use of buses or trains. It is worth taking time and trouble to find a view which moves and interests you; painting out of doors can be one of the most pleasurable of activities. Some people do not mind being observed at work, whilst others may prefer to find a secluded spot where they are unlikely to be disturbed. This is obviously a matter of individual preference.

Once you have decided upon your location, you must begin to consider how you will compose your landscape within the picture frame. Depending upon how high or low your eye-level is, you will have either a large area of sky or a greater expanse of land. It is generally better for the composition to divide your picture into two equal parts. You may find it useful to look at your view through a hole in a piece of card. This is an excellent device and widely used by artists to assist with the construction of their paintings. Cut a hole in a piece of thick paper or card. It need be no larger than a few inches across but should be in the same proportions as your canvas or board. Leave a generous border around the hole. This will allow you to view parts of the landscape in isolation so you can judge more easily whether they meet with your requirements. It is important to give some indication of the scale at which you are working. Imagine that the border of your painting is the outside edge of a box into which you are looking. Establishing the depth of your box will depend upon your having a clear idea of what is near, what is in the middle distance, and what is far away.

A full understanding of the rules of perspective will be particularly helpful here. Remember that it is not only by reduction in size that distant objects can be made to lie behind the picture plane. A reduction in tonal contrasts will also aid the illusion of depth as will the use of cooler colours than you have used for the foreground areas.

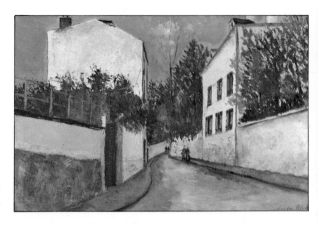

Strong architectural forms are a feature of the work of both the British artist J.S. Cotman and the French painter Maurice Utrillo. Cotman's *Viaduct (BELOW LEFT)* shows a strong sense of design, especially in the symmetry of the partial reflection of the bridge in the water. The large areas of flat colour convey the impression of strong sunlight. Utrillo's *Parisian* *Street (ABOVE)* is a strong, relatively simple composition. The lines of the centrally positioned street lead the viewer's eye into the picture. This is a good example of the application of the principles of perspective and vanishing points.

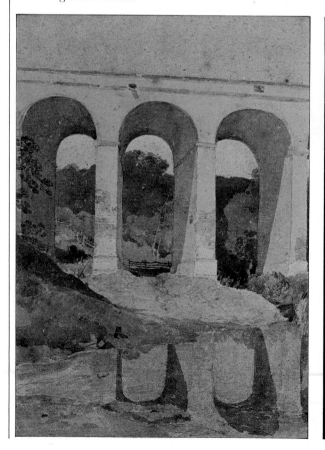

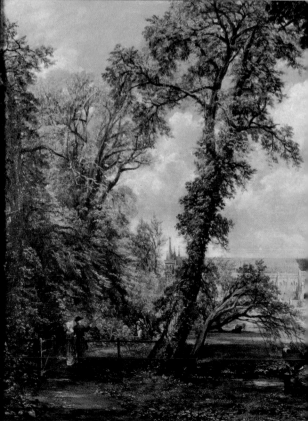

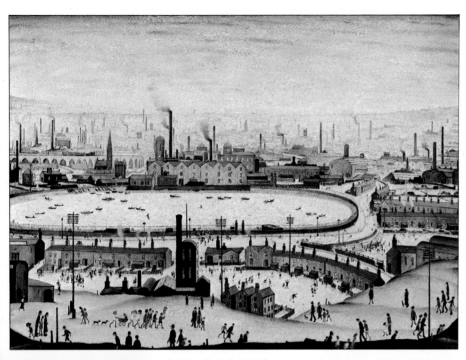

*The Pond* by L.S. Lowry *(LEFT)* is typical of his style. Small figures are seen scurrying about a bleak winter landscape. There is no obvious focus in the image, the viewer's eye being led in many different directions by the figures and the widely spaced buildings. Despite the warm colours of the brick, the overall impression is pale and cold. It is nonetheless worth looking in some detail at individual elements in the composition and working out how the many parts have been put together. The eighteenth century Italian artist Canaletto painted many scenes of both Venice and London. In comparison with the Lowry, this London scene *(BELOW)* shows clearly how an urban landscape has changed since the Industrial Revolution. Most of the buildings are low and the sky line is dominated by St Paul's Cathedral and the many church spires.

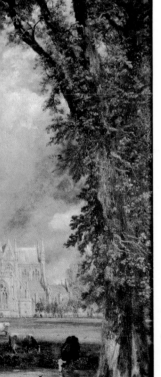

*Salisbury Cathedral* by John Constable *(LEFT)* is a good example of the use of a framing device around the main subject. The dark trees and foliage frame the brightly lit cathedral, helping to add depth to the composition.

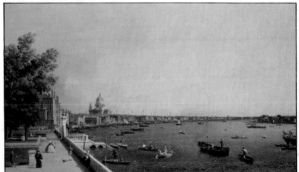

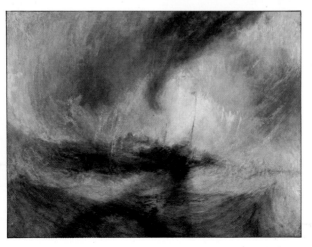

Turner has frequently been considered one of the main precursors of Impressionism. Painted in 1842, *Snowstorm (LEFT)* is an atmospheric depiction of a snowstorm at sea. The surface with its effect of broken colours was created by painting different layers of colour over one another and then dragging them into one another. Although the picture gives an almost abstract impression, the main lines of the composition can be followed – the swirls of the wind-tossed water and snow around the central ship.

# Figures in a landscape

Paint a picture of a group of two or more figures in a landscape setting. You may, if you wish, make separate studies of the figure group and then place it within the landscape. However, you will probably find it much easier to work directly from life. For this reason, it would be very useful if you could work with a number of other people, using one another as models. There are plenty of examples to be found where artists have used friends in their paintings.

**Preparation** The speed at which you work will, to a certain extent, dictate the sort of figure group that you use, but it will probably be a good idea to keep the poses fairly casual. The aim is to produce a piece of work within which there is harmony between the figures and their setting. This will partly depend upon the proportion of the canvas which your figures occupy and whether or not you place them in the foreground. A good way to establish depth is to position one group of figures close to the viewer, so that they appear to be actually on the picture plane, and then include another group in the middle distance. This is a favourite compositional device, as it leads the eye naturally into the painting.

There will probably be aspects of the view before you, which you will feel are unnecessary as part of your picture. You will probably know instinctively how to select from what you can see in order to achieve the right balance within your picture. Never forget you are the one who decides what to include, so remember you can distort wherever you feel that this would improve your composition.

You will notice, even if you are working on a clear blue summer's day, how very quickly the light changes. This happens particularly if there are clouds. You will have to decide how you intend to deal with this problem, which affects the figures especially. It may be that you can work quickly enough for the changing quality of the light not to matter. If you have time, there is no reason why you should not spend several days on the painting. This would probably enable you to deal with your figure content all within the same day. As long as you are aware that the problem exists, you may solve it in the way that best suits you.

Your finished painting should be one which has something to say about the people and something to say about the landscape. Neither should assume a greater importance than the other. To see whether you have achieved this, ask yourself what the painting would look like if you abstracted either aspect. If they are interdependent, then you will probably have been successful.

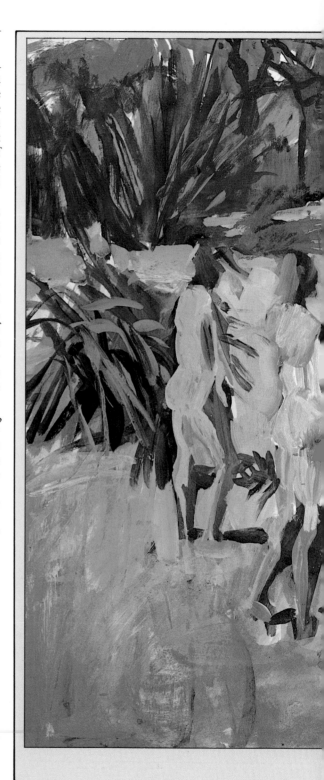

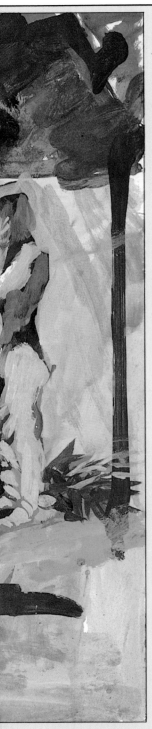

The artist's principal interest here is the intense quality of strong sunlight playing over the solid, rounded forms of the figures and the textural detail in the foliage. In order to record the impressions quickly and boldly, acrylic paints have been used to block in areas of vivid colour. The figures are defined in terms of broad masses of light and shade against similar treatment of the surrounding garden. The circular arrangement of the figure group is placed just off-centre within the rectangle to avoid a completely symmetrical division of the plane. This is anchored by the patch of green foliage behind the figure at left, which also provides a clear colour contrast. The heads of the figures rise almost level with the horizontal division near the top of the canvas, marked by a line of dark trees and bushes. A broader feeling of space might be created by bringing the central figure forward, or placing the figures so that they break the division between background and middle ground.

The painting creates overall a striking impression but on closer inspection seems rather hastily constructed, approximating the forms rather than describing them. The loose brushwork over the figures and in the foliage supplies an area of active interest. In the foreground on the left, however, the flat plane of grass is disrupted by the broken colour and vertical brushmarks, distracting attention from the figures without providing a definite contrast of colour or texture. As a colour study to form part of an investigation of the subject, this painting makes a stimulating record of certain aspects of the scene, but is not finally resolved as an image in its own right.

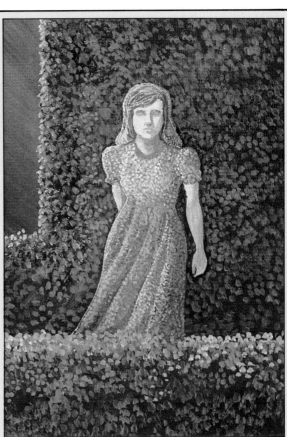

The predominance of one particular colour sets the mood of a painting, especially in figurative work. The blue-green hues and ghostly white highlights in this image contribute to an atmosphere of isolation and uneasiness. The blue tones are ambiguous, sometimes seeming cold and hostile, but occasionally broken by hints of warmer hues. The landscape is deliberately made anonymous, consisting only of two flat planes of dense foliage. The break in the hedge behind the figure reveals nothing further of the environment or its inhabitants. The attitude of the girl leaves uncertainty as to whether she is running away from something unseen or hesitating in front of the viewer. The composition is given unity by the overall patterning, seen in detail across the hedges and echoed more loosely in the dress. This is interrupted by and contrasted with the stark forms of the figure painted in light tones. The style of the painting is reminiscent of some Surrealist works, both in design and execution. Figures are portrayed in a representational but not wholly realistic manner. Since attention is centrally focused on the figure, it should be a strong, well defined image. Here the shapes of arms and head seem to depend upon the light tone to draw attention, and the forms are not fully convincing. The general distribution of tone follows a logical pattern, but the head does not sit squarely on the neck and the contour of arm and hand does not adequately describe the actual position of the limb.

# Landscape painting

When painting a landscape with figures, the focal point or area of interest within the picture is predetermined. Before you embark upon a painting which does not include figures, you must give careful consideration to the composition and think about what your focal point will be. Deciding where you wish to make the painting and the viewpoint which you intend to adopt should be thoroughly thought out. When looking for a suitable viewpoint, think about the way in which you would divide the canvas. What are the main compositional lines? Besides lines of hills, valleys and trees, what are the outstanding features of the landscape in front of you? If there is a piece of architecture of note—a castle or church, for instance—then this will be the obvious point around which to organize your composition.

**Preparation** A day spent in making colour notes can be of great assistance before you begin your painting. It will help you to get to know the landscape if you prepare several small sketches, spending no longer than one hour on each. Try adopting a stance from which you have a good view in all directions and make four separate drawings, turning through 90° for each. Compare these sketches and observe not only the differences but also the similarities between them. Once you have completed these, try doing another drawing of each of the views, paying particular attention to the way in which the light has changed since you completed the first drawing some hours earlier. Observe the way in which this affects the entire aspect before you, often changing the emphasis from one part of the view to another. Notice in particular how the changing light causes the colour and therefore the mood and atmosphere of the scene before you to alter.

Once you have spent a day or so in this way, you may feel that you are ready to begin work on the actual painting. Using the preparatory sketches, make your final decision about the viewpoint you intend to adopt. Your finished painting should have regard to harmony of colour and tone in the abstract sense, while at the same time leading the eye naturally into the distance implied by use of linear and atmospheric perspective.

How long you spend in the completion of this painting will depend very much upon what sort of image you feel you are setting out to make. If you intend to produce a realistic record of the view which you have chosen, even allowing for your own selectivity about and consequent rejection of certain elements in the view, you must expect to take several days over

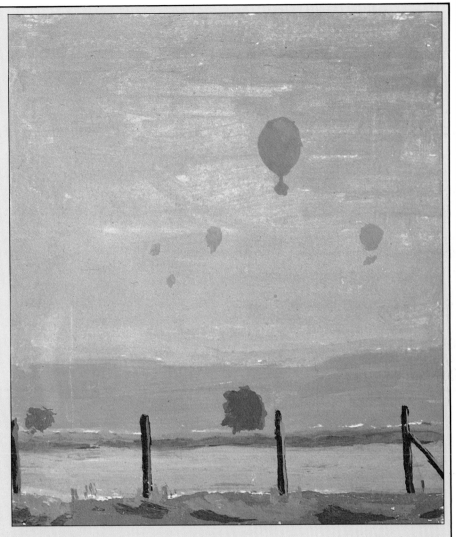

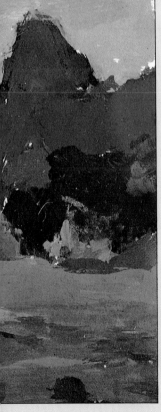

These three paintings by the same artist show three different approaches to very similar subjects. They were all painted in a very small format on board and mounted in large wooden frames so that the images were behind glass and surrounded by space which helped to focus attention on the image. All three show the artist's basic interest in general form and atmosphere rather than the detail of the scenes. They also demonstrate the use of blue tones to create an impression of distance. Interest in the first image (ABOVE LEFT) is created by the balance between the light strip of grass and the line of the sky. Two strong tree forms in contrasting colours dominate the middle distance. Look out for such features before you start work on your picture and adjust the image according to what seems best for your purposes. In the second (LEFT), the composition is based on the three dominant tree forms. Indeed, the artist has created an almost abstract patterning by not differentiating the space of the sky behind the trees. In the third (ABOVE), the general blue tonal range is dominant, and the artist makes good use of the forms of the balloons floating in the sky. Unlike the other two works where the horizon line is high and close, the horizon line in the balloon picture is very low and distant. Look carefully to see how this affects the balance of the painting. The low horizon line gives much greater emphasis to the sky.

it. In any case, if you are using oil paints in a fairly traditional manner, then you will need to allow time for each layer of paint to dry before you apply the next one. If, however, you intend to make a record of the more immediate aspects of the landscape—such as the effects of wind and weather—you will probably need to spend less time over the actual painting process, although your time for planning and preparation may be longer. Make sure that your intentions are clearly thought out before you begin to work.

To a certain extent, the size of your painting will be decided by what equipment and materials you are able to take with you. There is no reason, of course,

why you should not make extensive notes from life and take them back home with you where you may use them to produce your finished painting. The important British art historian Kenneth Clarke pointed out perceptively in his book *Landscape into Art* (1949) 'Throughout history, landscapes of perception have been small. Large landscapes, with all the artifice of construction, have been studio made.' If you decide to work at home then make sure that you have sufficient reference to inform your memory. Besides drawings and photographs, you should have copious colour notes.

Whichever way you work, try to make a painting of

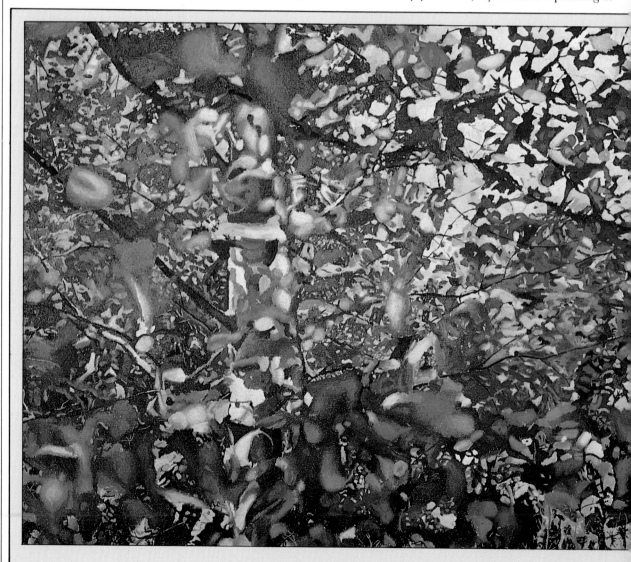

reasonable size, say not less than 36 inches by 24 inches (90 cm by 60 cm). This will allow you enough space to develop a composition which can clearly establish the travel between the foreground and distance. One final point—because vast tracts of the countryside are either cultivated or used as grazing land, it is quite unusual to find anywhere which completely lacks evidence of humanity. This can be used to your own advantage, because including flocks of sheep or fields of cattle, for instance, can give scale and add a point of interest to your painting, even when they are only seen as distant objects punctuating the landscape.

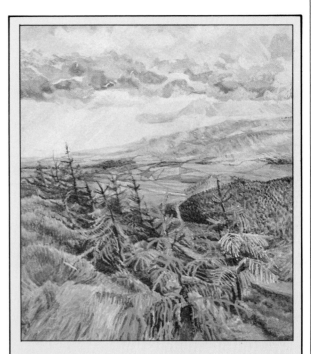

*The raggedness and huge scale of landscape are suggested by this painting. Although the landscape itself is practically contained within half the canvas space, the interwoven forms and graded colour imply distance and the undulation in the land. This is enhanced by the contrast of colour between land and sky.*

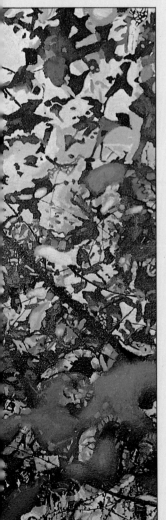

*Strong tonal contrasts within a harmonious colour range have been used here to illustrate the dappled effect of light passing through trees and foliage. The composition is given structure by the linear network of tree trunks and branches. This painting is a successful example of how a subject can be treated in an almost abstract manner without sacrificing clear references to actual objects. Landscape is a particularly suitable subject for this type of semi-abstraction, since the colours and organic shapes suggest a patterning approach. Oil paint is exploited here in thin, bright glazes, strong dark colours with surface sheen and patches of opaque light tones. The image successfully evokes the warm, pleasant atmosphere of a sunny landscape and the freshness of nature at close hand. It almost represents a symbolic expression of the spirit of landscape, but herein lies also the danger of this type of work. It may be tempting to develop a formula of representation which is sufficiently seductive to distract the artist from really looking closely at reality wherever it is encountered. In order for an artist to remain stimulated by the activity of painting, and in turn to stimulate the viewer, it is necessary to keep looking afresh at even the most familiar and often seen surroundings.*

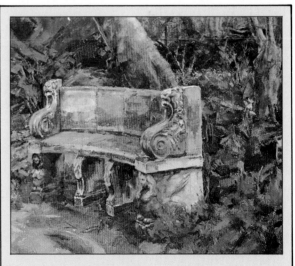

*The artist has shown considerable expertise here in handling the paint, exploiting the texture of brushmarks and paint over canvas weave to evoke the forms without laboriously drawn details. This type of subject can be tremendously appealing as it tends to express an air of mystery. It may be necessary to exercise careful self-discipline to avoid letting the subject do all the work for you. A picturesque painting may easily become sentimentalized.*

# Townscape

The landscapes discussed so far have only included natural landscapes of hills, trees, river valleys and so on. Loosely speaking, the category of landscape painting also includes townscapes and water-scapes, although in certain respects these demand a different approach.

**Preparation** For this, you should execute a painting, the major part of which is taken up by streets and buildings. The type of architecture you include at least partially depends upon what is conveniently available in the locality in which you live. Try to choose an area which is fairly urban so that the entire picture is filled with buildings. It is almost inevitable that you will also include in your painting a number of figures since it is quite unusual for a built-up area to be totally deserted. You may, of course, wish to create a strange and surreal atmosphere by deliberately excluding any signs of life from your picture.

If you are lucky enough to live in an area of outstanding architectural beauty, your approach to this exercise may be entirely academic. In any case, all students of the visual arts should have an interest in the history of architecture, and making numerous studies, both paintings and drawings, will help you increase your knowledge and awareness of your environment. It certainly is not necessary to confine yourself to painting only those buildings which you consider to be of architectural merit. Many artists have set out to do quite the opposite, wanting instead to depict life as it really is. These representations of everyday scenes and the life of ordinary people are known as genre paintings and have been popular since the sixteenth century. There are many modern genre painters who often concentrate upon the less obviously picturesque aspects of life although even the most industrial of landscapes is not without a certain beauty. Your own response to your surroundings is important and will certainly be apparent in the painting you make.

Whether you intend your painting to be a straightforward visual record or to make some form of social comment, you will have certain structural problems to deal with. In a picture of this sort, it is of primary importance that you are fully conversant with the workings of perspective. It is likely that you will have not one but several vanishing points and you will probably have to do a careful drawing of your chosen scene before you start painting. You should be particularly aware of the eye-level as it will be necessary to locate your various vanishing points here. Be prepared to spend time and trouble in getting this stage of your picture right as, if the structure is unsound, it will be

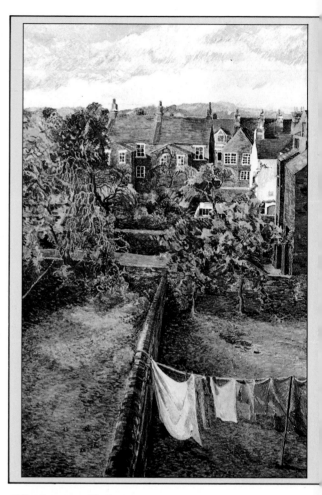

difficult to rectify later.

Besides the buildings themselves, you will find that there are numerous other details to be included, all of which will help to give your picture vitality and interest. There is bound to be a variety of street furniture such as telephone boxes, lamp-posts, pillar boxes and telegraph poles. The buildings themselves will have television aerials, telephone wires; there will be cars, lorries and buses moving in the streets, people on bicycles, cats, dogs, and so on. Have an eye for all these things, as, by making use of them, you will lend conviction to your finished piece of work.

You will notice that the effects of changing light upon buildings are very different from those observed in the open countryside. Because streets are often narrow, there may be bright sunlight on the upper part of the buildings whilst at ground level all is in shadow. You can make use of this sort of contrast to make lively tonal arrangements. Alternatively you might like to tackle the problems of painting the scene at night. The pools of

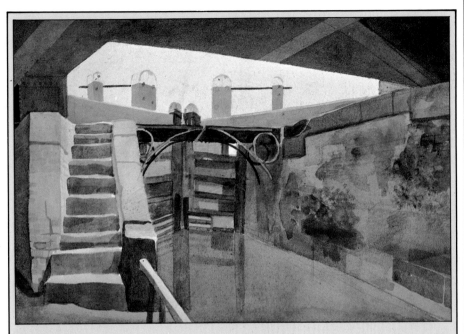

*This painting shows a balanced combination of rigid forms in the walls and houses with irregular shapes and rich texture in the surrounding landscape. The work is executed in tempera which is a medium requiring considerable patience on the part of the artist. Thinly glazed layers of colour are built up slowly to achieve the full intensity of the hue. It has, however, a plastic quality which has been put to use in the textural detail. The paint is also translucent and the finished areas of colour have a brightness which is not found in any other medium. This is apparent here over the whole picture plane. The space within the picture is defined at the drawing stage, rather than by colour recession. The composition has been carefully constructed and there is no area left inactive. It is an everyday subject, the type of scene which rarely inspires comment, but this treatment proves that even seemingly mundane views can provide the basis of a pleasing composition. Note how the artist has used the washing line in the foreground to enliven the design and add touches of complementary colours. The whole work is well balanced in both tone and colour and suggests tranquillity and domestic peace. The unity of the painted surface is preserved by linking blue and red-brown tones throughout the composition in addition to the broad areas of green.*

*The delicate tones of watercolour are particularly suitable for this painting of the stonework and wooden structure of a canal lock. The subject has been carefully observed and translated into the chosen medium. The artist has clearly recognized the charm of the scene and selected the essential features for the composition. The cramped spaces of the canal provide an unusual and interesting*

*arrangement of planes and varied surface texture. The clear white and grey down the lefthand side enhance the warm pink tones of the wall on the right, and both are set off by the green water between them. In order to preserve the delicacy of colour with this medium the paint should be laid in thin washes and not allowed to build up too thickly. The artist here shows considerable economy in this 'layering' technique,*

*which demonstrates how details of tone and shape can be suggested with a few brushstrokes.*

light thrown by street lamps, bright oblongs representing windows and doorways whilst the greater part of the picture is in darkness, can provide exciting visual stimuli, although being much more difficult to deal with convincingly.

---

# Water-scape

---

With the previous exercise your main concern was with structural complexity. It is the lack of structure which will prove to be the main problem here. Make a painting of a view which is largely dominated by water. If you live close to the seaside the obvious choice will be to make this the subject of your painting. However, any large area of water will be adequate for this exercise, as the main aim is to emphasize the change in mood that comes when the tonal values of landscape painting are reversed. It is conventional for landscape paintings to have the lightest tones in the sky. The ground area is almost always darker unless a winter scene with snow is depicted. This creates its own individual atmosphere.

**Preparation** Observe how an expanse of water reflects the sky above, and particularly notice the ways in which the reflection is similar and also different. Compare the colour as well as the tone, and note even the subtlest differences. Unless you include other elements in your painting, the successful representation of depth within the picture plane will depend upon your accurate judgement of tone.

However, there is no reason why you should not make boats or bathers, for instance, an important part of your picture. If you do this, or if you make a painting of a scene where there are trees or buildings close to the water's edge, pay attention to the way in which the repetition of shape by reflection makes an interesting and often abstract pattern. It is the way that shapes are echoed with only slight variations which has made water such an absorbing and fascinating subject to so many artists, past and present.

# STILL-LIFE PAINTING

The history of still-life painting is a fairly short one, stretching back only to the sixteenth century. Before this, groups of objects were painted only as a setting for the main subject matter. It was not until the demise of religious painting, which, in Northern Europe, followed the Reformation, that still-life became a subject in its own right. Many of the still-life paintings of this period were groups of objects chosen to remind the viewer of the transience of time, including such obvious devices as hour-glasses, skulls and books. Some made oblique Biblical references by depicting wine, water and bread as part of the group, or by using flowers or fruit with hidden religious meanings. Often, of course, the main purpose of the still-life painting was to demonstrate the skill and virtuosity of the artist.

Whilst most of the problems that must be dealt with in the painting of still-life are the same as those met with in the painting of figure and landscape, there are certain advantages. Inanimate objects do not need to rest or walk around, and there is little danger of your still-life group becoming shrouded in mist or rain. It is much easier to control the arrangements of tone and colour, and a matter of extreme simplicity to alter anything which does not meet with requirements. The selection of objects for still-life is an entirely subjective exercise, and it is often fascinating to see what other people choose to paint.

The first step is to find a corner where it is possible to enclose your still-life group partially and where it can remain undisturbed for as long as it takes you to paint it. This will allow you to keep your composition simple since the background can be either plain walls or drapes, and it also means that it will be much easier for you to control the lighting of your group. If you wish to work by natural light, you must bear in mind that you will only be able to paint during a fairly limited period of each day, otherwise the constantly changing tonal values will present great problems. The alternative approach is to set up a system of artificial light which, although many people find it less sympathetic than natural light, can be adjusted until exactly the right effect is achieved and may then be switched on for use at any time of the day or night.

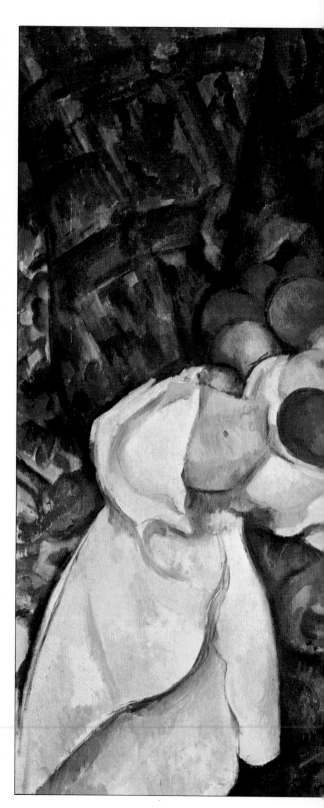

The arrangement of this still-life by the French artist Paul Cézanne shows how colours and textures can be combined to produce a rich and vivid image. The strong colours of the fruit contrast with the comparative paleness of the cloth, and both these elements are thrown into relief by the darker patterned cloth in the background, especially on the left.

The patterned jug takes up the colours of the background. Strong shadows in the foreground on the white cloth emphasize the three-dimensionality of the composition.

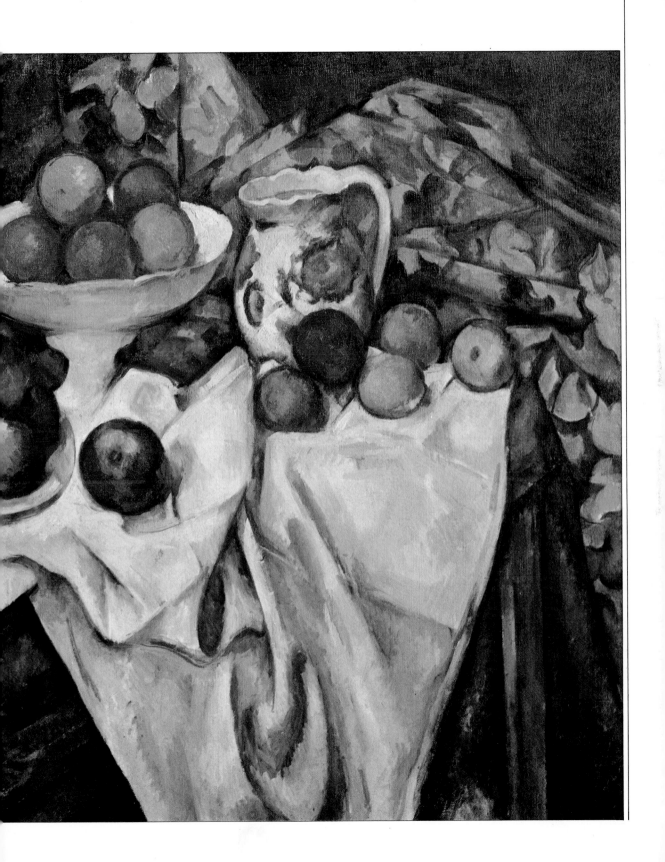

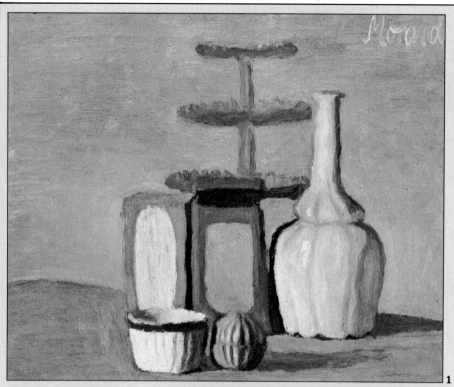

1

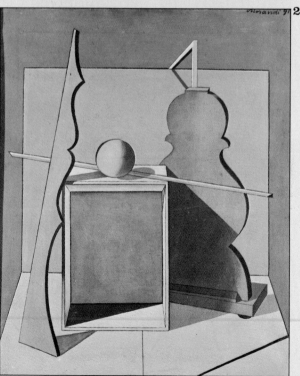

2

3

Some artists concentrate on one aspect of painting throughout their careers. The Italian artist Giorgio Morandi, for instance, painted mainly still-lifes. He also narrowed his focus further, using only a small range of colours and tones. Morandi stood mainly outside the artistic movements of his day, preferring to develop his own individual style and approach. This selection of paintings shows his concentration on strong, simple shapes in uncomplicated settings. One temporary influence was the work and ideas of de Chirico. This can be clearly detected in the juxtaposition and formal qualities of the picture space in Morandi's 1919 *Still-Life (2)*. This contrasts with the later work *(1)* where the artist has treated the strong simple shapes of the vases and other containers in a more realistic way.

The still-life of 1915 *(3)* shows a Cubist influence in the geometric treatment of the shapes in the composition. The long vertical strokes emphasize the vertical axis of the painting.

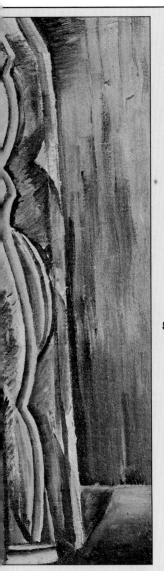

The background in the still-life of 1918 (4) is more prominent than in the other pictures. The geometric shapes of the background are balanced by the strength of the shadows. In all still-life painting, it is important to work out what kind of balance you wish to achieve between the subject and its setting. In this picture, it is clear that the objects are standing on a table, while in many of the others the background is less obvious. If your subject is on a table, how should you position it best – in the centre or, as in this example, to one side? Before starting to paint, examine your subject from several angles and, possibly, do a number of quick studies in pencil or charcoal to work out the pros and cons of various arrangements.

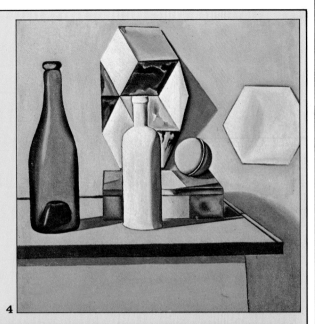

4

5

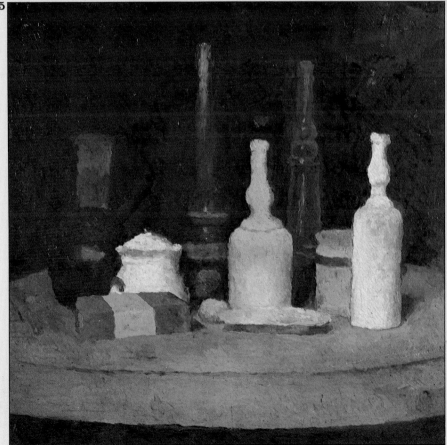

This picture (5) was painted in 1926 and is therefore the latest in this sequence. In order to help you with your own still-life painting, compare these five examples and give some attention to how the artist's approach and style has changed in treating very similar groups of objects. Look at Morandi's use of shadows. Where are they hard and where are they soft? What effect does this have on the overall effect of the image?

# Man-made objects

Collect a small number of man-made objects, which may if you wish be representative of a particular theme. Some obvious choices include sports equipment, gardening tools, kitchenware, and so on. Your choice of objects will inevitably evoke a certain atmosphere which can be further emphasized by the manner in which you paint. You may choose to treat this painting in an autobiographical way, deliberately selecting items for which you have a special affinity or interest.

**Preparation and painting** However you decide which items to include in your group, there are certain other considerations which must be remembered. Think about the scaling of your arrangement and, if you are including many small or highly detailed objects then these can be set off against a large and simple shape. Be aware of the interplay of colour and texture and set up your group in such a way that the basic character of each object is easily recognizable. If, for instance, you intend to include a piece of soft drapery, like a handkerchief or an article of clothing, make sure that you place it in a way which will demonstrate how it hangs in folds and takes on the shape of other objects over which it is laid.

For the purposes of this painting, try to create as convincing an illusion of reality as possible. You will be particularly aware of your brushstrokes and the way in which you lay the paint onto the canvas. In some areas, it will be possible to use the brush in wide, free strokes which can be used to emphasize those parts of the painting where a broad statement of tone and colour will act as a setting for more intricate detail. In other areas, it will be necessary to blend the colours on the surface of the painting carefully, so that the resulting texture is quite smooth.

Before you begin to paint, make sure that you have lit the group to the best advantage. If you are using natural light, try to set up your group in a position where there is only one main light source. Be particularly careful, if you are using artificial light, that you do not set yourself impossible problems. If your arrangement is made up of a number of objects with highly reflective surfaces, make sure that they do not create a too fragmented pattern of sparkling light; this could make it difficult for you to unify the picture. If this is the case, experiment with indirect lighting which will greatly cut down the number of reflections. To achieve this, place a screen between the light source and the still-life group so that it is lit by reflective light from the walls and other objects around.

You should consider these two approaches to still-life

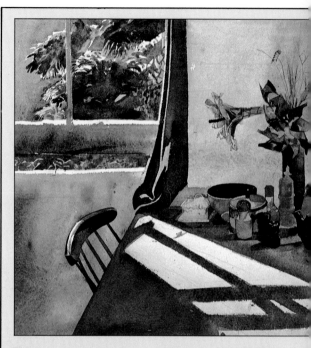

*The artist has here used an ordinary domestic scene as the basis of an unusual composition. The central position of the table, emphasized by the two windows placed one on each side, gives the design a symmetry which can sometimes be visually dull. This is avoided by including several features which draw the eye and enliven the design. The windows give on to different images, one describing broad masses of colour and light, the other having* *an open linear quality. The focal point is the bright pattern of sunlight striking the surface of the table. This makes a diagonal division across the table which underlines the arrangement of various objects in a triangular shape at the top of the table between the windows. The eye is given strong lines to follow as it travels round the painting. A further link is formed by echoing the line of the curtain in the angled shape cutting down the*

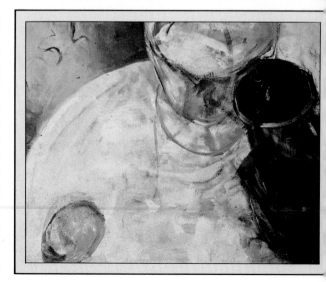

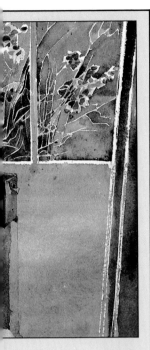

*right side of the picture. Watercolour washes are built up into strong tonal contrasts with plenty of detail added where appropriate.*

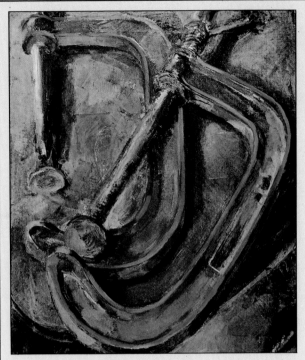

*This simple arrangement of two clamps was assembled to form the basis of an exercise in complementary colours. However, the artist has clearly become fascinated by the combination of linear shapes in the painting and has paid careful attention to the placing of the objects together and within the rectangle of the canvas. Thus strong areas of interest are developed across the picture plane — the interaction of curving outlines against the background and the manipulation of colour related to the spatial organization. The importance of negative space, the space around and between objects, is well illustrated here.*

*In this painting the objects are represented slightly larger than life size, which gives the artist the opportunity to handle the paint with freedom and energy, while preserving the recognizable shapes of the objects. The forms are given a more abstract quality by drawing them out beyond the edge of the picture plane so that the curving shapes are abruptly cut off. Predominant areas of black and white are given touches of colour, occasionally strongly emphasized. Outlines drawn in with a brush are not completely obliterated by subsequent overpainting. These traces keep the paint surface active, but the viewer is nonetheless able to pick out the true lines of the forms.*

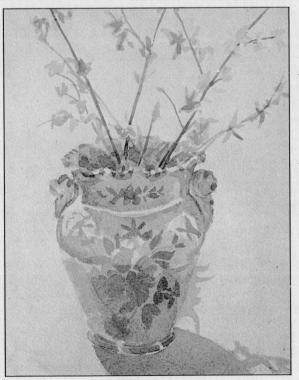

*A simple arrangement of flowers in a vase will provide many hours of study for an artist. An interesting exercise is to treat the same subject in several different media. Prolonged observation of one object sharpens the vision and changing the medium forces you to reinterpret the information each time. This delicate watercolour study contrasts the fragility of the flowers with the round, solid form of the vase. At the same time, the pattern on the vase relates directly to the flower forms, giving the composition unity. Although no background detail is given, the object is anchored in space by the cast shadow. The artist has chosen to run the image off the edge of the paper at top and bottom. If you work directly in watercolour without drawing first, be careful to check the scale of your work and its position on the paper, deciding at the start how much of the image you wish to include. There is also a danger of overdoing the delicacy of the colour, but build up slowly, as it is very difficult to remove colour once it has been laid.*

painting only as starting points. There are endless variations within the outlined themes which you should explore in some depth. Many artists confine themselves almost entirely to still-life painting, but whatever subject matter you find most interesting, studies of this sort can be informative and stimulating.

# Natural forms

Select a number of fruits and/or vegetables and place them either on a table top or within a simple container such as a basket or a fruit bowl. When choosing the objects, remember to give consideration to colour, shape and texture and think about how you would describe the subtle differences. Do not try to crowd too many objects into the space and try out a number of juxtapositions before beginning to paint. Become aware of the way in which the local colour of each object modifies that of its neighbour, and particularly observe these effects where the surface is a highly polished one.

**Preparation and painting** As with any composition, the negative shapes must be considered as carefully as the solid objects. When setting up your still-life group, therefore, it is important that you should look at it from the viewpoint which you intend to adopt.

When you are satisfied that you have arranged your selection of fruit and vegetables in the best possible way, you are ready to start work. Your chosen support should be no greater than 36 inches by 24 inches (90 cm by 60 cm), which means that you will be working at slightly less than life-size.

Remembering to apply the basic rules of picture composition which were discussed in 'Figure painting' (p 152–158), block in the main areas. How you develop the painting will obviously depend upon the medium you are using, but it is a good idea to indicate the tones early as this helps to establish the solid forms. Look carefully at the spaces left between the solid objects; these are the 'negative' shapes which are an important aspect of the composition within the picture frame. It helps at this stage for you to consider the abstract qualities of the painting. Once the main colour areas have been indicated, stop work and look at your picture from a distance. Try turning it upside down and sideways to see whether you have achieved a well balanced composition. This is the time to change anything which is not quite right, so if any of the negative shapes seem too pinched or ill-considered in any other way, then adjust your group accordingly. It is easier to alter things now, but do remember that it is possible to do so at any point during the making of your picture.

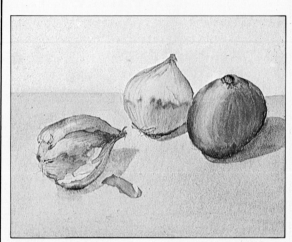

The shapes and spatial relationships in an arrangement of natural forms must be carefully considered. Pay particular attention to outlines and to the shapes of spaces between objects. This arrangement is made with three forms to avoid a blandly symmetrical composition. By placing one onion slightly apart from the others, a path is formed through the picture plane, leading from foreground to background. The irregular broken shape in the skin of the onion on the left emphasizes the smooth shiny colour and unbroken contours of the pair standing together. The illusion of three-dimensional space is rather disrupted by the line of dark colour across the onion in the centre. This falls very close to the line of the tabletop and prevents the form from standing out fully against the background.

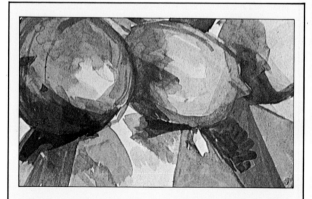

This arrangement of fruit has been translated onto the picture plane in an almost abstract design. This has been achieved by placing the objects in an even line, cut at both sides by the edges of the rectangle. The foreground broken into small coloured shapes defines no clear plane, though this is indicated by brief indication of cast shadows. The strong shadows on the forms break the surface colour and contour, although the distribution of tone suggests the roundness clearly. This painting is interesting because it is bold and colourful, but it seems the artist has sacrificed any real description of the fruits to formal considerations within the painting itself. This illustrates that there are many different approaches to even quite simple subjects, and the artist must be constantly taking decisions and examining the intentions behind each piece of work.

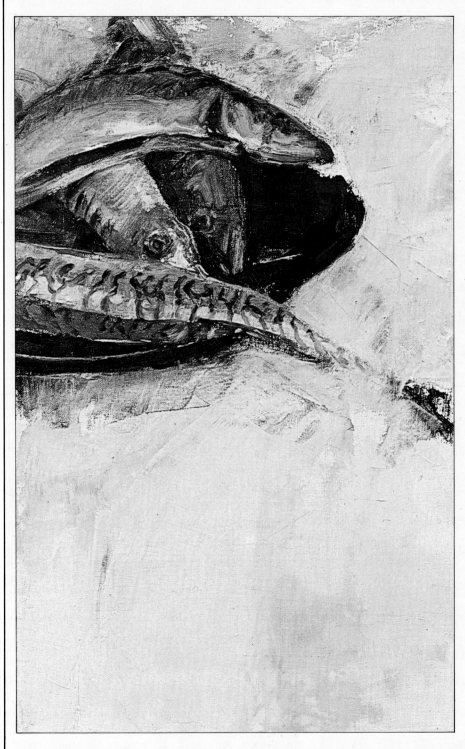

A well defined pattern of stripes on the fish skin complements the loose gestural marks in the surrounding area. The rectangle is divided roughly in half by the positioning of the fish, and this can sometimes separate the elements of the image. This danger has been quite successfully overcome here because of the activity of the paint surface as described above, and also partly due to the proportions of the rectangle itself, which is long and relatively narrow. The horizontal division is marked by the long fish tail sweeping across the canvas, but the line is not jarring since it is curved and the colour is broken towards the righthand side of the picture.

The painting works well in terms of design and surface texture. These considerations override concern for a wholly illusionistic representation. One can assume that the plate of fish rests on a flat, horizontal surface but the loose brushmarks give the foreground space a vertical emphasis and this is again reinforced by the shape of the canvas.

# ABSTRACT PAINTING

Many of the paintings which might be considered as 'abstract' are in fact figurative paintings albeit highly abstracted. The distinction between what is representative and what is abstract in any case is an extremely fine one, especially as it is difficult to look at any visual image without finding some kind of association with reality. This has been demonstrated in the Rorschach ink-blot tests where subjects are invited to describe what entirely arbitrary abstract shapes suggest to them. Any representational painting, however realistic, depends upon a certain amount of selectivity. It is by this process of selection and by the use of deliberate distortion that the artist is able to make a personal statement. Many painters use the figure, landscape or still-life as a starting point for paintings which, once completed, give no hint of their origins. Shapes and colours can be utilized in this way, using repetition and variation to develop a theme.

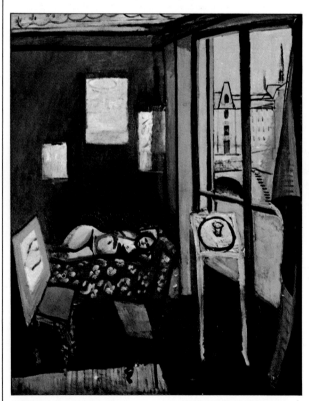

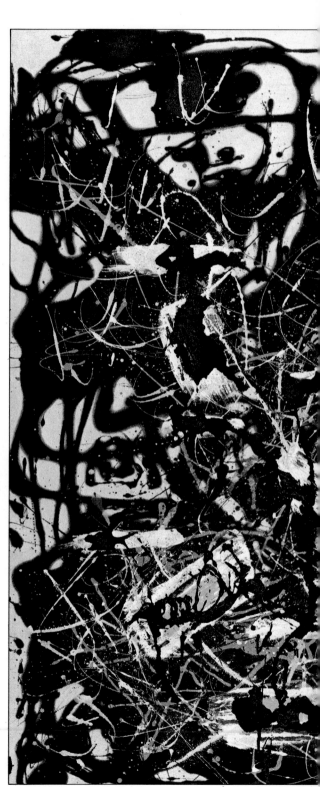

*Studio Quai St Michel* by Henri Matisse *(ABOVE)* is an image which is moving towards abstraction. The chair, bed and figure are still recognizable, but the picture concentrates more on the interplay of colour and line. The work of the American artist Jackson Pollock shows one highly 'individual approach to abstract painting. In *Untitled (Yellow Islands) (RIGHT)* the main colours are black and yellow on a white ground. Often laying his canvases on the floor, Pollock would drip, spatter and throw paint onto the surface, as well as applying it with brushes.

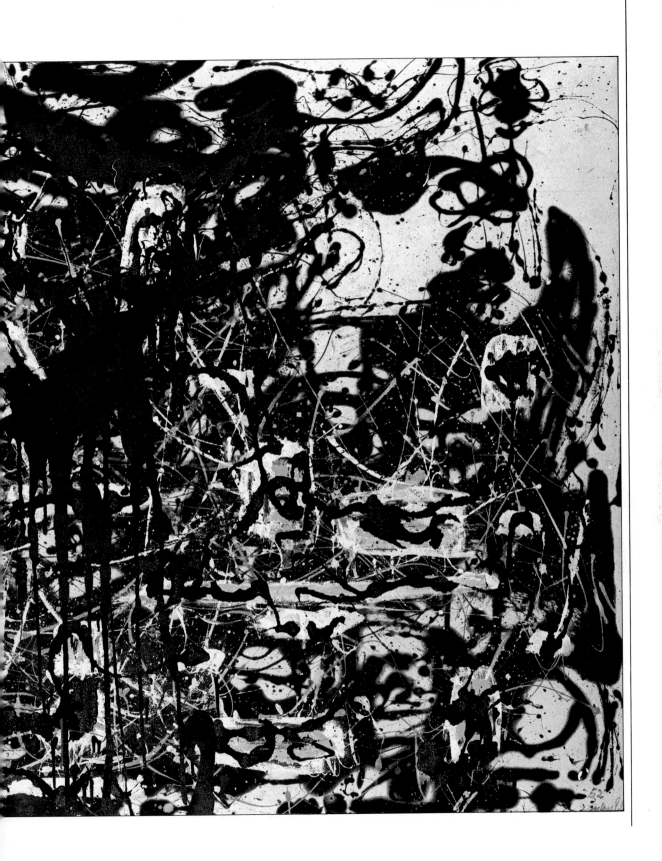

# Abstracting from natural forms

Find an interestingly shaped natural form and prepare a sheet of drawings from it. Some of the drawings should be entirely linear, whilst others should concentrate on the tonal aspects of the object. Suitable items to choose from might include bones, root forms, shells or pieces of wood, and should be sufficiently complex in form to offer a number of differing aspects. Those objects which enclose space will lend themselves very well to the exercise in hand. Having drawn the object from all possible viewpoints, begin to consider how you can use the shapes to construct a semi-abstract painting. Although your starting point may be very small, there is no need to allow this to influence the scaling of your painting. Something tiny and delicate can take on a new significance when greatly enlarged. A shell can become a deep cave, whilst an animal skull can take on the dimensions of a lunar landscape with hills looming over valleys. Once you have decided which of the

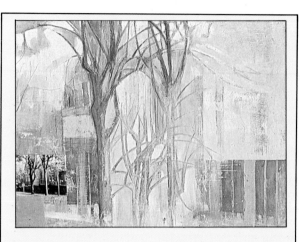

*Developed from a townscape, this acrylic piece shows well how an image can be moved towards abstraction. The trees are greatly simplified and are transformed into rhythmic compositional lines.*

*Horizontal and vertical lines give structure to the design. The colour concentrates more on unity than description.*

drawings you will use as a basis for your painting, begin to plan out the composition. You may find it easier to do this initially onto a large sheet of paper, although it is also possible to work directly onto canvas or board. Using your drawings for reference, simplify or exaggerate, select and adjust in any way which you feel appropriate. The resulting piece should retain a strong connection with the original object, but it will need to stand by itself as a harmonious arrangement of shape and colour.

It is possible to apply this method to any of the paintings produced for the previous exercises. A group of figures, still-life group or landscape can be seen in abstract terms by considering only the surface of the picture. This allows colour to be used solely to make a pattern which is aesthetically pleasing and releases the painter from the constraints of simulating depth within the picture.

This is something which greatly preoccupied such artists as Georges Braque (1882–1963) and Pablo Picasso (1881–1973) who were involved in the Cubist movement earlier this century. Until that time painters had been largely concerned with making the picture as though the scene were viewed through a window or other aperture. The Cubists, on the other hand, tried to build their images in many different ways, particularly as if the images were in front rather than behind the picture plane, thus eliminating traditional approaches to perspective.

Spaniard Pablo Picasso and Frenchman Georges Braque, working under the influence of the French

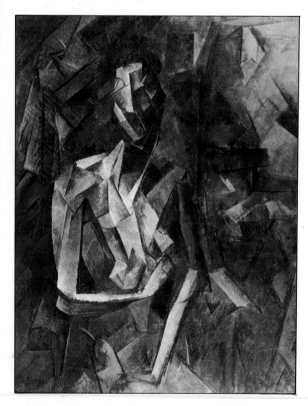

*Seated Nude* by Picasso *(ABOVE)* is an excellent example of one way of abstracting from natural forms. The curves of the body are depicted as flat surfaces. Despite this, the form still remains clearly recognizable as a figure. This is an example of the work Picasso did during his Cubist period.

artist Paul Cézanne (1839–1906), were the two major exponents of Cubism. This movement was in many ways a reaction against the concerns of Impressionism with the appearance of an object. The Cubists approach was more intellectual and concerned with the idea, not the appearance of reality. By making a conglomerate image of something from several different viewpoints, they were attempting to convey exactly what it would be like from any angle. In the early stages of Cubism, artists became so engrossed in the breakdown of form that they painted almost exclusively in monochrome. Only later did they again become interested in the very varied qualities, textures and colour of the paint they were using.

Using these considerations as your yardstick, make two or three paintings in a variety of media which should be of still-life groups or landscapes. Try making two representations of the same subject using a very limited palette for the first and then an arrangement of primary colours for the second. Observe how the change of colour alters the mood and appearance of the picture.

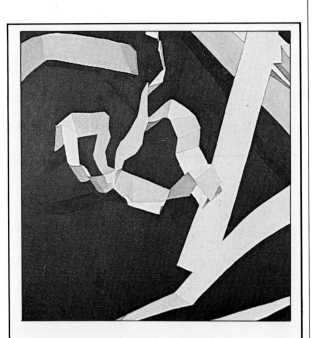

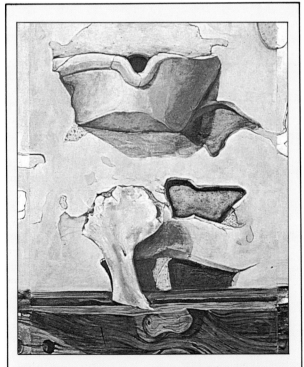

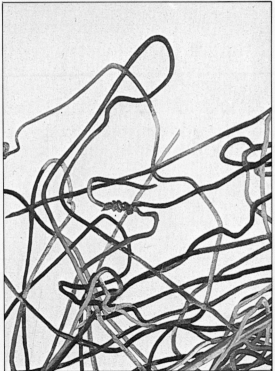

*The raw material for this interesting image was an old wall-mounted sink and conduit. The artist kept the colours fairly neutral, but also focused so closely on the subject that the image is almost abstract. The end effect is one of an overall pattern of interlocking shapes.*

*Both these images, painted in acrylics, show a strong sense of structure and abstraction. The basis for the first composition (TOP) was an arrangement of paper strips, while wire was used for the second (ABOVE). Both images show strong tonal contrast and the artist has paid special attention to where the materials join or overlap.*

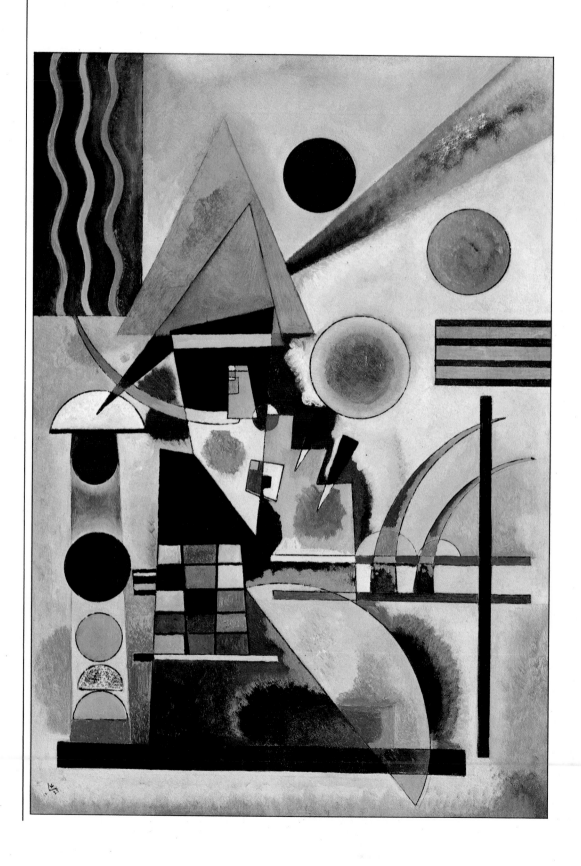

# Abstract colour field

Using a strong colour—red, green, blue or yellow, for example—cover the canvas or paper by flooding the paint on very generously. Into this colour field introduce strips, shapes and rhythms to combine into an agreeable whole. Think about the structure of your work even though it will be far less obvious than in the previous exercises. Decide upon a basic composition which is either symmetrical or asymmetrical and by use of colour and shape work upon achieving an overall balance between the various elements.

You should be familiar with the theory of colour discussed earlier and you can exploit your knowledge in this exercise. Begin by making quite simple colour arrangements, relating an area of yellow, for instance, to complementary violet, but do not be afraid to experiment with unlikely combinations.

With a painting of this sort, where interest is concentrated on the surface, it is important to consider the textural and three-dimensional qualities of the paint you are using. Decide whether you want a flat and smooth surface or whether you wish the pigment to provide not only colour but texture. It is possible to add fillers to your paint if you intend to lay it on thickly. Find out what effects you can achieve by adding sawdust or sand, for instance. If you wish to extend your paint in this way it would be as well to conduct a series of tests before actually using it for a finished piece

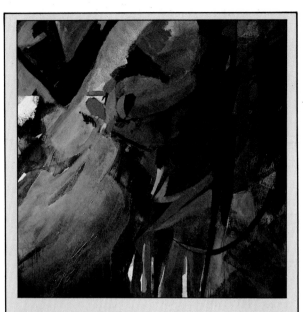

*This large-scale abstract was painted in oils. The size of the marks meant that the format had to be large to achieve a suitable balance in the image. Each of the marks on the canvas is made by an arm gesture rather than by a smaller movement of the hand or wrist. The range of the colour has been deliberately restricted, but within that range the artist has been very enterprising. If you are interested in this type of work, examine this example to see where the same colours have been used and how they have been varied. The impression of this image is one of richness and warmth.*

Many abstract artists have been fascinated by the interplay of geometric forms. In *Swinging (LEFT)*, for example, the Russian-born artist Wassily Kandinsky has combined distinctive geometrical shapes with strong colours. It is noticeable that various colours, especially the pink-purple and orange recur in different parts of the composition.

*Light Red over Black (RIGHT)* is typical of the work of the American abstract expressionist artist Mark Rothko. Large rectangular areas of colour are characteristic. He often painted them in a series of thin washes layered upon one another. This produced the hazy outlines to the shape which often appear almost to float above the background colour.

of work. Make sure that you know what will happen to your mixture when it has completely dried as, if it lacks a certain amount of elasticity, there is a danger that it will crack away from the surface of the painting.

These are only a few aspects of the wide and important field of abstract painting. Obviously there are numerous other approaches to this type of painting with which you may care to experiment at first hand. You should, in any case, produce more than one answer to each of the briefs given, making your paintings as lively and varied as possible.

# Abstract painting based on a grid

The logical continuation of Cubism was to divide the picture area with rigidly geometrical forms and flat areas of colour. The Dutch painter Piet Mondrian (1872–1944), whose particular brand of abstract painting was known as Neo-Plasticism, made pictures with divisions of black lines drawn along the vertical and horizontal and filled in with primary colours so that the effect was rather like that of a stained glass window.

Using graph paper for your working drawings, devise a picture based upon a grid, making it as simple or as complicated as you wish. Just as with representational paintings certain divisions are more pleasing than others, you will find this to be the case with abstract pictures also. You might try making a composition based entirely upon divisions and subdivisions along the Golden Section, arranging large passages of cooler hues as a contrast to smaller but more stridently coloured areas. Alternatively concentrate upon variations of one particular colour from your palette, using others only to modify and adjust. Do not forget that, although you are not concerned with tone in order to create an illusion of space, it can still be used to alter the values of the colours which you are using.

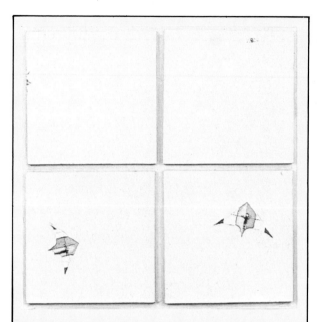

*This work was painted on four square canvases arranged in a grid. Although the image of hang-gliders is not in itself abstract, the sense of abstraction is very strong. This effect is created at least partly by the changes in scale, which are also used to suggest movement. This sense of movement contrasts with the rigidity of the format of the work, and a* *tension is created between these two elements. This is an interesting attempt to develop an image which is moving towards total abstraction.*

The Swiss artist Paul Klee was extremely innovative in the techniques and approaches he used. Many of his pictures are based on grids, but he uses them in widely varying ways, not allowing himself to be dictated to by the shapes on the grid. In the watercolour *Motif of Hammamet (RIGHT)*, the effect of the geometrically based shapes is enhanced by the texture of the paper which shows through and by the artist's subtle use of tonal contrasts. Klee was a very prolific artist, often working on many pictures at one time, as photographs of his studio clearly show.

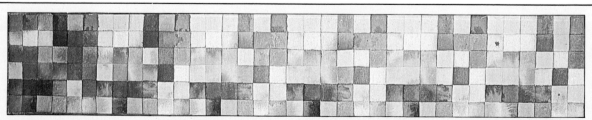

*The colours for this oil painting were selected in an arbitrary way by throwing dice. Using the tightly structured grid format, the artist was trying to produce an image* *which combined randomness with a fixed form. The grid holds the arrangement of the colours closely together. When doing the painting the artist used masking tape to* *enable him to paint the lines very straight. This is a useful aid for other kinds of painting too. Note how the artist has created variations within the colours he has chosen.* *This adds much visual variety to the image. The picture is a creditable attempt to use the strict structure imposed by the grid in an interesting and personal way.*

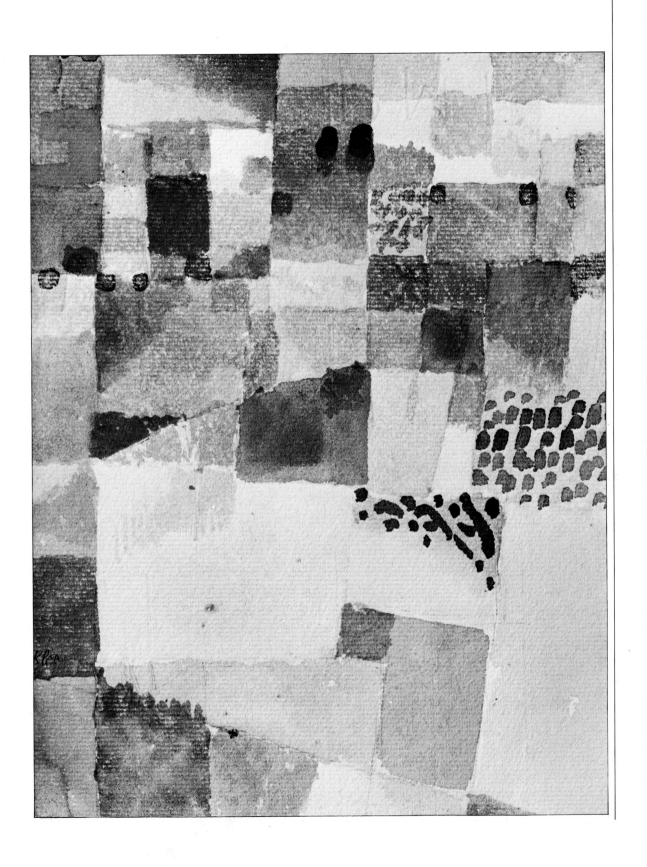

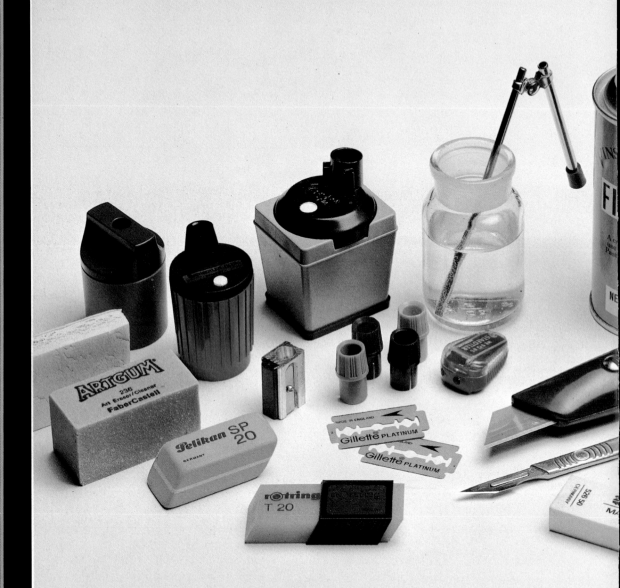

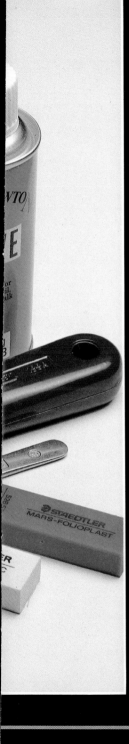

# APPENDICES

•

PRACTICAL HINTS

•

GLOSSARY

•

INDEX

•

## Painting equipment

The quality of the equipment you use for any kind of painting or drawing is very important. It is much better to have a small selection of high quality equipment which will last you many years than to buy a large range of cheaper materials which will be less satisfactory to use.

Apart from brushes, paint and supports you will find the following useful for oil painting: palette knife, palette and an easel. In addition, a number of small containers for holding oil, turpentine and so on and a mahl stick (which you can easily make yourself) will also be of use. For watercolour painting you will need a different type of palette, one with indentations more suitable for mixing watercolours than the flatter kind of palettes for oil work. Easels for watercolour painting are also different. Although often expensive, an easel is invaluable for holding your work steady at the angle you want. A painting kit can provide a useful selection of equipment for the beginner.

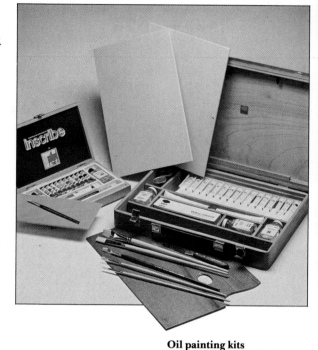

### Oil palettes
The traditional painter's palette is a flat piece of wood with a thumb-hole and an indentation at one end for the fingers *(4, 9)*. These are intended for easel painters, so that the whole range of colours can be laid out ready for instant use. Small dip-pers *(3, 5)* can be attached to the palette to hold oil or turpentine. Palette boxes *(1, 2)* are useful for outdoor work as they can be closed up and carried with the colours remaining in place. Recessed palettes made of plastic *(6)* or aluminium *(7)* and paper palettes *(8)* are also useful.

### Oil painting kits
Boxes containing the basic equipment for oil painting are available in a whole range of sizes. This can be an expensive way of buying paints, but such kits can prove convenient, especially if you intend to paint in the open air.

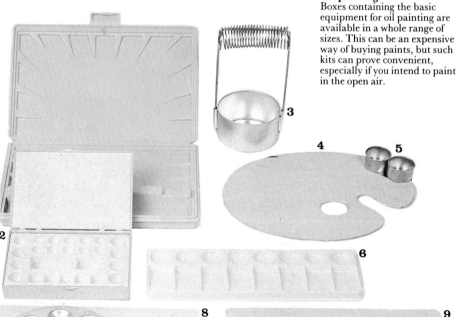

**Mahl stick and palette knives**
(*RIGHT*) A mahl stick (*1*) is used as a rest for the hand which holds the brush to steady it especially when painting details. It consists of a length of bamboo with a cushion at one end. The stick is held across the canvas with the cushioned end resting lightly on the surface. Palette knives (*2–7*) of different shapes are used principally for mixing up paint on the palette though they are often used to apply paint to the canvas, especially when an impasto effect is required.

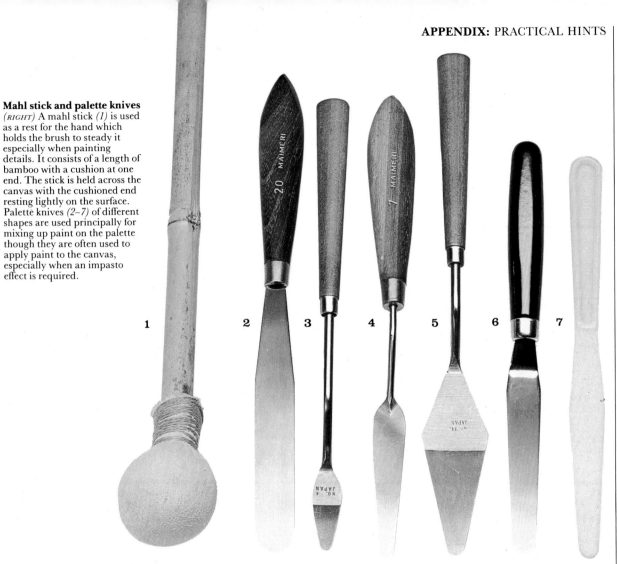

**Palettes** Recessed or well palettes (*4, 5, 6, 7*) must be used for mixing watercolour. These mean that any quantity of water can be added and that the colours will not flow into one another. Exactly which type you use is a matter of personal choice. The larger thumb-hole palette (*1*) is obviously the most useful for outdoor work, while the separate small pots (*2, 3*) have a much greater capacity.

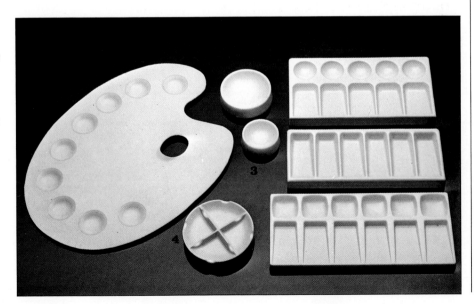

# Brushes

The quality of your paint brush is determined by the quality of the bristle, while the type of mark it makes depends on the thickness and length of the bristle and the way in which the bristles are inserted in the metal ferrule, which holds them in place. For oil painting, the main types of brush are flat, filbert and round. Brushes for oil painting are usually made from hog's hair. For watercolour painting, sable is the preferred material. All brushes are made in a very wide variety of thicknesses and widths.

It is well worth spending extra to obtain good quality brushes for your painting as, although a high quality brush will not guarantee that you will produce a high quality painting, it is much more difficult to paint well with a poor quality brush, especially if you are doing fine and detailed work.

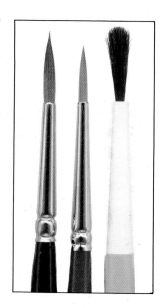

**Selecting suitable brushes**
Good quality brushes can be very expensive but they are a good investment and will last if well kept. This illustration (*LEFT*) shows (from *LEFT* to *RIGHT*) a good quality sable brush, a synthetic round hair brush and the poor quality type sometimes included in paintboxes. It is clear that the good sable brush has the best shape and will be the most versatile. Brushes are made for different purposes and in a range of sizes and prices. Those shown (*BELOW*) are all suitable for use with watercolour: (from *LEFT* to *RIGHT*) blender, fine synthetic roundhair, mixed fibre round, ox hair round, squirrel hair round, sable fan brush (for careful blending), sable bright, sable round, fine sable round. Round hair brushes can be used as points or with bristles spread.

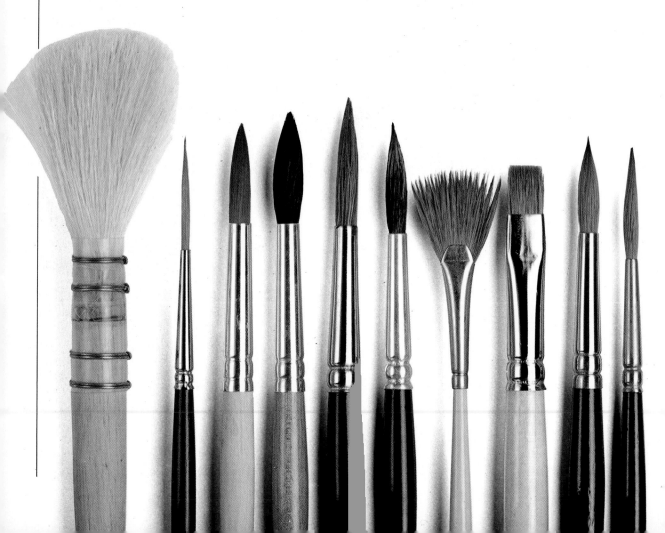

As sable brushes are soft, they are not always strong enough to manipulate thick oil paint, but may be good for spreading thin glazes. Hog's hair is the best quality bristle for oil painting, but many new synthetic brushes are on the market and these may well

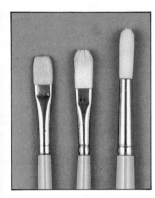

be found more than adequate, especially for artists who wish to experiment with different shaped brushes to find the most suitable for their purposes. Flat brushes are firm and give a clean mark. By using both flat and tip of the bristles, you can work on quite intricate detail and complex contours with flat brushes. Small round hair brushes are also good for detail but the larger sizes tend to splay out so are best for spreading broad areas of colour. The choice between short haired flat brushes, known as brights, and the rounded flat filbert may only be a matter of personal preference. Every artist will need a selection of broad and smaller brushes, especially if working on large canvases. It is best to start with a small range of assorted shapes and sizes and build up the collection as you define your specific needs. The selection shown (*RIGHT*) are (*TOP* to *BOTTOM*) sable fan, red sable round, synthetic round, synthetic bright, hog's hair flat, hog's hair filbert, Russian sable bright, synthetic flat, red sable bright.

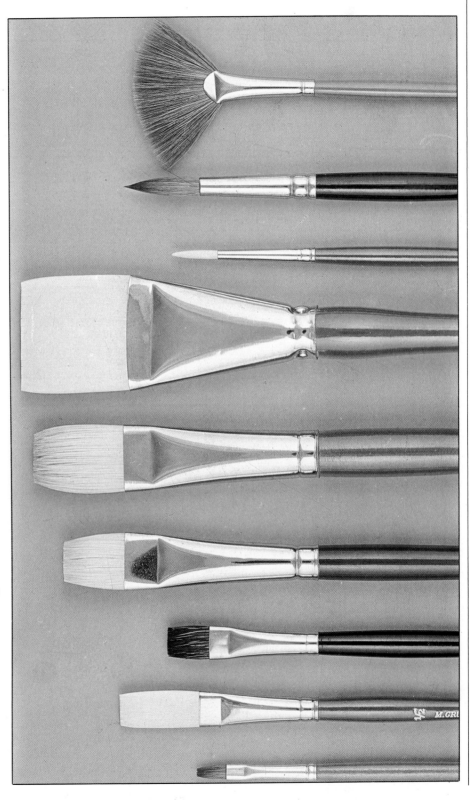

# Preparing supports

There are four main types of support for painting and drawing: wood, paper, fabric and metal. The most commonly used are paper and fabric. The great advantage of paper is that it is cheap. Furthermore, it is light and easy to prepare. It can be used for any medium, although it is not commonly used for oil painting. The term 'canvas' applies to any stretched fabric. An artist's canvas can be made from linen, cotton, unbleached calico, twill or duck. In a sense, it is the most inconvenient support for painting on because it needs considerable preparation. It has to be mounted onto a frame and then primed. However, ready-made canvases can be bought and you may find this convenient, albeit more expensive.

Wood has a longer history than canvas. Make sure that you only use well-seasoned wood which has been properly treated, otherwise it will warp and crack. Wooden supports need to be battened at the back in order to prevent any buckling. Metal plates have been used since before van Eyck. In recent years, artists have experimented with zinc and aluminium.

## Stretching a canvas

Despite the advent of commercially produced canvases and boards for oil and acrylic painting, it is still cheaper and more satisfactory to stretch canvases according to your own requirements. Fine woven linen is regarded as the best canvas, but cotton duck is often used as it is sturdy and cheaper, although it has a coarser texture. Stretched fabric puts tremendous pressure on its support, especially if it gets wet during painting, and wooden stretchers must be strong and firmly jointed. If they are not absolutely secure the whole canvas will very soon warp noticeably and will not hang properly on a wall. The great advantage of stretched canvas over the various types of board as a painting support is that it is very much lighter for handling, hanging and storing. The canvas can be pinned around the back of the stretcher, but it is easier and more convenient to secure it with a strong staple gun and this is a real necessity for any serious painter over a period of time, and is endlessly useful in other ways for general studio work.

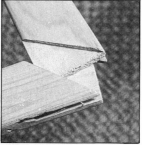

**Stretching a canvas**
**1.** Form an L-shape by fitting two sides of the stretcher together. Repeat with other sides and join.

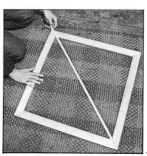

**2.** Check the right-angled corners of the stretcher by measuring the diagonals. If they are equal the stretcher is square.

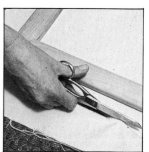

**3.** Lay out the canvas and put the stretcher down on it. Cut the canvas to overlap by at least 1½in (3.75 cm) on each side.

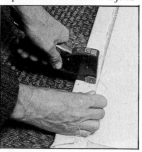

**4.** Pull the canvas evenly over the stretcher and staple it in the centre of each side. Work along the sides to secure it.

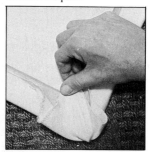

**5.** Smooth the canvas over each corner and staple it to the wood at the centre of the overlap. Keep the corners taut.

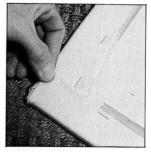

**6.** Make the corners neat by folding over the remaining flaps of canvas and stapling them down firmly.

## Cradling a board

A board used as support for a painting which is intended to last should be cradled, that is, strengthened with wooden battens on the back. This is somewhat laborious and makes the board heavier, but without this support the board will certainly warp and may even crack. It is necessary to judge how much bracing the board will need, as it may be necessary to have quite a complex network of battens reinforcing both right-angles and diagonals. Wherever possible use screws to secure the battens as this is much more reliable than glue.

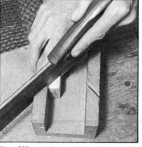

**Cradling a board**
**1.** Cut battens to a suitable length, slightly shorter than the board. Mitre the battens.

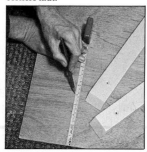

**2.** Place the battens on the back of the board and mark positions. Drill holes into the battens for screws and mark the points.

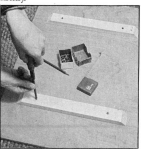

**3.** Place the battens on the board, aligned to the marks and parallel to the sides. Screw them firmly to the wood.

## Sticking muslin to board

Some artists prefer the rigid surface of a board to the give of canvas, but would rather work on to the surface texture of a fabric. This can be solved by sticking muslin to a piece of board to give the surface the tooth of fabric. Muslin is a suitable material to use, giving a fine texture over the board, but being also light enough to adhere firmly. Muslin is easily found in small shops or stores which carry a range of fabrics.

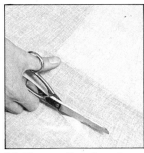

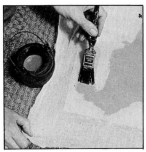

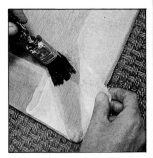

**Sticking muslin to board**
**1.** Choose a board of suitable weight and cut muslin to overlap 2in (5 cm) all round.

**2.** Smooth out the muslin over the board so the overlap is even and brush over it with glue size. Eliminate any creases as you work.

**3.** Turn the board over and fold down the overlapping fabric. Glue it to the back of the board, tucking in the corners.

## Squaring up

A painting may evolve in many different ways and some artists start work directly on their canvas without preliminary drawings. For a subject which requires basic definition, it may be necessary to transfer the outlines of a previously prepared drawing or design to the canvas, and this will probably involve a change of scale. Squaring up provides guidelines on the canvas proportionate to those on the drawing, enabling you to reconstruct the design accurately.

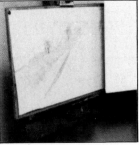

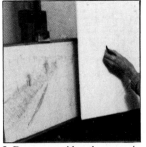

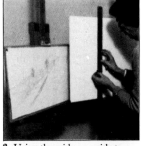

**Squaring up**
**1.** Complete the rough drawing of the subject on paper and rule a light grid of squares with a pencil.

**2.** Draw up a grid on the canvas in direct proportion to that on the drawing. Keep the two side by side for reference.

**3.** Using the grid as a guide to position, draw up the outlines and main features of the subject onto the canvas.

## Stretching paper

Paper is the best support for gouache and watercolour and can also be used for acrylic paints, but to take oils it must first be well primed. So that the paper will not buckle and pull out of shape when soaked with paint, it should be stretched onto board. The paper is wetted thoroughly to remove some of the dressing and it expands. It is firmly taped down while wet and, as it dries, it contracts tightly across the board. It will then return to its tautness as it dries out after wet paint has been applied.

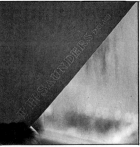

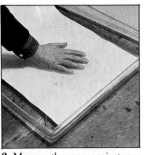

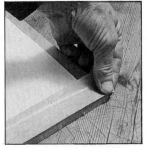

**Stretching paper**
**1.** Papers have a rough and smooth side so choose which to use.

**2.** Measure the paper against your drawing board and trim it carefully to leave enough margin of board for the tape.

**3.** Fill a clean dish or sink with water and immerse the paper. Thick watercolour paper may need a longer time to soak.

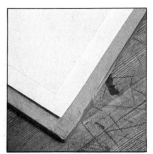

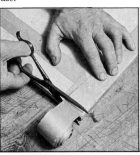

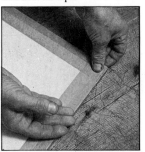

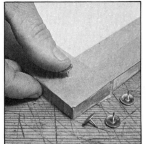

**4.** While the paper soaks, cut lengths of adhesive paper tape measured along each side of the board.

**5.** Lift paper and let surplus water drain off. Lay it flat on the board and run damped paper tape along one side.

**6.** Tape the opposite side of the paper with damp paper tape and repeat for the other two sides. Keep the paper flat.

**7.** The paper must be dried naturally, as forcing may split it. For extra strength, push in a drawing pin at each corner.

# Framing

Any painting or drawing which you wish to display will need to be framed. This will not only improve the look of the picture but will also help preserve it. Framing is not difficult; it simply requires the right tools, care, and time.

In order to frame your own pictures, you will need a metal ruler, a tenon saw, a hand drill, a claw hammer, a mitre clamp or saw guide, a punch or awl, pinchers, set-square and a G-clamp. Your first task is to choose a suitable moulding for your picture. Mouldings are made from a whole variety of materials and come in a wide range of designs. Obviously, you need to choose a moulding which will suit the picture. A very heavily gilded frame would, for example, look incongruous around a delicate pencil drawing.

The other ingredients in a frame are the glass at the front and the backing behind. With oil paintings, these two things are not really necessary. With watercolour painting and drawings they are essential. Backing should always be hardboard, never cardboard, which is too soft, nor plywood, which warps.

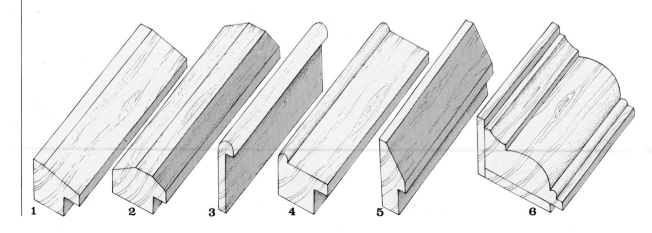

**Tools**
A number of tools are necessary for framing, but these are mostly useful for other types of work also. A suitable sized tenon saw (5), corner clamps (13), drill (14), hammer (9), chisel (1), pin punch (10), bradawl (19), pliers (16,18), G-clamp (17), file (20), and a strong pocket knife (2) form the tools for cutting and assembling the frame. To trim drawings and cut mounts, you need a sharp craft knife (11), ruler (6) and set square (21), scissors (12), pencils (3,4) and adhesive tape (15). Glass cutting tools (7,8) are available in different sizes.

**Mouldings** Plain wood mouldings are easily cut and pinned and come in several shapes and widths: box (1), reverse slope (2), half round or hockey stick (3), raised bead and flat (4), box (5) and a composite architrave and planed wood moulding (6).

When framing watercolours and drawings you might want to give them window mounts. These not only enhance the display of the picture but also help protect it by holding it clear of the glass.

The first step in making a frame is to measure the picture. Remember to add more if you intend incorporating a window mount. Never cut until you have got the measurements absolutely right. If you are framing a canvas, you must allow an extra ¼in (6mm) all around to allow for expansion and contraction in temperature changes. If necessary, the canvas can be wedged in with cork spacers or veneer pins.

## Cutting glass

Glass cutting tools are quite easy to handle, but it is essential to cut the glass with one clean stroke and it is not possible to make the cut accurately a second time. If possible, practise with the tool on small offcuts of glass until you are confident of the action of the tool. Use common sense in handling the glass. Picture glass is quite fine and fragile and liable to snap unexpectedly, but with care cutting need not be hazardous. Avoid putting any pressure around the edges.

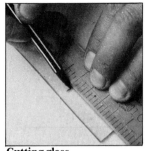

**Cutting glass**
**1.** Mark the glass with the required dimensions using a set square and ruler for accuracy.

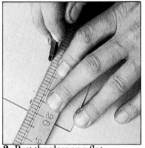

**2.** Rest the glass on a flat, supportive surface and position the ruler between the marks. Guide the tool along the ruler.

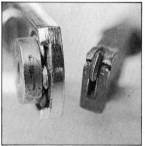

**3.** The head of a glass cutting tool is set so that the wheel which makes the cut is centred but distanced from the edge.

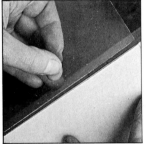

**4.** Place the score in the glass along the edge of a table and let the glass drop, snapping it gently along the cut.

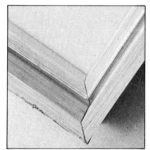

**5.** Make sure the glass is cut a fraction smaller than the inside of the frame so it is not wedged in.

## Assembling the frame

Well cut mitres are essential to good frame making. If the moulding is cut at an incorrect angle, however slightly, the frame will be warped and the corners untidy. Simple details make a difference here. Use a sharp pencil to mark up the measurements so the saw cut can be accurately placed. Keep the saw keen and make sure it does not angle while making the cut. Use clamps to hold the corners while they are glued and pinned or they will be pushed out of true.

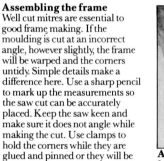

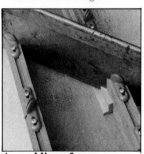

**Assembling a frame**
**1.** Place the moulding in a mitre board or clamp, and cut through one end to make the first angle.

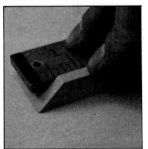

**2.** Measure the length of one side of the frame along the inside of the rebate of the moulding from the mitred end.

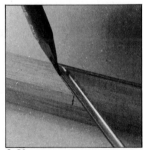

**3.** Use a set square to measure a 45° angle and mark up the cutting point for the second mitred end.

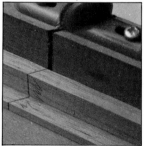

**4.** Before cutting, mark the waste side of the cut so that the saw can be accurately placed. Make the second cut.

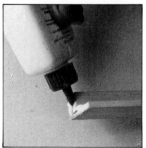

**5.** Repeat this process until you have cut all four lengths of moulding required for the frame. Apply glue to the mitres.

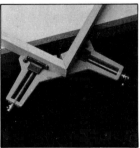

**6.** Make two sides of the frame into an L-shape and secure them in a corner clamp. Make sure both pieces lie flat.

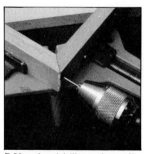

**7.** Use a hand drill to make small holes into each side of the corner. Use panel pins to secure the joint.

# GLOSSARY

## A

**Abstract art** An art form which is not dependent upon a fundamentally naturalistic approach to the subject matter for the expression of form, space and colour.

**Abstract Expressionism** A form of *abstract art* which originated in America in the 1950s in which the artist involved chance and the subconscious in the creation of the painting.

**Achromatic** A term which is applied to a light or a tone which contains no colour.

**Acrylic paint** Paint which comprises of pigment which is bound with a synthetic resin. Acrylic paints can be diluted with water and yet dry within minutes. Once dry, they do not change in colour or texture. They are opaque and dry to an even matt finish. They do not deteriorate or change colour markedly when exposed to atmospheric conditions. Acrylic paints can be used on a wide variety of surfaces. Acrylic paints were developed in the 1920s and 1930s. They became more readily available after the Second World War and are now very popular with artists, both professional and amateur, because of their versatility.

**Additive mixing** When coloured light is mixed, the wavelengths of each colour are combined so that they become lighter. This is known as additive mixing. If the three light primaries (red, green and blue) are mixed, the combining wavelengths create white light.

**Advancing colours** Warm, strong colours which give the impression of being near the spectator. These colours seem to advance while cool colours appear to recede.

**Alla prima** A method of painting by which all the pigments to be included are laid on the painting surface in one layer and during one session.

**Aerial perspective** see *perspective.*

**After-image** The opposite or complementary colour which is seen after the retina has been focused for 30 seconds or more on a particular colour. For example, after looking at a red area for some time, you will see a green after-image if you transfer your gaze to a neutral coloured surface.

**Aquarelle** A drawing which is coloured with watercolour washes.

**Aqueous** Refers to pigments or media which are soluble, or can be suspended, in water.

**Atmospheric perspective** see *perspective.*

## B

**Binder** In painting, any liquid medium which, when mixed with powder pigment, forms paint.

**Binocular vision** see *monocular vision.*

**Blocking in** A technique which is employed during the formative stages of a painting when the artist describes roughly and approximately the composition of the painting.

**Bright** A flat brush.

**Broken colour** In colour theory, a colour which is made by mixing two secondary colours. Broken colours tend towards grey and their chroma is low. The word tertiary is sometimes used to describe these colours but it is becoming increasingly obsolete. In painting, broken colour refers to various techniques in which several colours are used in their pure state rather than being blended or mixed. Usually the paint quality is stiff and thick and, when the paint is dragged across the surface, layers beneath show through. This term can also refer to Pointillist techniques.

**Brushes** Crucial tools to the painter, the best oil painting brushes are made from hog's hair while the best watercolour brushes are made from sable. Brushes are made in a very wide variety of shapes including flat, round, filbert or fan.

## C

**Cadmiums** In painting, brilliant and permanent pigments prepared from cadmium sulphate.

**Canvas** The most commonly used surface for painting in oils. It is stretched on a wooden support and then it is treated with a ground before the application of pigment. Pigments adhere well to its surface because of the texture created by the weave of the material.

**Centre line** The line of vision which extends from the spectator's eye to the object being scrutinized.

**Chalk drawing** A drawing which is done using pastel or crayon.

**Chamfer** A symmetrical bevel cut in a right-angled edge or corner.

**Charcoal** Wood, often vine, which is reduced by burning so that it can then be used for drawing. Because the wood is charred the line which it produces has a powdery quality. It needs to be made permanent on the drawing surface through the application of a fixative.

**Chiaroscuro** The literal translation of this Italian term is light-dark, but the term has come to mean the skilful exploitation of light and shadow within a painting. Rembrandt and Caravaggio are artists particularly associated with the use of chiaroscuro.

**Chroma** The term used to describe and measure the purity of a colour. Neutral grey, for instance, has no chroma while pure red can be said to contain much chroma.

**Collage** Derived from the French verb *coller* meaning 'to stick', collage is the technique of pasting cloth, paper or other materials onto a canvas or surface. It was first used by the Cubist artists.

**Colour sphere** A sphere which is designed and laid out for charting and measuring colour. Hue is measured around the circumference of the sphere, chroma across the diameter and tone vertically, from one pole to the other.

**Complementary colours** Pairs of colours which are widely separated on the colour sphere. Violet and yellow or red and green are complementary colours.

**Composition** The term which is applied to the arrangement of form and colour in a painting.

**Cone of vision** The field of vision in which everything can be reasonably clearly seen when the eyes are looking in one direction. This field extends for only about 40°. Outside of this field everything becomes increasingly blurred.

**Contour** The outline of a form in a painting or drawing.

**Cover** This term refers to the capacity of a pigment to obscure an underlying surface. It is also applied to the capacity of a pigment to extend by given volume over a surface.

**Crayon** Powdered pigments which are bound, usually with wax, so that they form a hard stick. Crayons come in a wide variety of colours.

**Cross-hatching** A technique whereby pencil or some other medium is drawn or laid down in a series of criss-crossing strokes to build up tone. It is a technique which is used mostly in drawing for defining shadow and depth.

**Cyan** A light secondary colour which is made by mixing the light primaries green and blue.

As a result, cyan is a brilliant blue-green hue.

# E

**Eye-level** The horizon line when drawing perspective. Vanishing points are placed along this line. It should not be confused with the horizon line which represents the meeting of earth and sky.

# F

**Fat** A term which describes paint which contains a high proportion of oil.

**Fat over lean** A painting technique which allows the bottom layer of paint to dry before further application. 'Fat' paint is mixed with oil to create a thick paste while 'lean' paint is thinned with a diluent such as turpentine to make it dry more quickly.

**Ferrule** The metal attachment on a brush for holding the hairs or bristles.

**Figurative art** Representational art as opposed to abstract art.

**Filbert** This is one of the main types of brush for oil painting. A filbert is shaped slightly at the tip so that it produces a smooth, rounded stroke. The other main types of brush are flat and round.

**Fixative** Thin varnish, either natural or synthetic, which is sprayed on drawings, especially work in pastels or charcoal, to give them protection.

**Flat** This type of brush is used for both broad strokes which can be produced by the flat of the brush and fine lines or dabs of paint which can be made with the side of the brush. Flat brushes are a versatile tool for any artist, especially for painting in oil or acrylic.

**Foreshortening** The means of representing the apparent diminishing of distance or length as an object recedes from the viewer.

**Fresco** A method of wall-painting on a plaster ground. True fresco was much used in Italy from the thirteenth to the sixteenth centuries. First, the *arriccio* is applied and upon this the design, or *sinopia*, is traced. An area small enough to be completed in one day – the *giornata* – is covered with a final layer of plaster, the *intonaco*. The design is then redrawn and painted with pigments mixed with water. Giotto was one of the masters of this time-consuming, demanding painting technique. Fresco is relatively little used today.

**Fugitive** The term is applied to paints which are short-lived in colour or intensity, due to inherent defects or the action of natural forces, especially sunlight.

# G

**Genre painting** A type of art which depicts scenes from everyday life. Two of the better known genre painters are the Dutch artist Vermeer and the Spaniard Velazquez.

**Glaze** A transparent film of pigment which is laid over a lighter surface.

**Gouache** An opaque, water-based paint. Unlike watercolour, it is possible to work from dark to light, adding white to lighten the colours rather than thinning the medium with more water. Nevertheless, water-thinned gouache can be used for painting large, graduated washes.

**Graphite** A form of carbon which is compressed with fine clay and used in the manufacture of pencils.

**Grisaille** A grey underpainting which is laid down for subsequent colour glazing.

**Ground** A prepared surface on which the colours of a painting are then laid. It is applied to the paper, canvas or any other surface on which a painting is to be done. A ground heightens the brilliance of colours, stops chemical interaction between the paint and the support, and prevents absorption.

**Gum arabic** A soluble gum which is obtained from the acacia plant. It is used as the binding agent in watercolours, gouache and pastel.

# H

**Hessian** A form of canvas which generally has a coarse, thick weave. It is usually used as a support for oil paints.

**Horizon line** Imaginary line on the picture plane which corresponds to the place where the horizontal line which is level with the eye meets the picture plane.

**Hue** The colours which are found on a scale ranging through red, orange, yellow, green, blue, indigo and violet. There are about 150 discernible hues.

# I

**Impasto** A technique whereby paint is applied very thickly.

When paint is thick enough to create lumps and reveal distinct brushstrokes, it is said to be heavily impasted.

**Isometric projection** A pictorial projection used in producing a three-dimensional representation of an object when all three faces are equally inclined to the plane of the projection. All the edges are foreshortened equally.

# L

**Lean** Used to describe paint which possesses little oil in relation to pigment.

**Local colour** The inherent hue of an object or surface when it is not modified by light, atmosphere or adjacent colours. The local colour of a tomato, for instance, is red.

# M

**Magenta** A light secondary colour which is made by mixing the light primaries red and blue. Magenta is identified as a pink-purple colour.

**Medium** The liquid into which a pigment is ground in the preparation of paint. The medium binds the particles of the pigments together and to the ground. It also makes it possible for the pigment to be applied to a surface. Oil, for instance, is the medium of oil paint while gum arabic is used for watercolour paint. In a less technical sense, the medium refers to the actual material used for painting or drawing, such as pencil, crayon or oil paint.

**Mixed contrast** The creation of a colour by the mixing of an after-image with a hue. A yellow after-image imposed on a blue field will produce the appearance of green.

**Modelling** In painting and drawing modelling is the process of depicting light and shade on objects so that a three-dimensional effect is achieved.

**Monocular vision** Vision with one eye. When measuring distances and relative proportions, the draughtsman must use monocular vision to avoid seeing double images. Binocular vision is the normal stereoscopic vision which employs two eyes.

## O

**Oblique projection** A pictorial projection in which the plan or side elevation is drawn and the all the other elevations projected from it in parallel lines at 30° or 45°.

**Oil paint** A paint which consists of pigment mixed with an oil medium such as linseed or poppy oil. These oxidize in the air and form solid skins in which the colour is evenly distributed. The paint surface can be made more opaque or transparent, more matt or more gloss, according to the proportions and type of oil or thinner added.

**One-point perspective** see *perspective.*

**Opacity** The power of a pigment to cover or obscure the surface to which it is applied.

**Orthographic projection** A pictorial projection of a three-dimensional object in which there is no convergence of parallel lines.

## P

**Painterly** A term applied to a painting style in which objects and masses are defined through colour and tone and light and dark rather through contours and linear means.

**Palette** A slab on which colours can be mixed. It can be made of wood, metal, glass, china, marble or paper. The word is also used to denote the range of colour at an artist's disposal.

**Palette knife** A flexible knife which is used for mixing paints on the palette or for applying them to a painting surface.

**Pastel** Pastels are dry colours. Powdered pigments are mixed with just enough gum to bind them together. They are made up into sticks, known as pastels, and are used like crayons. They are opaque, so that mixing is done either by cross-hatching or juxtaposing dots of different colours. The major problem associated with pastel drawing is making the pigments adhere to the chosen surface. A fixative has to be applied after the drawing is finished to protect the fragile surface.

**Perspective** Any graphic technique which creates the impression of depth and three dimensions on a flat surface or on a form which is shallower than the one which is represented (for instance, stage scenery). Linear perspective is the means of creating the sensation of depth through the use of converging lines and vanishing points. Aerial perspective creates this sensation by imitating modifications of colour which occur as a result of atmospheric effects. One-point perspective refers to a linear system of perspective which has one vanishing point. In a two-point perspective system there are two vanishing points.

**Picture plane** The imaginary vertical plane on which the drawing is plotted. It is in effect the window through which the artist views the world.

**Pigment** Any substance which, when mixed with a liquid, creates a colour which can be used for painting. Pigments are generally organic (earth colours) or inorganic (minerals and chemicals).

**Plein-air** Term for a painting which is done out of doors rather than in a studio.

**Primary colours** Colours which cannot be made by mixing others. There are two sets of primaries – light primaries, which consist of red, blue and green and pigment primaries which are red, blue and yellow. When mixed, the light primaries produce white (light) while the pigment primaries produce black.

## R

**Resin** Substance which is obtained from coniferous trees and used in media and as varnish. Synthetic resins are now available.

## S

**Sable** A weasel-like animal whose hair is used for making fine soft brushes. These are usually used for watercolour painting.

**Saturation** A technical term used by artists to describe the degree of purity in a colour. This is established by comparing a sample of the colour with a colourless area of equal brightness.

**Scumble** To apply a thin, often broken, layer of paint over a darker surface.

**Secondary colour** A colour which is made by mixing two primary colours.

**Sepia** A dark brown pigment which is extracted from the cuttlefish.

**Simultaneous contrast** The instantaneous increase or decrease in the intensity of colours when they are perceived in adjacent positions. When two complementary colours are placed next to each other their intensity and brightness appears to be enhanced. When two colours which are not diametrically opposed on the colour sphere are juxtaposed they have a modifying or cancelling effect on each other.

**Size** A gelatinous solution such as rabbit skin glue, used to prepare the surface of a support for priming and painting.

**Stipple** A method of drawing or engraving which employs a series of dots rather than lines.

**Stretcher** The wooden frame on which a canvas is stretched. Stretched canvas is less prone to change with atmospheric variations and less susceptible to damage than unstretched canvas.

**Study** A carefully done drawing or painting which is a preparation for a more complex or finished work.

**Subtractive mixing** When coloured pigments are mixed they absorb light from each other and become darker. This is known as subtractive mixing. The mixing together of the three primaries (red, blue and yellow) creates black.

**Successive contrast** The enhancing or modification of a colour by the imposition of an after-image upon it. Its effect is similar to that of simultaneous contrast though the period of time before it takes effect is longer.

**Support** The term applied to any material, whether it be canvas, wood, board or paper, which is used as a surface on which to paint or draw.

# T

**Tempera** This term describes a type of binder added to powdered pigment, but now refers to the egg tempera paints which were popular until the late fifteenth century. Being a quick-drying medium, tempera is difficult to work with but it dries to an almost impenetrable surface. You can make tempera by mixing powdered pigment with an egg solution. All painting supports must be sized to provide a suitable surface.

**Tertiary colours** see *broken colours*.

**Tone** The measure of light and dark. It is often referred to as value.

**Tooth** The degree of roughness or coarseness in texture of paper or canvas which helps the medium to adhere to the surface.

**Two-point perspective** see *perspective*.

# V

**Value** see *tone*.

**Vanishing point** When parallel lines are viewed obliquely they appear to converge. The point at which these lines meet is known as the vanishing point.

## T

Turner, J.M.W.:
*Jetty* (sketch) *68–9*
*Norham Castle 31*
self-portrait *22*
*Snowstorm 179*

Utrillo, Maurice:
*Parisian Street 178*

Vanishing points 33, *36*, 38
invisible *36*
Vasari 16
Velazquez, Diego:
self-portrait *20*
Veneziano:
*The Academy in Rome 10–11*
Vermeer, Jan:
dealing with distortion 174
*The Music Lesson 163*
Viewing point *see Station point*

Wright, Joseph:
*Academy by Lamplight 12*
Wallis, Alfred:
*St Ives Harbour 30*
Watercolour paints 149
Watercolour paper 83
Watercolour wash drawing 83
Water-scape project 187, *187*
preparation 187

## V

Value *see Tone*
Van Eyck:
self-portrait *20*
Van Gogh, Vincent:
pen and ink landscape *31*
reed-pen landscape *81*
use of Japanese drawing style
80

## U

Uccello:
urn (use of grid system) *42*
Uglow:
*A Standing Nude 42*

## W

Wooden panels 151

## Z

Zoffany, Johann:
painting of English Royal
Academy *14–15*

# ACKNOWLEDGEMENTS

**Key:** **t** – top; **b** – bottom; **c** – centre; **l** – left; **r** – right.
**p 8** Winslow Homer: By courtesy of the British Library; **p 10–11** Veneziano: By courtesy of Cambridge University Press; **p 12** Joseph Wright: Yale Center for British Art, Paul Mellon Collection; **p 13** Quadal: Vienna-Akademie der Bildenden Künste; **p 14** Zoffany: Reproduced by gracious permission of Her Majesty the Queen; **p 15** Phillips-Fox: Art Gallery of New South Wales, Sydney; **p 16** Lemaistre: By courtesy of Phaidon Press; **p 18** Michelangelo: Metropolitan Museum of Art, NY, Purchase 1924, Joseph Pulitzer Bequest; **p 20–23** Van Eyck: National Gallery, London; Leonardo: Biblioteca Reale, Turin; Bosch: from Codex de la Bibliothèque d'Arras (Giraudon); Titian: Prado, Madrid; El Greco: Metropolitan Museum of Art, NY; Velazquez: Uffizi (Scala); Rubens: Albertina, Vienna; Rembrandt: National Gallery, London; Reynolds: Tate Gallery, London; Gainsborough: National Portrait Gallery, London; Ingres: Uffizi (Scala); Delacroix: Uffizi (Scala); Turner: Tate Gallery; Courbet: Musée Petit Palais, Paris (Cooper Bridgeman Library); Munch: National Gallery, Oslo; Cézanne: National Gallery, London; Gauguin: Norton Simon Collection, Los Angeles; Matisse: Statens Museum fur Kunst, Copenhagen; Picasso: Philadelphia Museum of Art, A. E. Gallatin Collection; Mondrian: Collection Haags Gemeentemuseum, the Hague; Léger: Musée National F. Léger, Biot; Lowry: Private Collection; **p 28** Muybridge: Kingston upon Thames Art Gallery; **p 29 l** Horniman Museum (Michael Holford); **r** British Museum (Michael Holford); **p 30** Wallis: Tate; Martin: Tate; **p 31** Van Gogh: British Museum; Turner: Tate; Canaletto: **r** Reproduced by gracious permission of Her Majesty the Queen; **l** By courtesy of the Fogg Art Museum, Harvard University, Bequest of Grenville L. Winthrop; **p 42** Uglow: Tate; **p 46** Hockney: Private Coll. (© David Hockney, courtesy of the Petersburg Press); **p 48** Goodman: Museum of Modern Art, NY; **p 65** Rembrandt: National Gallery, London; **p 66** Rosa: L'Ecole des Beaux Arts, Paris; Guercino: British Museum; Matisse: Baltimore Museum of Art; **p 68** Turner: British Museum (John Freeman) **p 69** Michelangelo: Ashmolean Museum, Oxford; **p 74** Seurat: Yale University Art Gallery; **p 76–7 t** Michael Holford; **b** British Museum (Michael Holford); **p 77** Victoria and Albert Museum, Crown Copyright; **p 78** Michelangelo: Reproduced by gracious permission of Her Majesty the Queen, Windsor Royal Library; **p 79** Leonardo: Reproduced by gracious permission of Her Majesty the Queen, Windsor Royal Library; **b** Leonardo: Biblioteca Reale, Turin; **p 80** Degas: National Gallery, London; **p 81** Van Gogh: Museum of Art, Rhode Island; Mondrian: Collection of The Solomon R. Guggenheim

Museum, NY (R.E. Mates); Hockney: © David Hockney 1973, courtesy Petersburg Press; **p 98–9** Michelangelo: British Museum; **p 100 t** and **c** Leonardo: Reproduced by gracious permission of Her Majesty the Queen, Windsor Royal Library; **b** Constable: Victoria and Albert Museum, Crown Copyright; **p 101** Rembrandt: Staatliche Graphische Sammlung, Munich; **p 102** Dürer: Metropolitan Museum of Art,NY, Robert Lehman Collection, 1975; **p 103** Dürer: Albertina, Vienna; Cézanne: Courtauld Institute Art Galleries, London; **p 106** Rowlandson: Henry E. Huntington Library and Art Gallery; Hogarth: Pierpont Morgan Library, NY; **p 108** Blake: Courtesy of the Fogg Art Museum, Harvard University, Gift of W. A. White; **p 108–9** Blake: Tate; **p 112** Gozzoli: Museum Boymans-van Beuningen, Rotterdam; Brueghel: Albertina, Vienna; **p 113** Delacroix: **tl** Musée des Beaux Arts, Dijon; **tr** Dubant Collection, Paris; **c** Musée des Beaux Arts, Poitiers; **crt** Musée des Beaux Arts, Rouen; **crb** Rouen; **b** Courtesy of the Fogg Art Museum, Harvard University; **p 114 t** Musée des Beaux Arts, Besançon; **b** Louvre, Paris; **p 114–5** Dubant Collection; **p 115 tl** Dubant Collection; **tr** Musée Bonnat, Bayonne; **cl** Rouen; **cr** Marillier Collection; **b** Louvre, Paris; **p 118** Degas: Metropolitan Museum, NY; **p 120** Motherwell: By courtesy of the artist, photo by Steven Sloman; **p 140** Seurat: Art Institute of Chicago; **p 146** Van Gogh: Tate; **p 153** Degas: Bulloz, Paris; **p 157** Botticelli: National Gallery, London; **p 159** Piero: Uffizi (Scala); **p 161** Matisse: Tate; **p 162** Giotto: Scala; **p 163** Vermeer: Reproduced by gracious permission of Her Majesty the Queen; **p 164** Ingres: Louvre (Bulloz); **p 165** Bonnard: Phillips Collection, Washington; **p 168–9** de la Tour: Musée de Rennes (Snark); **p 172** Spencer: National Trust, Sandham Memorial Chapel; **p 173** Delacroix: Louvre (Snark); **p 173** Brueghel: Kunsthistorisches Museum, Vienna; **p 176** Leonardo: National Gallery, London; **p 177** Gauguin: National Gallery of Scotland (Tom Scott Photography); Palmer: Ashmolean Museum; **p 178** Cotman: Victoria and Albert Museum, Crown Copyright; Utrillo: Courtauld Institute Art Galleries; **p 178–9** Constable: Victoria and Albert Museum, Crown Copyright; **p 179** Lowry: Tate; Canaletto: Reproduced by gracious permission of Her Majesty the Queen; Turner: Tate; **p 189** Cézanne: Jeu de Paume, Paris (Bulloz); **p 190 t** Morandi: Milan Gallery of Modern Art (Scala); **b** Coll. Jesi, Milan (Scala); **p 190–1** Private Collection, Milan (Scala); **p 191 t** Coll. Dr. Orombelli, Milan (Scala): **b** Collection della Ragione, Florence (Scala); **p 196** Matisse: Phillips Collection, Washington; **p 196–7** Pollock: Tate; **p 198** Picasso: Tate; **p 203** Klee: Kunstsmuseum, Basel (Hans Hinz).